Before I started marketing "My Amazing Discovery" I sent it to experts and others for review. Read for yourself and find out what they said.

WHAT THE EXPERTS SAY:

If this book had been written by anyone in the USA it would be interesting, inspiring and serve as a useful guide to business success. But it was authored by a man who could not speak, read or write a word of English when he arrived in America seven years ago. Mr. Honek lived under Communist rule during the first 29 years of his life, where almost all businesses were owned by the government. That in itself translates his story into inspiration and hope for everyone, but this book goes far beyond inspiration as the author walks you through each step of his progression to achieve the success he now enjoys. His chosen business was mail order, and the primary product is information. The author's ability to master mail order techniques and procedures in such a short period of time is nothing short of amazing, but even more amazing is that he has used what he learned so successfully, and now shares his acquired wisdom with readers in this remarkable book. He covers advertising, publicity, record keeping, taxes and legal aspects. He even includes appropriate magazines and newspapers for advertising, a ZIP code directory and an extensive glossary. The book itself has been beautifully and expertly written, typeset and bound with a colorful coated cover. This is probably the newest book published on mail order and most likely the best such book to come along during the past ten years.

Stew Caverly / Stew's Reviews — *Pennsylvania*
Writer - Publisher - Columnist
Direct Response Counselor and Copywriter

I have read your book, "My Amazing Discovery," and would highly recommend it to anyone who is even thinking about the mail order business. You have documented the things you learned from experience and this information could save the beginner a fortune. It's a lively book, easy to read and understand.

To the mail order newcomer I say, buy "My Amazing Discovery," read it and use it in your business. It will save you a fortune and help you make one.

Lee Howard — *Florida*
Marketing & Advertising Consultant

Your book, "My Amazing Discovery," is a very inspiring personal story and also very informative . . . It covers mail order from A to Z!! This is MUST READING for anyone who desires to achieve success in any aspect of the mail order business!

Andre' Gilliam, Publisher / Editor — *California*
Mail-Courier Express Magazine

Everyone is looking to be successful in business and you, Walter V. Honek, have made it possible with "My Amazing Discovery." Any entrepreneur, whether just starting or a seasoned veteran can make the sky the limit at obtaining success by following the information in your book. You have laid-out all the precise details and even covered topics that some have forgotten. This is truly a total business between two covers.

Charles Resser — *New York*
Advertising

What a great book! Where was this masterpiece when I started out more than nine years ago?! Anyone serious about making money in this fabulous business MUST have this book in their library. If this book had been available when I got started, I would have saved thousands and thousands of dollars and countless hours of trial and error. I also can't begin to imagine how much more money I would have made and how much faster I would have made it! And this comes from someone who's used to taking in more than $100,000 a month!

I consider myself an expert, but I was reminded of important money-making lessons I had forgotten and learned new techniques from your book.

This is the greatest business in the world as far as I'm concerned and perhaps the last hope for the "little guy" just starting out. And with your new book, they can get the best start possible because you show them everything they need to know to get started properly and even how to avoid potential problems.

Armed with this valuable knowledge, I really believe anyone could start with less than a few hundred dollars like I did, and go on to make millions if they so desire.

Don Mikrut — *Illinois*
Entrepreneur

Your book, "MY AMAZING DISCOVERY," is a college education for the beginner wanting to start his own Mail Order business. This book gives you primary instructions in an "A," "B" and "C" method that any one who follows these directions cannot go wrong and will find themselves with super bank balances . . . having much fun cre-

ating the business. I recommend any new entrepreneur seeking success in the Mail Order business to register at this university.

Leonard Murray Enterprises — *California*

Using the methods outlined in this great book, I have gone from $300 to over $6,500,000 in less than 4 years! I know this may sound unbelievable—but it's the God's honest truth! . . .

Eileen K. Rohleder — *Kansas*
Entrepreneur

I would recommend your book to anyone going into the mail order profession, or even an established dealer, as we have learned much valuable knowledge and plan using many of your techniques discussed in your book "My Amazing Discovery." It is an invaluable source of information for the mail order dealer and definitely a much needed publication in the mail order community.

Steve & Rose Brown — *Kentucky*
Mail Order News

. . . I have read your book, "My Amazing Discovery" and find that you have written a very complete and detailed description of every facet of the business and from a "Hands-On" point of view. You tell it like it is and leave nothing to the imagination. This is must reading for anyone interested in going into the mail order business and contains plenty of information that even seasoned mail order operators should take note of.

Donald H. Perry — *California*
Entrepreneur

"My Amazing Discovery" is much more than a how-to book on mail order marketing. If there was a university course on the subject, this would be the textbook. The instruction goes beyond the basics to give you the details you need to successfully make money with direct response sales. I especially liked the wealth of resource material, complete with over one hundred important names and addresses. To top it off, it was truly enjoyable reading. I highly recommend it to beginner and pro alike.

David Thurman — *Nevada*
Prosper Publishing

After analyzing your book, "My Amazing Discovery — A True Rags To Riches Story," I must say that you thoroughly and completely detail what it takes to be successful in mail order. I highly recommend everyone read your book.

Larry Chiappone — *New York*
Mail Enterprises, Inc.

"My Amazing Discovery" is a TRUE inspiration to all! Those wishing to start their own business need to read your book to see for themselves that it can definitely be done. Those that are in business need to be reminded of many of the points in your book. Thank YOU!

Linda Enterprises — *Texas*

I guess it is the secret dream of every American to be able to "retire" from their office job, and be able to work out of their home. It's true. Home based businesses are growing at a tremendous rate each year. And why not? There are very few businesses which allow a person to start on a shoestring and with hard work and determination be able to amass a personal fortune. Walter is one person who has made his own dream come true. And, by reading his own personal success story, others can follow the same formula to gain their own financial independence. All the information and sources for supplies are included which will help anyone avoid making the typical beginner mistakes. If you are serious about starting a home based business of your own, then do yourself and your business a big favor by reading a copy of "My Amazing Discovery" FIRST!

Mary Anderton — *Alabama*
Executive Director — Direct Mail Order Association, Inc.

I have read your book "My Amazing Discovery" and I find it a very good book for anyone thinking about going into the mail order business. The information is easy to read and understand and very useful in operating a daily business by mail. If read and applied the book could save the beginner in mail order a lot of time and money.

Larry C. Martin — *Texas*
P & L Publishers

Your book, "My Amazing Discovery" provides the reader with a much needed first hand grasp of vital information and insight into mail order procedures. This well written book is an asset and incentive to all of our aspiring endeavors.

J & W Enterprises — *Michigan*

"My Amazing Discovery" is an informative book suited to both mail order entrepreneurs as well as anyone with an interest in starting their own business. It is well written and serves not only as an outline, but also as a guide to the ups and downs of direct mail marketing. A must for everyone in business or thinking of starting their own business.

Jeanne Lelli — *Ohio*
Lelli Printing & Advertising

"My Amazing Discovery" is a winner! Author Walter Honek has written an excellent up-to-date course on the basics of creating a successful mail order business. Lots of good concise, clear directions and advice. I recommend it.

Gerald "Gery" Carson — *Nebraska*
Publisher

"My Amazing Discovery" by Walter V. Honek is an EDUCATION in mail order. A practical book for students and old timers about the MAIL ORDER BUSINESS . . .

Litton Anderson — *Maryland*
Anderson Opportunity Newsletter

WHAT THE READERS SAY:

I thoroughly enjoyed your book "My Amazing Discovery." As I read I was reminded of its practical one-step shopping feature. You cover all the information needed to succeed in this business. Your book is easy to read and understand. You share and identify a genuine approach which taps the future global business opportunities through mail. As an experienced entrepreneur you were able to establish a thorough framework for a person to begin a successful business through mail.

Having grown up under a different political and economic system from the author, I sensed our common hopes and goals. By sharing your misfortunes and successes with the reader we see success for what it is — a commitment to a goal. I will use the valuable information the book gave me.

Roger E. Lamb — *Texas*

. . . The subject matter is laid out clearly making the book easy to read and understand. Readers will appreciate the wide range of business facets that you discuss. You have covered all necessary areas to assist the reader in being successful in their ventures. The reader needs to simply read this book, implement the ideas, be persistent and success will follow.

Robert G. Hamm — *Wisconsin*

"My Amazing Discovery" contains usable information on making money. It is really a true rags to riches story. You certainly do share your experience and knowledge.

Mark Bobowicz — *New Jersey*

I have read almost every book available concerning copyrighting and operating a successful mail order business. No one book can match your priceless work of devotion. "My Amazing Discovery" is the most comprehensive, uncluttered and straight shooting how-to succeed at selling information through the mail book available today! Your revealing book shows with extraordinary clarity how anyone with a burning desire can master the art and science of the best business in the world — selling information through mail order! Your book, "My Amazing Discovery," has empowered my mind to do great works!

Doyle Chambers — *Texas*

I found your book to be extremely informative. This kind of practical advice can only be learned from experience. Your success story should motivate anyone reading this book. It is a very detailed invaluable book, at a bargain basement price for the contents.

Gene Turk — *New Jersey*

I'm very impressed with your new book. Your book is great! Simple to read and to apply. Well worth the money.

Dr. Craig D. Sanford — *Florida*

I've read your book "My Amazing Discovery" and without question, it is a "must read" book on how to succeed against all odds in the mail order business.

A.F. Dandre — *Illinois*

. . . Reading your book "My Amazing Discovery" has given me the inspiration to continue in mail order. I wish I'd had it two years ago as it could have saved me thousands of dollars in mistakes. This is very well written, easy to understand with useful information that should be in the hands of anyone thinking of going into mail order. It is a true mail order guide for anyone. . .

J.S. Stroud — *Georgia*

. . . It's about time someone came out with the right "how to" book for mail order. I think the book is GREAT! This information is worth a million bucks! Thanks again! You have a real winner there!

David Herrick — *Texas*

My Amazing Discovery

Walter V. Honek

Beta Books Cataloging-In-Publication Data

Walter V. Honek

MY AMAZING DISCOVERY

Third Edition - 1994
BETA BOOKS CATALOG NUMBER: **WSKP-601-7516-273-18**

This manual is designed to provide information regarding the subject matter covered. It is sold with the understanding that the author and publisher disclaim any responsibility for any liability or loss associated with the use, content or subject matter of information provided herein, or otherwise. The author and the publisher are not engaged in rendering legal, accounting or other professional service. If legal, accounting or other expert assistance is required, the services of a competent professional should be sought.

Published by Beta Books

COVER DESIGN: STEVE RAYMOND

TYPESETTING: AUSTIN DESIGN STUDIO

CAMERA WORK: AD PRINTING COMPANY

PRINTING: BOOKCRAFTERS

INTERNATIONAL STANDARD BOOK NUMBER: **0-9630806-0-1**

Printed and bound in the United States Of America 10 9 8 7 6 5 4 3
A B C D E F G H

Dedication

"My Amazing Discovery" is based on my true story—my experience. It is dedicated to all readers who have a sincere desire to learn how to make their dreams become a reality.

I hope "My Amazing Discovery" helps promote the creation of small businesses which are the cornerstone of the free enterprise system in the United States and our country's best hope for a bright and prosperous future.

Table of Contents

PART I

My Story

PART II

What I Have Learned Since I Got Started

PART III

APPENDIXES

Part I

MY STORY

CHAPTER 1

Introduction

You are reading "My Amazing Discovery," which is about me, an ordinary person who wanted and achieved something more out of life—financial independence. I will tell you my incredible story, I will reveal all the information about my secret, my amazing discovery, what it is, what I have learned since I got started and the mistakes I made so that you do not have to repeat them.

I will relate to you my experiences and the knowledge and opinions I have gained since I got started. Please read "My Amazing Discovery" from cover to cover, perhaps more than once, so you can get the complete benefit of my experiences and knowledge. Some of the many important lessons you will learn are about the mistakes I made and exactly what to do not to repeat them because I do not want you to make the same mistakes I made. The purpose of "My Amazing Discovery" is to help you in two ways. To help you succeed if you desire success and also to help you avoid all the mistakes I made so that you can avoid potential problems.

I have to tell you from my heart that I would have been the happiest person on earth if I had been lucky enough to have had a book like "My Amazing Discovery" when I got started. I believe I would have made a lot more money and avoided all of the mistakes I made if that had been the case. I did not have a book like "My Amazing Discovery" because I could not find a book like it anywhere. That is a reason why I wrote "My Amazing Discovery"—to provide you with valuable and complete information. So once again, I advise you to read "My Amazing Discovery" from cover to cover.

Life was not always rosy for me as I am sure it is not rosy for many of you. I have often asked myself why most people do not live very successful lives. In my opinion, most people do not achieve great success in their lives because they do not believe they can achieve great success. Most people do not believe in themselves.

If you do not believe in yourself, it will be hard for you to achieve success. This is why, before I write about how I made big money in the United States, I will write my story. In my opinion, after reading my story, people who right now do not believe in themselves will begin to do so.

You may think: "If he can be successful, so can I!" or "If he could do it, so can I!" Believing in yourself is a key to making your dreams come true. Once you believe in yourself, anything is possible.

I lived in Europe, in Czechoslovakia, under the communist boot for the first 29 years of my life. I only finished nine grades of regular school and four years of vocational high school. When I arrived in the United States about seven years ago I could not speak, write or read English. During my first years in the United States I worked for a few dollars per hour and despite everything I was able to achieve my success. Looking back at the tremendous obstacles I had to overcome, I can not help feeling that if I could achieve such success, anyone else can also.

MY STORY IS AN AMERICAN DREAM COME TRUE

My amazing discovery is a celebration of the free enterprise system. It is a true rags-to-riches story. It is a story of an American dream come true. However, I am getting ahead of myself. Let's start from the beginning.

Chapter 2

From Communism To Free Enterprise

Most Americans take their personal freedom and the free enterprise system for granted. This is because most Americans were born in this wonderful society of ours which gives us both personal freedom and the free enterprise system. It is only natural that when you are born with something, you take it for granted. I did not experience personal freedom and the wonders of free enterprise until I was almost thirty years old. As a result, I really appreciate the society we live in.

I Lived In Communism For 29 Years

I was born in Czechoslovakia in 1955. At that time my father worked as a car mechanic for a big government owned company. Communists were in power in Czechoslovakia so there was practically no free enterprise and no personal freedom. Almost all businesses were owned by the government. My father always dreamed about having his own car repair business but because of the circumstances he had to retire without ever having a chance to achieve his dream.

My mother was a clerical worker for another big government company. She also had a dream she was never able to realize. She always dreamed of having her own bookkeeping service but this was a dream that she could never realize in a communist country.

MY PARENT'S HOPES AND DREAMS FOR ME

Since I was the oldest son, my parents hoped that someday I would escape from the clutches of communism and realize the dreams they could never realistically hope to achieve. We had a number of distant relatives and friends who lived in Western Europe. They told my parents that I could realize the dreams my parents had for me in Western Europe because of the capitalist economic system.

My parents knew that they would miss me terribly if I left Czechoslovakia but for the sake of my future they hoped that some day I would escape to Western Europe and live out the dream of prosperity and freedom.

MY GRANDPARENTS

Both my mother and father had to work all day just to make ends meet so I spent a great deal of time during my youth at my grandparent's home. When I was in my early teens, my grandmother, who had retired, told me stories about the life in freedom she and my grandfather had enjoyed before the communists came to power in 1948.

My grandfather worked in his own, privately owned shoe repair shop and was making enough money to support his family. My grandmother was able to stay at home and raise children. They enjoyed having freedom of speech and religious freedom. Unfortunately, when the communists took over in 1948, all of this came to an end.

The communists took my grandfather's business from him and forced him to work for a large, government owned machinery company as an unskilled laborer. Despite the fact that they had a need for experienced, skilled shoe repairmen to work in their large government owned companies, they forced my grandfather to work with machinery he had no experience with. Shortly after he had started working for the government, he became ill.

CHURCHES WERE NOT USED FOR PRAYING BUT AS MEETING PLACES

My grandfather's illness was so severe he was unable to work. When he suffered his grave illness, my grandmother wanted to go to church to pray for him. However, the communist authorities had already closed the church and the communist secret police were guarding it to prevent people from worshipping.

Inside the church (and many other churches all across Czechoslovakia) communist party officials were meeting and celebrating the success of their looting campaign. As soon as the communists took power, they changed the currency in order to make people's savings worthless. In addition, they also confiscated almost all private possessions people like my grandparents had spent their entire lives earning.

The communists met inside the churches and divided up what they had stolen from the people. The communists thus overnight became rich at the expense of the people who were non-communist.

MY GRANDMOTHER

The communist government forced my grandmother to work in the state owned agriculture fields surrounding her small town. She had to work from dawn until late in the evening and sometimes the communists did not even give her enough time to eat lunch.

Listening to my grandmother's stories at an impressionable age elicited very bitter feelings toward communism. I knew that I did not want to live my whole life under the communist boot.

My Early Years

I have only nine years of basic school and four years of vocational high school. I did not even complete regular high school. In Czech language, regular high school is called "Gymnazie Skola" and it encompasses grades ten through thirteen. At that time the Czechoslovakian communist government did not want to pay for regular high school education for all the students from grades ten through thirteen. Regular high school was more expensive for the government than vocational high school.

The only way a student could obtain a regular high school education was to pass a standard test at the end of ninth grade. I was a poor student and I did not pass the test.

I was only 15, so I could not go to work. The communist government did not even give me a choice of which vocational high school I could attend. Instead, they assigned me to a vocational high school for locksmiths. One of the reasons they did this was that I was not a very good student.

I did not want to be a locksmith. As a matter of fact, I hated the idea. Unfortunately, there was nothing I could do.

I finished the vocational high school for locksmiths, but in those four years I learned very little. I failed my final exams the first time and had to stay in vocational high school an extra two months, almost the whole summer. I managed to pass my final exams the second time. I was looking forward to getting a fairly good job in my vocation but instead I got another bad surprise.

Instead of giving me a job as a skilled locksmith, the communist government in its infinite wisdom forced me to go to work 3000 feet under the ground as an unskilled coal miner. I had absolutely no previous experience as a coal miner or a wish or desire to become one.

All the money the communist government spent on my four years in the vocational high school went down the drain. Naturally, what little hope I had for my future went down the drain also.

My Life As A Coal Miner

I worked for a coal mining company for about nine years. Because I was completely unskilled, in the beginning I had to do the hardest work. Later, after I got some experience doing the work, I got promoted to a foreman. As a foreman I had a number of people under me. At that point the people under me had to do the hardest work.

Even though I no longer had to do the hardest physical labor, I was not happy because I had to spend most of my time attending endless, meaningless meetings. Only ten percent of the time in those meetings was spent discussing our work. The other ninety percent of the time I had to listen to endless discussions about the communist philosophy and how the Western capitalist countries were supposedly destroying their economies and abusing their workers.

I COULD NOT EXPRESS MY TRUE OPINIONS

These meetings were doubly difficult for me. First of all, I do not enjoy spending countless hours discussing politics. Second, and even more important, I did not agree with the communist philosophy of the people around me. I had to be very careful about everything I said because I knew that if I ever told them what I really thought about communism, they would put me in prison.

People who are lucky enough to be born and raised in a free society do not know what it is like to be unable to express your true beliefs in public. As time went on, it became increasingly difficult for me to participate in those meetings and keep lying convincingly.

THE COMMUNISTS FORCED ME TO LEAVE MY OWN COUNTRY

After a number of years of working for the coal mining company, the communist party members asked me to join the party. I simply could not do it. I hated communist ideology, their oppression and hypocrisy.

My refusal to join the communist party was very insulting to the communists and they threatened me with the loss of my job as a foreman. When I saw that they had cornered me like a rat, I decided that some way, somehow, I had to leave my country.

The communists let me know in no uncertain terms, that if I wanted to keep my foreman's job, I had to become one of them. I did not like the prospect of becoming a stooge of the party. I hoped and wished I could find a place in the world where my opportunity in life would be in my own hands.

The situation became very bad for me. The communists started to accuse me of being anti-communist. This placed me one step closer to prison. Only God knows what would have happened had I decided to stay in my own country.

How I Got To The United States

I gave my future much thought and decided that I could find the best opportunities in the United States. I knew that people in the United States had been free for two hundred years. I desperately wanted to be free too. I also knew that there was a free enterprise system in the United States. I desperately wanted to control my own destiny and dreamed of owning my own business and achieving financial independence in the United States.

Finally, I decided I had to take action. I could not go directly to the United States because the communist government in Czechoslovakia did not allow people to immigrate. I came up with a plan. I took my family on a vacation to Yugoslavia.

The Czechoslovakian communist government allowed its people to take vacations in Yugoslavia because Yugoslavia was also a communist country. I knew that once in Yugoslavia, we could probably cross the border into Italy with relative ease. This is exactly what happened.

We crossed the Yugoslavian-Italian border without too much trouble and to my delight I was finally free from communism. Then all that remained was to find a way to get to the United States. I registered with the immigration office in Italy and asked for political asylum in the United States.

After almost four months of waiting, I was told that I had a sponsor and that therefore I could immigrate to the United States. When I heard the news, I was the happiest man on earth. We boarded an Italian airplane and soon after that we were standing on United States soil in New York City. From there I flew to Texas to meet my American sponsor who found me a job.

I have lived in the United States for about seven years and I am still surprised how many people here do not understand why communist governments all over the world are collapsing. I hope that at least a few of them discover some of the reasons why while reading this chapter.

My Search For A Financial Secret In The United States

When I arrived in the United States, I did not speak English. I also could not read or write English.

I worked as an unskilled laborer because I was without a skill that could earn me more money. I had to do any work available for me to support my family. I worked as a machinist and any work that was given to me, in a junk yard, repairing fences, cleaning and so on.

I was glad to be a free man living in the United States but I could see that I would not achieve my financial dreams while working for other people. So, I began to look for a secret—a way to make my financial dreams come true.

Before I discovered my secret, my amazing discovery, I purchased a lot of money making offers through the mail. I tried many of them. But I never made any money, I even lost money.

The last money making offer I purchased was about mail order. I received a booklet a few pages long. I instinctively knew that the author's little advice on how to write an advertisement would not be enough to become successful. At that time it finally hit me—I discovered my amazing discovery. I started to use my own idea, my amazing discovery and I wrote an advertisement.

My Amazing Discovery

What led to my amazing discovery was my fascination with the fact that up until that point I had been one of the purchasers of information by mail and therefore knew from personal experience how purchasers think before they make a decision to purchase information by mail.

In a nutshell, the following is my secret—my amazing discovery and it has worked beyond belief: in order to write a successful advertisement, I always put myself in the place of the potential purchasers of my information. After I write each sentence or paragraph of my advertisement, I always read it and ask myself the following question: "If I was a potential purchaser, would this sentence or paragraph help persuade me to make a purchase?" If my reaction to the sentence or paragraph from the viewpoint of the potential purchaser is positive, I keep the sentence or paragraph and continue writing the advertisement.

To put it broadly, my secret, my amazing discovery is how to write a successful advertisement and you can find more about this in Chapter 4, "How To Write A Successful Advertisement." To put it even more broadly, my secret, my amazing discovery is how to write a successful advertisement and just about all the information contained in "My Amazing Discovery" including what I have learned since I got started.

YOU ARE IN A BETTER POSITION THAN I WAS WHEN I DISCOVERED MY AMAZING DISCOVERY

Since you, the readers of "My Amazing Discovery" are also purchasers of information by mail like me, you can put yourself in the place of the potential purchasers of your information and thus write a successful advertisement like I have.

In fact, you are in a better position than I was when I discovered my amazing discovery because you have "My Amazing Discovery" in front of you to guide you and give you the complete benefit of my success. By reading "My Amazing Discovery" you will also learn about the mistakes I made so that you do not have to repeat them. In addition, you will learn what I have learned since I got started. Once again, please read "My Amazing Discovery" from cover to cover, perhaps more than once, so you can get the complete benefit of my experience and knowledge.

My First Year In Business

After I discovered the real secret and put it into action, the money started rolling in. It came like lightning from the sky. It almost made me think I had a money machine at home.

I had never imagined so much money in my life because I always worked for only a few dollars per hour. This can not be, I thought I was dreaming. It was not a dream but reality. It made the American dream come true. I made over $300,000 the first year.

When I came to the United States, I certainly did not expect that in the near future I would publish and sell information by mail and make that kind of money in my first year in business!

I worked at home by myself and because I did not speak, read or write good English I felt I needed somebody to help me with things I thought I could not do by myself. After about seven or eight months in business, I saw a competitor's advertisement in a magazine with an address geographically close to me. So, I contacted the magazine and got the name and telephone number of the person running that advertisement.

We talked on the telephone, met personally and discussed plans about getting into business together. We contacted each other on the telephone about once a month after that. At the very end of my first year in business we did a very small direct mail project together to find out if we could work together in the future. Because this project was done at the very end of my first year in business, we did not make a profit from it that year. The profit I made in my first year in business in 1989 came from display advertisements I ran on my own, by myself.

I MADE A MISTAKE THAT KEPT ME FROM PERHAPS DOUBLING MY INCOME MY FIRST YEAR IN BUSINESS

As I already mentioned, I waited too long (almost the whole year) during my first year in business to start doing direct mail by renting mailing lists. At that time I was already aware of the fact that some successful mail order operators entire business consisted of direct mail which meant that direct mail was very lucrative. Unfortunately, despite the great success I was enjoying with display advertising, I was reluctant to expand into direct mail also.

This was a big mistake. I have learned since then that direct mail by renting mailing lists is at least as profitable as display advertising. So, looking back at my first year in business, I believe I could have perhaps doubled my net income if I had gone into direct mail by renting mailing lists within 30-45 days of starting my business.

ANOTHER FIRST YEAR MISTAKE COST ME PERHAPS $100,000

I believe that another first year mistake cost me perhaps $100,000 or even more. I did not even use my own, in-house mailing list to do direct mail during my entire first year in business. I have since learned (see Chapter 11, "Direct Mail Advertising") that my own mailing list performs much better than any mailing list I have ever rented.

Chapter 3

The Power Of Belief

Before I made my amazing discovery, I wondered how other people achieved success. By reading various magazine and newspaper articles I discovered that no matter how they made their money, all rich people seemed to share one common trait: belief in oneself.

Belief In Oneself

I learned that over the years, numerous books have been written about this very idea. Some of the books have been autobiographical. Other books have been written by writers who studied and analyzed the success stories of various rich people, looking for the common thread, the trait all the rich people seemed to share. Almost without exception the writers concluded that the common trait is belief in oneself.

I came to the same conclusion, that belief in myself would be an absolutely necessary ingredient to my success. I decided that without this belief, success would probably be almost impossible for me to achieve.

IT WAS NOT EASY FOR ME TO BELIEVE IN MYSELF

But I also knew that attaining this belief would not be easy, after all, as you have already learned by reading "My Amazing Discovery," I was an immigrant who could not read, speak or write English well. I had only a vocational high school education which I did not even complete in the United States but Europe.

I began to start believing in myself and thus feel like a winner after reading the articles about positive thinking several times. The reason I am including my rags-to-riches story in "My Amazing Discovery" and the purpose of this chapter is to persuade you, the readers, to start believing in yourselves.

HOW I OVERCAME FEAR OF SETBACKS

I knew that in order to become successful I had to take action. What was preventing me at first was the fear of setbacks. I was afraid. I was afraid of failing. I was afraid of making a fool of myself. I was afraid of disappointing my family.

By reading the articles on positive thinking, I learned that taking action is the key to overcoming fear of setbacks, the key to getting started. This knowledge released me from the fear trap I was in and I was able to take the first all-important steps on the road to success.

EVERYONE FEARS SUFFERING SETBACKS

Everyone fears suffering setbacks in the game of life. Because of this fear many people refrain from taking action, thereby giving up on their chance to succeed. In order to overcome the fear of setbacks, you must accept that setbacks are a part of life.

In my opinion, it does not matter if a person is young, middle aged or old, a businessperson, a laborer, a secretary, a professional athlete, a politician, a government worker or a financially independent individual—everyone has to face and deal with setbacks in life.

It is easy to feel great and achieve great things when everything is going your way. Unfortunately, life is not a bowl of cherries. Everyone also has to face setbacks.

FACING SETBACKS

Facing setbacks is not easy, but it can be done. When faced with a setback, most people fall apart. They feel sorry for themselves, blame others for their misfortune, fail to realistically analyze the situation, fail to learn from the experience and/or simply give up. In short, they stop believing in themselves.

In my opinion, how each one of us deals with setbacks to a large extent determines how well we do in life. Let me share with you how some famous people whose careers I followed have dealt with setbacks in their lives. Read how they faced setbacks and still managed to achieve their goals. One thing you can be sure of, they never stopped believing in themselves.

Muhammad Ali

Muhammad Ali retired from boxing more than ten years ago but he is still probably one of the most famous people in the world. He is certainly the most widely recognized athlete of all time. Those of us who followed his incredible career remember that in addition to all of his triumphs and accomplishments, he faced some devastating setbacks in his career.

ALI'S EARLY SUCCESS

On February 25, 1964 Ali, at the age of 22, won the heavyweight championship from Sonny Liston when Liston failed to answer the bell for round seven of their fight. From 1965 to 1967 Ali successfully defended his title nine times.

During this time Ali coined the now famous phrase: "Float like a butterfly, sting like a bee, you can't hit what you can't see." At a very young age he became not only the most talented heavyweight champion of all time, but also a poet.

ALI'S INCREDIBLE DEFENSIVE TALENTS

Ali's boxing style was all of his own. He defied the boxing traditionalists who insisted a boxer must hold his hands high to protect himself at all times in the ring. Ali did just the opposite, boxing with his hands hanging down by his side.

He was able to get away with this unorthodox style because he had two defensive talents never before or after equaled in the boxing ring. First, Ali had incredible foot speed. He was so quick afoot that he would spend entire three minute rounds never throwing a punch of his own. Instead, he simply danced around his opponents, his hands dangling by his side, taunting and daring his opponents to hit him.

His frustrated, angered opponents would throw fast, hard punches at Ali and hit only air. They became even more frustrated when Ali employed his second incredible defensive talent. Ali had an unbelievable ability to snap his head back in the last split second before an opponent's punch could land on his head.

ALI'S INCREDIBLE OFFENSIVE TALENTS

Ali was not just an extraordinary defensive boxer. He also had incredible hand speed. I will never forget seeing a videotape of the young Ali throwing stunning combinations that were so fast my eyes could not follow them. You can imagine my shock and disbelief when the announcer said: ". . . and now, let's see that combination in real speed." It was only then that I realized that Ali's hands were so fast that my eyes were not able to follow a slow motion replay!

Many boxing experts agree that Ali possessed faster foot and hand speed than all the heavyweights before and after him and even boxers eighty pounds lighter than him.

ALI'S FIRST SETBACK

In 1967, at the age of 25, Ali was stripped of the heavyweight title when he refused on religious grounds to go to Vietnam. He was not allowed to pursue his chosen career for three and a half years. Those would have been his best years as a professional boxer.

ALI'S FIRST COMEBACK

Ali could have permanently retired during that period of time. But he did not. His goal was to regain the heavyweight title. Ali knew he could achieve his goal because he believed in himself. He was finally able to resume his career late in October of 1970. He defeated Jerry Quarry and then, a few months later, Oscar Bonavena.

ALI'S SECOND SETBACK

On March 8, 1971, Ali stepped into the ring with the reigning heavyweight champion, Joe Frasier. They fought 15 exciting, competitive rounds and Frasier knocked Ali down with a brutal left hook in the 15th round.

I doubt that any other fighter in history could have gotten up after being hit with that punch. But Ali was the greatest fighter of all time and his courage and ability to take a punch are legendary. Ali got up and finished the 15th round.

Unfortunately, when the judges' decision was announced, he heard the bitter news: he had suffered his first defeat as a professional. Ali made millions of dollars from this fight. After his first defeat he could have easily said that he lost because he was robbed of the best years of his career and then announced his retirement from boxing. Did he retire after his first defeat? No. Did he stop believing in himself? No.

ALI'S SECOND COMEBACK AND THIRD SETBACK

Ali continued to fight and in 1973 he suffered not only his second defeat but also a broken jaw in his fight with Ken Norton. Norton broke Ali's jaw in the second round. The pain must have been excruciating and surely any other man would have quit then and there. But Ali did not quit. He fought Norton for ten more rounds. Ten more rounds of having to endure hits on his already broken jaw!

Despite this incredible feat of courage, Ali lost that fight on a split decision. This was his second defeat as a professional and the critics all proclaimed that Ali was finished as a fighter. Some even called for his retirement from boxing.

ALI'S THIRD COMEBACK

So what did Ali do? Did he quit? No. Later in 1973 he defeated Norton in a rematch and then in January of 1974 he avenged his only other defeat by winning a unanimous decision over Joe Frasier.

On October 30, 1974, more than seven years after he was unjustly stripped of his heavyweight title outside the boxing ring, Ali regained the heavyweight title by knocking out George Foreman in the eighth round. Despite his setbacks, Ali continued to believe in himself. He refused to allow his setbacks to keep him from achieving his goal.

Ronald Reagan

Ronald Reagan went from being a movie actor to becoming the Governor of California in 1966. In 1970 he was re-elected as Governor. In 1976 he challenged President Gerald Ford for the Republican Party nomination. Reagan knew he had a difficult task ahead of him because it has historically been very difficult for a challenger to deny an incumbent president his party's nomination.

REAGAN'S FIRST POLITICAL SETBACK

The New Hampshire primary was Reagan's first test of the 1976 campaign. He made a crucial mistake by following the bad advice of John Sears, his campaign manager. Sears advised Reagan to leave New Hampshire the weekend before that primary in order to campaign in Illinois. Reagan then paid the price for his campaign manager's mistake. He lost the New Hampshire primary by less than 1500 votes.

Losing the New Hampshire primary was a terrible setback for Reagan. To make matters worse, Reagan then lost the primaries in Florida and Illinois. The news media began to write his political obituary. They thought Reagan's presidential ambitions would never bear fruit.

REAGAN'S FIRST POLITICAL COMEBACK

But Reagan would not quit. He pulled out all the stops for the North Carolina primary. He campaigned day and night and did not repeat his earlier mistake in New Hampshire: he did not leave the state the weekend before the primary. His determination, hard work and ability to learn from a previous mistake paid off. He won the North Carolina primary.

Winning that primary brought him credibility as a viable candidate and badly needed money to run his campaign. He ran against President Ford in primaries and caucuses all across the country, winning two of the biggest primaries: Texas and California.

REAGAN'S SECOND POLITICAL SETBACK

At the Republican National Convention in Kansas City, Reagan lost the Republican presidential nomination to President Ford 1,187 votes to 1,070. Despite Reagan's gallant effort, he had lost a bitterly close race.

Losing the nomination was a tremendous disappointment and a big political setback for him. Once again the news media wrote his political obituary. But Ronald Reagan believed in himself. He did not give up on his dream to become president of the United States.

REAGAN'S THIRD POLITICAL SETBACK

Four years later he ran for president again. He was a big favorite to win the Republican nomination for president. Unfortunately, on his way to the nomination, he suffered a serious setback: he lost the first presidential contest, the Iowa caucuses to George Bush.

A big reason Reagan lost the Iowa caucuses was that, like in 1976, he again followed some bad advice of John Sears, his campaign manager. Sears believed Reagan would win Iowa easily, so he hardly had him campaign there and even kept him out of a crucial debate. Once again Reagan had to pay the price for listening to John Sears.

Because of his shocking loss in the Iowa caucuses, only weeks before the nation's first primary in New Hampshire, Reagan went from being a big favorite to being an underdog.

He also soon learned that his campaign was spending way too much money that early in the presidential campaign. At that pace, they were bound to run out of funds before the big primaries only a few months down the road. Worse, he knew that losing to George Bush in New Hampshire at the heels of his defeat in Iowa could mean the end of his presidential aspirations.

REAGAN'S SECOND POLITICAL COMEBACK

Reagan was determined not to lose. He did not repeat his previous mistakes. He campaigned unceasingly and won the New Hampshire primary. Before the polls closed the day of the primary he fired John Sears, his campaign manager.

Reagan went on to win the Republican nomination and later defeated President Carter to become the fortieth president of the United States. Despite his setbacks, Reagan continued to believe in himself. He refused to allow his setbacks to keep him from achieving his goal.

How I Face Setbacks

Since I started believing in myself I have faced many setbacks. Every setback has been different, but my approach to facing each setback has remained the same. I have done four things.

1. I analyzed the situation and then tried to learn from the experience. I believe that every experience, no matter how bad or negative it seems at first, can be turned into something positive if you learn from it.
2. I tried a different route or approach to my goal. I believe it is better and more efficient to come up with a new approach than to try again the one that has already failed.
3. I simply doubled and tripled my efforts to succeed and this has always worked for me. I know in my heart that no matter what happens, I can not afford to give up because that is the sure way to lose everything.
4. Despite all of my setbacks, I have continued to believe in myself. I refuse to allow the setbacks to keep me from pursuing my goals.

So far in my business experience, no one has been able to truly defeat me, to truly derail me from my chosen path and goals. The reason is that I am a fighter.

I Am A Fighter

Since I started believing in myself, I have become a fighter. I simply can not accept defeat. Even if and when I lose (and I think everyone loses sometimes) I know that the defeat is only temporary. I know that defeat is really only a state of mind. So, I try to learn from the defeat in order to win the next time. I also try to learn from my mistakes so that I do not have to repeat them.

I can not quit. The word quit is not in my vocabulary. No matter what problems I have faced and still may face in my business, I have eliminated the option of giving up.

I Regard Business As War

Readers of military textbooks are familiar with the concept called "the path of least resistance." The world's greatest military leaders applied this concept time and time again. The idea behind "the path of least resistance" is that in war (and I believe also in business) it is far better to attack your enemy (or to overcome your obstacles) indirectly rather than directly.

A direct attack means that you are attacking your enemy straight ahead where he is expecting you to attack. In war, this is where the enemy amasses his troops. In business, this is where the obstacles you must overcome to reach your goals are situated.

The more effective strategy in business as well as war is using the indirect approach—"the path of least resistance." An indirect attack is a flanking attack, going around the enemy or obstacles.

War should be fought to win and I fight in business to win. I do not believe in sitting back and turning on the cruise control because that can lead to a second place finish.

My Desire To Succeed

I believe that my desire to succeed has been one of the keys to my success. My desire to succeed is so real that I can almost taste it. I wake up almost every morning and go to bed almost every night with the desire to succeed strongly on my mind. Sometimes, when I think that all my day's work is done, I say to myself: "there must be something else I should do." I then look around in order to find something else to do.

I Must Have Balance In My Life

I do enjoy relaxing. I enjoy swimming in my pool, going to the beach, sunbathing and playing in the ocean. I enjoy many other things in life. I believe that to be successful I must have balance in my life. But before I enjoy myself I try to remember to remind myself that what I am about to do is a fruit of my desire to succeed.

I Am Never Completely Satisfied

No matter how good a job I do, before I walk away from it I always think to myself: "I know I can do this better. If I just change this and that. . . ." Despite this, I am never completely satisfied with my work. One of the benefits of writing "My Amazing Discovery" has been to remind me of the mistakes I have made so that I do not have to repeat them.

Praise

I praise people when conducting business. I also praise my family members. I believe that they need as much or even more praise than other people. When I praise my family members, they feel better about themselves and our relationship improves. That gives me even more energy to pursue my goals.

In my opinion, my belief in myself, my desire to succeed and my willingness to praise people have been keys to my success.

Chapter 4

How To Write A Successful Advertisement

Before you start writing your advertisement study very carefully United States Postal Service, 39 U.S. Code 3005, Figure 10.7 which you will find at the end of Chapter 10, "Tax, Record Keeping And Legal Aspects." Before you run your advertisement, consult a lawyer who is an expert in mail order so that he can review your advertisement and the information you are selling to make sure that they are not in violation of various federal provisions regarding advertising. Please note that I wrote ". . . consult a lawyer who is an expert in mail order. . . ." because from my experience, a lawyer whose specialty is not mail order does not have the expertise necessary to review the advertisement and information being sold by mail.

"My Amazing Discovery" can teach you how to write a successful advertisement but I can not give you legal advice regarding advertising because I am not a lawyer. However, there is something I can do to help you even regarding this point. I can state the following: to the best of my knowledge, the lawyers listed in "Legal Aspects To Consider Regarding Advertising" in Chapter 10 are experts in mail order and therefore have the expertise necessary to review advertisements and information being sold by mail. Once again, I have to tell you that I would have been the happiest person on earth if I had been lucky enough to have had a book like "My Amazing Discovery" when I got started. I believe I would have made a lot more money and avoided all of the mistakes I made if that had been the case. It took me two and a half years to find lawyers whose specialty is mail order and who therefore have the expertise necessary to review my advertisements and the information I am selling by mail. They can do the same for you.

Let me get started teaching you how to write a successful advertisement. When writing your advertisement, keep in mind that each sentence or paragraph is important in the success of your advertisement. Write a sentence or a paragraph. Put yourself in the place of the potential purchasers of your information.

Read the sentence or paragraph and ask yourself the following question: "If I was a potential purchaser, would this sentence or paragraph help persuade me to make a purchase?" If the answer is yes, keep the sentence or paragraph and continue writing the advertisement. If the answer is no, rewrite the sentence or paragraph, perhaps you will come up with something better.

If you do not come up with something better, ask family members for their opinion. Consider their opinion and write it down. Perhaps they will come up with an idea or a word or two to make the sentence or paragraph better.

Put yourself again in the place of the potential purchasers of your information. Read the sentence or paragraph one more time and ask yourself the same question again: "If I was a potential purchaser, would this sentence or paragraph help persuade me to make a purchase?"

You can also ask your friends the same question. If they answer no, ask them why. Try to get an explanation from them. Listen to the advice of everyone you talk to and always keep the best parts which everyone likes. This way, if everyone you talk to likes what is written, there is a chance that your potential customers may like it also. Continue writing your advertisement and repeating this process.

Identify And Think Like Your Potential Customers

You must identify your potential customers (purchasers) before you start writing your advertisement. Since I decided to sell information on how to make money and since I had been one of the purchasers of such information it was easy for me to identify my potential customers. They had to be opportunity seekers, people like me. People who were looking for solutions to their financial problems.

IDENTIFYING YOUR POTENTIAL CUSTOMERS IS EASY

Identifying your potential customers is easy because it is common sense. For example, if the information you will sell deals with gardening, your potential customers are gardeners. If the subject of your information is golf, your potential customers are golfers. If your information is about tennis, your potential customers are tennis players.

Once you have identified your potential customers, you have to decide if you should start writing a successful advertisement before or after you obtain or write the information you will be selling. For more on obtaining and writing information, see Chapter 6, "Selling Information By Mail."

I prefer to start writing my successful advertisement before the information I will obtain actually arrives or before I write my own information. At this point I know what the information will be about and I have already identified my potential customers so I am eager to start writing the advertisement. I use this approach because it saves time.

Some mail order experts prefer to use this approach also. Melvin Powers, who has sold millions of books, most of them by mail (see Chapter 5, "The Greatest Business In The World") is an expert who usually writes the advertisement before he writes the information.

The Benefit

By thinking like your potential customers, you can find out what they want. Potential customers are individuals with various wants and desires but they all have one thing in common. Before potential customers purchase your information they will want to know how they can benefit from it. No matter what type of information you are selling, whether it is about how people can make more money, or how they can have a more beautiful lawn, your advertisement has to show them that they can benefit from purchasing your information.

If your advertisement fails to show them the benefits, they will not place an order. Honestly, would you order something if you could not see benefit from it?

It is human nature to want to know what the product or information can do for you before you make the purchase. As I am writing these words I am reminded of a line in a song that was a big hit a few years back. To the best of my recollection the line was: "what have you done for me lately?"

The point here is not the last word, "lately" but the first six words "what have you done for me . . ." This is very much like the classic line "what's in it for me?" Before human beings will buy anything, they want to know the answer to this question.

Put Yourself In Your Customer's Place

Now that I have stressed the importance of letting the potential customers know what your information can do for them, it is time to find out what else they want besides this knowledge. To find out, you must try to think like them, you must put yourself in your potential customer's place.

MOST OF MY CUSTOMERS ARE ORDINARY, AVERAGE PEOPLE LIKE ME

I prefer to sell information geared toward ordinary, average people. I do this for two reasons. First, I am an ordinary, average person and this makes it easy to put myself in my potential customer's place in order to find out what they want.

Second, I figure that ordinary, average people comprise over 70% of the population. I want the number of my potential customers to be as high as possible. The reason for this is obvious, the greater the number of potential customers, the more information I can sell.

SELL INFORMATION GEARED TOWARD PEOPLE LIKE YOURSELF

You should sell information geared toward people like yourself. You should do this even if you are a highly educated professional instead of an ordinary, average person like me.

You have two reasons for doing this. First, this makes it easy to put yourself in your potential customer's place so you can find out what they want. Second, if your potential customers are highly educated professionals you can charge a lot more money for your information than I can for mine.

THE MOST IMPORTANT ADVERTISING OBJECTIVE

The most important advertising objective is to persuade your potential customers to place an order and to do so immediately after they read the advertisement. Many so called mail order advertising experts place most of the emphasis on what the potential customers will think about the advertisement and not on what is really the most important objective—persuading the potential customers to place an order immediately.

Five Advertising Objectives

There are five advertising objectives you should be aware of. These objectives comprise a formula which you ought to follow when writing your own advertisement.

1. Capture the potential customer's attention.
2. Show the potential customers the benefits of your offer.
3. Prove to the potential customers that you can really provide the benefits.
4. Persuade the potential customers to place an order immediately.
5. Make it easy for the potential customers to place an order.

Objective number one "Get the attention of the potential customers" is the job of your advertisement's headline. A really good headline also shows the potential customers the most important benefit (partially achieves objective number two).

Objectives two through four are achieved in your advertisement's "copy" or "body." Objective number five involves the order form or coupon. You should make it easy for the potential customers to place an order.

The Potential Customer's Response

The previously discussed formula is designed to lead the potential customers down the road to placing an order. Let's see how this works.

1. The headline captures the potential customer's attention.
2. The capture of the potential customer's attention leads him to the first paragraph of the advertisement.
3. The first paragraph entices the potential customers to read the copy of the advertisement.
4. The advertisement copy shows and proves to the potential customers the remaining benefits of your offer.
5. The advertisement copy persuades the potential customers to place an order immediately.
6. The order form or coupon makes it easy for the potential customers to place an order.

Advertisement Layout

The advertisement's layout helps the headline in capturing the potential customer's attention. Often, advertisers try very hard to make their advertisements look balanced or even symmetrical. This is a mistake.

BALANCED ADVERTISEMENTS

The columns in a balanced or symmetrical display advertisement all look alike. All the columns have subheads in similar places followed by similar amount of advertisement copy. Advertisements which are balanced, or worse, symmetrical, look exactly the way most other advertisements look and the potential customers therefore immediately recognize them as advertisements.

UNBALANCED ADVERTISEMENTS

Advertisements should actually be unbalanced because this attracts more attention. When working on the layout, you should strive to create unbalanced, non-symmetrical looking advertisements. Having a photograph occupy space in one or two columns (but not all the columns) of an advertisement is perhaps the most effective method of unbalancing an advertisement to attract more attention.

The columns in unbalanced display advertisements all look different. They have subheads in different places in each column and the amount of the advertisement copy following the subheads differs from column to column.

WHY UNBALANCED ADVERTISEMENTS ARE MORE EFFECTIVE

Unbalanced advertisements are more effective than balanced advertisements because they look as if they were created by the advertiser instead of by an advertising agency. Potential customers prefer to read advertisements written by the advertiser because common sense dictates that the advertiser knows more about what he or she is selling than an advertising agency.

STUDY YOUR COMPETITION

Competition fuels free enterprise economies. Consumers are always looking for a better or cheaper product in their never ending need to consume. Someone is always trying to make a profit by inventing a better mouse trap.

Having The Best Product Does Not Guarantee Success

However, inventing the best mouse trap does not always translate into tremendous profits for the inventor. The reason this is true is advertising. With poor advertising the best mouse trap ever invented may only be half as successful as a really lousy mouse trap which has great advertising.

Study Mail Order Advertisements

You should not fear your competition. In fact you should be glad that they are there because this means they are making money. Visit your local bookstores and libraries and look at mail order ads your competition uses in newspapers and magazines. You can also write to the publications listed in Chapter 7, "Display Advertising" for sample issues of their magazines.

Your competition runs ads to make money so only successful ads run month after month. Your local library should also have back issues of magazines. Look through six months of back issues to see if the same ads appear in the publications.

I have included some successful mail order ads in "My Amazing Discovery" to help you to learn. Study the headlines, the layouts, the words used in the copy, the guarantees and the coupons.

Study Your Competitor's Advertisements But Do Not Copy Them

You should study your competitor's advertisements but never copy them. A reason you can not copy them is that all advertisements are automatically copyrighted once they are published. You can not copy copyrighted material because it is illegal. The person whose copyright you violate can sue you for copyright infringement.

Conclusions You Can Draw

If you notice a number of advertisements for similar information, this means the advertisers must be making sales. This can be translated into an opportunity for you. An ad selling similar information could also work for you.

PRICE

Study your competitor's ads to find out what price they charge for information similar to yours. You should do this to avoid under-pricing your offer.

LEARN FROM YOUR COMPETITION

Do not view competition as a negative. You should view them as a positive because you can learn from them. Mail order is growing by leaps and bounds and there is room for more competition because the market is huge.

THREE REASONS WHY I WELCOME COMPETITION

In my business, I definitely look at competition as a positive. As a matter of fact I welcome competition for three reasons.

1. Even though I have very successful experience in the mail order business, I still learn from my competition. I believe a person should always seek to learn, to improve.
2. My competitors keep the public aware of the importance of the type of information I sell. I believe this public awareness makes my own advertisements a little bit more effective.
3. I am always renting my competitors' names for direct mail purposes. The more sales they make, the more customer names they have and the more names I can rent. Naturally, the more names I can rent the more money I can make.

THE HEADLINE

The headline is by far the most important element of the advertisement because it captures the potential customer's attention. By doing that, the headline achieves the first objective of an advertisement. An advertisement which fails to capture the potential customer's attention with its headline can not be very successful.

How Important Is The Headline?

How important is the headline in an advertisement? In my opinion, the headline is perhaps 80% of the advertisement. All the other elements combined add up to 20%.

The reason for this is really simple. If your headline does not capture the attention of the potential customers, nothing else will. If you do not capture their attention, they will not read your advertisement copy. If they do not read your advertisement copy, they will not place an order (no matter how good your advertisement copy is).

In summary, the advertisement with the greatest copy ever can not be very successful if the headline fails to capture the attention of the potential customers.

The Headline Must Stop The Potential Customers

The headline must stop the potential customers from turning the page of a publication. If the headline does this, it has captured the potential customer's attention, which is the main objective of the headline.

If the headline fails to stop the potential customers from turning the page of a publication, then those potential customers will most likely fail to place an order. The reason for this is that it is highly unlikely that potential customers will flip back to your advertisement once they have already passed over it.

THE HEADLINE MUST BE EYE CATCHING AND MUST SHOW THE MOST IMPORTANT BENEFIT

The headline must be eye catching. It must reach out and grab the potential customers' attention. A good headline must also show the potential customers the most important benefit of your information (what your information can do for them). By achieving these two objectives the headline induces the potential customers to read the copy of your advertisement before turning the page.

The Headline Must Be Easy To Read

If your headline is to stop the potential customer from turning the page before reading at least the headline of your advertisement, the headline must be easy to read. Do not make your potential customer strain or squint in order to read your headline or for that matter, your advertising copy. Few potential customers are willing to make that kind of effort in order to read your advertisement.

How Many Words In A Headline?

I am undecided on the issue of how many words a headline should contain. On the one hand I believe that headlines should have a limited number of words. I like short, concise headlines.

On the other hand I also believe that what the headline states is more important than how many words are actually in the headline. A word of caution regarding longer headlines. If you want to use a longer headline, make sure it is easy to read. Keep in mind that bigger type (print) is easier to read than smaller type. The more words you use in your headline, the smaller the type must be.

Successful Headlines

Let's look at some successful headlines.

EVERYTHING YOU ALWAYS WANTED TO KNOW ABOUT SEX BUT WERE AFRAID TO ASK

CREDIT CARD SUCCESS SECRETS

THE SECRET OF MAKING PEOPLE LIKE YOU

HAVE YOU EVER TAKEN A PRACTICE SWING AT A DANDELION?

GET MILLIONS IN THE GREAT GRANT GIVE-AWAY

HOW TO MASTER THE ART OF SELLING ANYTHING

HOW TO MAKE A FORTUNE RENOVATING HOUSES

THE SECRET TO PERFECT PUTTING

$25,000 FOR A FEW HOURS WORK DOESN'T SEEM FAIR

67 REASONS WHY IT WOULD HAVE PAID YOU TO ANSWER OUR AD A FEW MONTHS AGO

HAVE YOU EVER BOWLED A STRIKE AND SAID, "I'VE GOT IT!"?

THE SECRET OF HAVING GOOD LUCK

THE GREATEST STORY EVER TOLD

HOW TO FLATTEN YOUR TUSH

161 WAYS TO A MAN'S HEART—IN THIS FASCINATING BOOK FOR COOKS

SECRETS TO A LIFE OF LUXURY

THEY ALL LAUGHED WHEN I SAT DOWN AT THE PIANO—BUT WHEN I STARTED TO PLAY!

HOW TO MAKE LOVE TO A SINGLE GIRL

HOW TO MAKE LOVE TO A SINGLE MAN

THE AMAZING DIET SECRET OF A DESPERATE HOUSEWIFE

WOULD YOU LIKE TO HAVE A PHOTOGRAPHIC MEMORY?

CAN YOU AFFORD NOT TO BE A MILLIONAIRE?

YOU CAN LAUGH AT MONEY WORRIES—IF YOU FOLLOW THIS SIMPLE PLAN

YOU CAN GET EVERYTHING YOU'VE EVER DREAMED ABOUT

WITH NO PREVIOUS EXPERIENCE YOU CAN LEARN AT HOME IN YOUR SPARE TIME

THE POWER OF POSITIVE THINKING

WHOSE FAULT WHEN CHILDREN DISOBEY?

HAVE YOU EVER SAID, "I JUST CAN'T SEEM TO CONCENTRATE"?

HOW TO MAKE A FORTUNE TODAY STARTING FROM SCRATCH!

DISCOVER THE FORTUNE THAT LIES HIDDEN IN YOUR SALARY

MAIL ORDER ADVERTISING COPYWRITER CAN HELP YOU PUT MORE DOLLARS IN YOUR MAIL BOX

HOW TO WIN FRIENDS AND INFLUENCE PEOPLE

HOW TO WRITE A HIT SONG AND SELL IT

OHIO MAN DISCOVERS THE SECRET OF HOW TO ESCAPE THE AMERICAN RAT RACE

WHY SOME PEOPLE ALMOST ALWAYS MAKE MONEY IN THE STOCK MARKET

GET RICH IN IMPORT-EXPORT STARTING TODAY

HOW I MADE A FORTUNE WITH A "FOOL IDEA"

WHICH OF THESE $2.50-TO-$5 BEST SELLERS DO YOU WANT—FOR ONLY $1 EACH?

Conclusion About Headlines

In conclusion, the very least your headline must do is to get the attention of the potential customers. A really good headline also shows the potential customers the most important benefit of your information. By achieving these two objectives the headline induces the potential customer to read the copy of your advertisement before turning the page.

SUBHEADS

Subheads (sub headlines) are short lines of print usually set apart from the rest of the advertisement copy by blank space above and below each subhead. Subheads can me made to stand out even more by using bold print, larger type size and/or using all capital letters.

Subheads Should State The Most Important Benefits

The main purpose of subheads is to entice and lead the potential customers into reading further into the copy of the advertisement. Therefore, it is very important that the subheads state the most important benefits.

SOME POTENTIAL CUSTOMERS MAY NOT READ THE ADVERTISEMENT COPY

There is another reason why it is very important that the subheads state the most important benefits. Some potential customers are lazy readers and may only read the headline, what is below the photograph or illustration, the subheads and the coupon. For the benefit of the laziest potential customers, your headline and your subheads should persuade such potential customers to place an order immediately.

Subheads Break Up The Advertisement Copy

Another purpose of the subheads is to break up the advertisement copy. This makes the advertisement more effective for two reasons. First, some potential customers are intimidated by long advertisement copy and subheads make the advertisement appear to be easier to read.

Second, by breaking up the advertisement copy, subheads also make it easy for your potential customers to scan your advertisement when they first look at it. You should leave some blank space above and below each subhead because this helps to break up the copy.

It is not important where potential customers start reading your advertisement, what is important is to get them to read it. For example, when reading a sales letter, some potential customers may not be very interested in the first two pages and may want to start reading on page three or four.

Introduce Your First Subhead Early In The Advertisement

You should introduce your first subhead early in the advertisement. Do not write three or more paragraphs before introducing the first subhead. If you do this, you run the risk that the potential customers will lose interest and stop reading your advertisement. One or two paragraphs and then your first subhead is a good rule to follow.

Sometimes, if the copy of the advertisement is very long, you can effectively use the first subhead on top of the copy, immediately below the headline. The first subhead then appears almost as a sub headline. The only purpose of the first subhead is to entice and lead the potential customers into reading further into the copy of the advertisement.

Use Subheads To LeadThe Potential Customers To Order

Your subheads should be like street or highway signs leading the potential customers to do what you want them to do to order. An excellent example of this is the Mark Haroldsen advertisement, Figure 4.2.

Subheads usually lead the potential customers to order by leading them to the coupon. The coupon should make it easy for them to place an order. Notice that the Mark Haroldsen advertisement did not have a coupon. His advertisement was tremendously successful, but I believe that having a coupon would have improved his results.

ADVERTISEMENT COPY

The advertisement copy (the body of the advertisement) is the part below the headline which is used to communicate your offer to the potential customers. Advertisement copy is a very important element of the advertisement because it is responsible for achieving advertising objectives two through four:

2. Show the potential customers the benefits of your offer.
3. Prove to the potential customers that you can really provide the benefits.
4. Persuade the potential customers to place an order immediately.

Use Long, Dense Advertising Copy

You should use long, dense advertising copy because it seems to be most effective. An excellent example of long, dense advertising copy is Joe Karbo's famous "Lazy Man's Way To Riches" advertisement, Figure 4.1.

The First Paragraph

The first paragraph of the advertisement is very important because it usually determines whether the potential customers will read the remainder of the advertisement copy. The first paragraph should therefore consist of exciting, short, easy-to-read sentences to entice the potential customers to read on.

The first paragraph should follow up on the idea expressed in the headline and summarize the benefits of your offer. The objective of the headline is to capture the potential customer's attention. The objective of the first paragraph is to hold the potential customer's attention—to entice him to read the paragraphs which follow.

Three Approaches To Writing The First Paragraph

The first paragraph should entice the potential customers to read the copy of the advertisement. There are three basic approaches you can use to achieve this objective. The three approaches are: a shocking statement, a story and a news story.

A SHOCKING STATEMENT

The first paragraph of Mark Haroldson's "How To Wake Up The Financial Genius Inside You" advertisement is a shocking statement. It reads: "If hours, efforts, or brains are not what separates the rich from the average guy who is swamped with debts and very little income then what is?" See Figure 4.2.

The Lazy Man's Way to Riches

'Most People Are Too Busy Earning a Living to Make Any Money'

"... *I didn't have a job and I was worse than broke. I owed more than $50,000 and my only assets were my wife and 8 children. We were renting an old house in a decaying neighborhood, driving a 5-year old car that was falling apart, and had maybe a couple of hundred dollars in the bank.*

Within one month, after using the principles of the Lazy Man's Way to Riches, things started to change – to put it mildly.

- *We worked out a plan we could afford to pay off our debts – and stopped our creditors from hounding us.*
- *We were driving a brand-new Thunderbird that a car dealer had given to us!*
- *Our bank account had multiplied tenfold!*
- *All within the first 30 days!*

And today ...

- *I live in a home that's worth over $250,000.*
- *I own my "office". It's about a mile and a half from my home and is right on the beach.*
- *I own a lakefront "cabin" in Washington. (That's where we spend the whole summer – loafing, fishing, swimming and sailing.)*
- *I own two oceanfront condominiums. One is on a sunny beach in Mexico and one is snuggled right on the best beach of the best island in Hawaii.*
- *I have two boats and a Cadillac. All paid for.*
- *I have a net worth of over a Million Dollars. But I still don't have a job ..."*

I used to work hard. The 18-hour days. The 7-day weeks.

But I didn't start making big money until I did less—a *lot* less.

For example, this ad took about 2 hours to write. With a little luck, it should earn me 50, maybe a hundred thousand dollars.

What's more, I'm going to ask you to send me 10 dollars for something that'll cost me no more than 50 cents. And I'll try to make it so irresistible that you'd be a darned fool not to do it.

After all, why should you care if I make $9.50 profit if I can show you how to make a *lot* more?

What if I'm so sure that you *will* make money my Lazy Man's Way that I'll make you a most unusual guarantee?

And here it is: I won't even cash your check or money order for 31 days *after* I've sent you my material.

That'll give you plenty of time to get it, look it over, try it out.

If you don't agree that it's worth *at least a hundred times* what you invested, send it back. Your *uncashed* check or money order will be put in the return mail.

The only reason I won't send it to you and bill you or send it C.O.D. is because both these methods involve more time and money.

And I'm already going to give you the biggest bargain of your life.

Because I'm going to tell you what it took me 11 years to perfect: How to make money the Lazy Man's Way.

O.K.—now I have to brag a little. I don't mind it. And it's necessary—to prove that sending me the 10 dollars ... which I'll keep "in escrow" until you're satisfied ... is the smartest thing you ever did.

I live in a home that's worth $250,000. I know it is, because I turned down an offer for that much. My mortgage is less than half that, and the only reason I haven't paid it off is because my Tax Accountant says I'd be an idiot.

My "office," about a mile and a half from my home, is right on the beach. My view is so breathtaking that most people comment that they don't see how I get any work done. But I do enough. About 6 hours a day, 8 or 9 months a year.

The rest of the time we spend at our mountain "cabin." I paid $30,000 for it—cash.

I have 2 boats and a Cadillac. All paid for.

We have stocks, bonds, investments, cash in the bank. But the most important thing I have is priceless: time with my family.

And I'll show you just how I did it—the Lazy Man's Way—a secret that I've shared with just a few friends 'til now.

It doesn't require "education." I'm a high school graduate.

It doesn't require "capital." When I started out, I was so deep in debt that a lawyer friend advised bankruptcy as the only way out. He was wrong. We paid off our debts and, outside of the mortgage, don't owe a cent to any man.

It doesn't require "luck." I've had more than my share, but I'm not promising you that you'll make as much money as I have. And you may do better; I personally know one man who used these principles, worked hard, and made 11 million dollars in 8 years. But money isn't everything.

It doesn't require "talent." Just enough brains to know what to look for. And I'll tell you that.

It doesn't require "youth." One woman I worked with is over 70. She's travelled the world over, making all the money she needs, doing only what I taught her.

It doesn't require "experience." A widow in Chicago has been averaging $25,000 a year for the past 5 years, using my methods.

What *does* it require? Belief. Enough to take a chance. Enough to absorb what I'll send you. Enough to put the principles into *action*. If you do just that—nothing more, nothing less—the results *will* be hard to believe. Remember—I guarantee it.

You don't have to give up your job. But you may soon be making so much money that you'll be able to. Once again—I guarantee it.

The wisest man I ever knew told me something I never forgot: "Most people are too busy earning a living to make any money."

Don't take as long as I did to find out he was right.

Here are some comments from other people. I'm sure that, like you, they didn't believe me either. Guess they figured that, since I wasn't going to deposit their check for 31 days, they had nothing to lose.

They were right. *And here's what they gained:*

$260,000 in eleven months

"Two years ago, I mailed you ten dollars in sheer desperation for a better life ... One year ago, just out of the blue sky, a man called and offered me a partnership ... I grossed over $260,000 cash business in eleven months. You are a God sent miracle to me."

B. F., Pascagoula, Miss.

Made $16,901.92 first time out

"The third day I applied myself totally to what you had shown me. I made $16,901.92. That's great results for my first time out."

J. J. M., Watertown, N.Y.

'I'm a half-millionaire'

"Thanks to your method, I'm a half-millionaire ... would you believe last year at this time I was a slave working for peanuts?"

G. C., Toronto, Canada

$7,000 in five days

"Last Monday I used what I learned on page 83 to make $7,000. It took me all week to do it, but that's not bad for five day's work."

M. D., Topeka, Kansas

Can't believe success

"I can't believe how successful I have become ... Three months ago, I was a telephone order taker for a fastener company in Chicago, Illinois. I was driving a beat-up 1959 Rambler and had about $600 in my savings account. Today, I am the outside salesman for the same fastener company. I'm driving a company car ... I am sitting in my own office and have about $3,000 in my savings account."

G. M., Des Plaines, Ill.

I know you're skeptical. After all, what I'm saying is probably contrary to what you've heard from your friends, your family, your teachers and maybe everyone else you know. I can only ask you one question.

How many of them are millionaires?

So it's up to you:

A month from today, you can be nothing more than 30 days older – or you can be on your way to getting rich. You decide.

Sworn Statement:

"On the basis of my professional relationship as his accountant, I certify that Mr. Karbo's net worth is more than one million dollars."

Stuart A. Cogan

Bank Reference:

Home Bank
17010 Magnolia Avenue
Fountain Valley, California 92708

Joe Karbo
17105 South Pacific, Dept. 8X-R
Sunset Beach, California 90742

Joe, you may be full of beans, but what have I got to lose? Send me the Lazy Man's Way to Riches. *But don't deposit my check or money order for 31 days after it's in the mail.*

If I return your material – for *any* reason – within that time, return my *uncashed* check or money order to me. On that basis, here's my ten dollars.

Name ____________

Address ____________

City ____________

State ________ Zip ________

Figure 4.1 Joe Karbo's advertisement.

A STORY

An excellent example of the story approach is Joe Karbo's "The Lazy Man's Way To Riches" advertisement. Karbo gets into his story from the first sentence of the first paragraph: "I used to work hard. The 18-hour days. The 7-day weeks." See Figure 4.1.

Advertisement Advertisement

How To Wake Up The Financial Genius Inside You.

"I Have Helped More Than 250,000 People Discover Exactly How To Achieve Financial Freedom."

THE DIFFERENCE

If hours, efforts, or brains are not what separate the rich from the average guy who is swamped with debts and very little income then what is?

I learned the answer to that question from an old fellow in Denver. This fellow worked in a drug store stocking the shelves. Very few people knew that he had $200,000 in the bank, all of which he had earned starting from nothing.

Within a year after meeting him, I was told and shown the same thing by a young man who had recently earned over a million dollars. By this time, I began to realize that what I was being shown was truly a remarkable and workable way to grow rich.

THE BEGINNING

I began to apply the principles and methods I had been shown. The results were amazing. I couldn't believe how easy it was, in fact it seemed too easy.

But then I met an elderly lady (83 years old) who, although not very smart, has made $117,000 using the same formula.

I then figured my beginning wasn't luck.

For three and one half years, I worked hard to refine and improve on the formula that I had been shown, so that it would be easy to get quicker results.

As I did this, my assets multiplied very rapidly (160% per year) to the point that I didn't have to work any longer.

MORE LEISURE

I guess I am bragging now, but I did start spending a lot of time in our back yard pool, traveling around the country, and doing a lot of loafing.

Then one day a friend asked me how he could do what I had done.

So I began to outline the formula that I had improved to show him really how simple it was, and how he could do the same thing.

By the next time he approached me, I had written almost a complete volume on the easy way for him to copy my results.

EASY TO READ

I wrote this in simple, straight-forward language so anyone could understand it.

This time my friend's questions were very specific. (He had already begun buying properties with the formulas I had been giving him.) Now he had a property he wanted to buy, but was out of cash. How could he buy it?

I not only showed him how to buy without cash, but by the time the deal was complete, he had $5,000 cash in his pocket to boot.

I also showed him how to buy a $26,000 property for $75 down.

ANYONE CAN

You can do exactly what I did, or my close friends have done; in fact, you may well do it better. (I began doing this in my spare time only.)

It doesn't matter where you live or the size of your town or city, my formula will show you exactly how to:

- Buy income properties for as little as $100 down.
- Begin without any cash.
- Put $10,000 cash in your pocket each time you buy (without selling property.)
- Double your assets every year.
- Legally avoid paying federal or state income taxes.
- Buy bargains at ½ their market value.
- Allow you to travel one week out of every month.

When you send me a check or money order for $10, I will send you all my formulas and methods, and you are free to use them anywhere and as often as you would like.

Mark O. Haroldsen became a millionaire in four years because he found a way to harness inflation to his benefit. Now it's your turn! *"I've found"* says Haroldsen, *"that most people just need a specific road map to follow... they can do what I've done."*

One of many unsolicited comments on my material:

"... when it came I read it. Then I read it again, and have read it about once a week since it came. No magic. No secrets. A plain, easy-to-understand, 1-2-3 way for anybody with a little patience and common sense to become totally independent within a reasonable length of time. The one book I've been looking for for at least fifteen years..."

—Jerry Donaho, Valdez, Alaska

IT'S GUARANTEED

Now if you were a personal friend of mine, I know you would believe me and not need any kind of guarantee, but since you don't know me personally, I will guarantee that you will be completely satisfied and that my formula will work for you if you apply it. I will back up that guarantee by not cashing your check for 30 days, and if you for any reason change your mind, let me know and I will send your uncashed check back.

You may ask, why am I willing to share my formula for wealth? Well, simply because those of you who order my material will be helping to increase my net worth.

You shouldn't care if I profit as long as you profit. I guarantee that you'll be satisfied that my methods will help you or I'll send your money back!

"FINANCIAL FREEDOM"

To order, simply take any size paper, write the words "Financial Freedom", and send your name and address, along with a check for $10.00 to Mark O. Haroldsen, Inc., Dept. G-397, 2612 So. 1030 West, Salt Lake City, Utah 84119

If you send for my materials now, I will also send you documents that will show you precisely how you can borrow from $20,000 to $200,000 at 2% above the prime rate using just your signature as collateral.

By the way, if you feel a little uneasy about sending me a check or money order for $10.00, simply postdate it by 30 days which will completely eliminate your risk.

*M3 © Mark O. Haroldsen, Inc 1978

Inquire at your local bookstore for Mark Haroldsen's "How to Wake Up the Financial Genius Inside You."

Figure 4.2 Mark Haroldsen's advertisement.

A NEWS STORY

Some advertisements are written as if they were a news story. Typically, the news story approach involves a question and answer format. This format starts from the first paragraph and continues until the end of the advertisement when the advertiser asks for the order.

Showing And Proving The Benefits

Benefits are the reason people buy anything. As an example, a person purchasing a daily newspaper for 25 cents is making that small purchase because of a perceived personal benefit.

Perhaps the purchaser wants to know about the details of a story on the front page, or perhaps he or she wants to know who won a certain sporting event the previous day. It is also possible that those things hold no interest for the purchaser and that he or she purchased the newspaper to find out at which theaters a new hit movie is playing. Or, perhaps the purchaser just wants to read the comics or find out about the weather forecast.

SHOWING BENEFITS: A MAGAZINE COVER EXAMPLE

I am looking at the cover of the July/August 1991 issue of Income Opportunities magazine. The cover offers a number of benefits for the potential customers who may be looking at magazines in bookstores. The benefits are there to entice potential customers to purchase the magazine.

Let's look at just some of the benefits offered on the cover of this one issue of Income Opportunities:

EARN $80,000/YR. OR MORE: DROP—IN BABYSITTING SERVICE

TEENS: HOW TO MAKE LOTS OF COOL CASH THIS SUMMER

$1,000 EVERY WEEKEND: KID'S ENTERTAINER

16 WAYS TO BIG PROFITS IN FOOD FOR AS LITTLE AS $500

HOME BUSINESS: BIG MONEY FROM CUSTOMERS WITHOUT ADVERTISING

ADVERTISEMENT COPY OBJECTIVES

The advertisement copy has to achieve two important objectives regarding benefits. Those objectives are advertising objectives two and three:

2. Show the potential customers the benefits of your offer.
3. Prove to the potential customers that you can really provide the benefits.

BENEFITS SHOULD BE SPECIFIC

Be specific when you show the potential customers the benefits of your offer. Do not use vague terms or generalities when describing the benefits.

Also, throughout the advertisement copy, stress all the benefits of your offer, not just the benefits you believe are the most important. The benefits you perceive to be small could be big in the eyes of the potential customers.

PROVE YOU CAN PROVIDE THE BENEFITS

Prove to the potential customers that you can really provide the benefits. The simple listing of all the benefits of your offer is enough proof to some potential customers. Some customers may accept your claims because your advertisement appears sincere.

Keep your claims credible. If your claims appear to be unbelievable, admit it. This approach can be good strategy for two reasons. First, it can put you on a more personal, one-on-one level with your potential customers. Second, such admissions can also give you credibility.

You can also prove to the potential customers that you can really provide the benefits by using testimonials.

Testimonials

It is one thing for you to write a good advertisement. It is another thing for one of your previous customers or a person who is an identifiable authority to write something favorable about the information you are selling.

Potential customers are more likely to believe what one of your previous customers or an identifiable authority says than what you say. This is why it is a big plus for your advertisement if you can include testimonials from your previous customers or identifiable authorities.

WRITTEN PERMISSION IS THE STRONGEST TESTIMONIAL

The strongest testimonials include the names and addresses of the satisfied customers. To be able to use their names and addresses, you must have their written permission allowing you to use their testimonial. The Federal Trade Commission requires that you keep the written permission on file.

CAN YOU USE THE TESTIMONIAL WITHOUT WRITTEN PERMISSION?

What happens if a satisfied customer sends you a favorable letter (testimonial) but does not write that you can use his testimonial? You can still use the testimonial, but you can only use the satisfied customer's initials and the city and state he or she is from. This type of testimonial is slightly less credible than the one with written permission to use the testimonial.

Use A Notary Public's Seal or Sworn Statement For Your Claim

You can use a notary public's seal in an advertisement to add credibility to your claim. You can also use sworn statements from your accountant, lawyer or banker. Joe Karbo successfully used such a statement: "On the basis of my professional relationship as his accountant, I certify that Mr. Karbo's net worth is more than one million dollars. (signed) Stuart A. Cogan." See Figure 4.1.

The Money-Back Guarantee

The money-back guarantee is an important element of the advertisement copy. There are several reasons why all mail order operators should offer a money-back guarantee to their customers.

MY MOTTO: BE FAIR TO YOUR CUSTOMERS

I always offer a money-back guarantee to my customers. My number one reason for doing this is my own belief that all mail order operators should be fair to their customers.

Let's be perfectly fair and realistic. The customer will be purchasing information by mail sight unseen, because the mail order operator is not operating a bookstore where the customer can look through any information before he or she purchases it. Therefore, the only way to be fair to the customer is to offer a money-back guarantee. This way, the customer can look through the information (like in a bookstore), and if he or she does not like it, he or she can return it for a refund.

ANOTHER REASON FOR OFFERING A MONEY-BACK GUARANTEE

Another reason for offering a money-back guarantee to mail order customers is that the money-back guarantee gives a mail order operator credibility in the eyes of the potential customers. The money-back guarantee helps gain the potential customer's trust which you must be able to achieve in order to be successful.

The potential customers feel safer in ordering when they know you guarantee what you sell. The money-back guarantee reinforces the idea that the potential customer risks nothing by ordering from you.

DO NOT PUT UNFAIR CONDITIONS ON YOUR MONEY-BACK GUARANTEE

You should not put unfair conditions on your money-back guarantee. An unfair condition would be that the customer has to do something else in addition to returning the information in order to receive a refund.

That "something else" could be that the customer has to actually apply the information you are selling and show you proof that he or she applied it. I consider this an unfair condition because it forces a customer to do something he or she may not want to do.

NEVER GUARANTEE SOMETHING YOU CAN NOT CONTROL

You should be very careful when wording your guarantee. The reason for this is that you should never guarantee something you can not control regardless of the potential for success.

For example, never say something like this in your advertisement: "Read my information. I guarantee it will reduce your golf score by ten strokes." You can not make a guarantee like that. The simple reason is that you have no control over such a guarantee because it is up to the reader of your information to reduce his golf score.

Perhaps after reading your information, the reader will only reduce his golf score by two strokes. Or, the reader may reduce his or her golf score by five strokes. The reader may even reduce his or her golf score by fifteen strokes!

Persuade The Potential Customers To Place An Order Immediately

Advertisement copy is responsible for achieving advertising objective number four: persuade the potential customers to place an order immediately. As discussed earlier in this chapter, this is the most important advertising objective.

Let's discuss various methods you can use to achieve advertising objective number four.

USE KEY WORDS AND PHRASES

Using certain key words and phrases can make your advertisement copy more persuasive. Here is a list of key words and phrases:

YOU
FIRST TIME
HOW TO
MAKE MONEY
DISCOVERY
BETTER HEALTH
INCREDIBLE
SAVE MONEY
NOW
IMPROVE
BE YOUR OWN BOSS
WEALTH
MONEY
ACT NOW
EASY
JUST ARRIVED
SECRET
YOU ARE IN LUCK
SEX
I WANT TO SHARE
MODERN
AMAZING
VALUE
LOW COST
LOVE
IT'S HERE
FREE
SIMPLE
MONEY BACK
SPECIAL
HURRY
AT LAST
COMPARE
LAST CHANCE
NEW
ORDER NOW
QUICK
SEXUAL POWER
FOUND
QUIT WORK

YOUR ADVERTISEMENT SHOULD BE EASY TO READ

Write your advertisement so that even a ten year old child could understand it. This is not because your potential customers are not smart, but because most of them will not give your advertisement their full attention.

If you make your advertisement difficult to read and hence force potential customers to study it carefully, your advertisement will probably not succeed. Why? Because most potential customers are not interested in taking the time to study your advertisement. So, make your advertisement simple and easy to read.

When your advertisement is finished and you are unsure if it is easy to read, ask an average ten year old child to read it. If the ten year old tells you he or she has problems understanding parts of the advertisement, rewrite those parts so that he or she can understand them.

Avoid using long and difficult to understand words. Try to avoid using long sentences. If you write a very long sentence, try to break it up into two sentences.

YOUR ADVERTISEMENT COPY SHOULD BE CONVERSATIONAL

Write your advertisement as if you are talking to a potential customer. If you write in this manner, the potential customers will feel as if you are speaking to them directly when they read your advertisement.

USE THE WORD "YOU" A LOT

You should use the word "you" in your advertisement as much as possible. Remember, the most important advertising objective is to persuade the potential customers to place an order immediately. The word "you" speaks directly to each individual potential customer.

REPEAT KEY WORDS AND PHRASES

Do not hesitate to repeat key words and phrases. Repeat them as often as necessary. When you are writing your advertisement copy, do not ever try to replace a key word with a synonym. This will only confuse the reader—the potential customer. Use the key words and phrases over and over again. They are proven winners and they can make your advertisement successful.

WRITE IN THE "ACTIVE" VOICE

You should write your advertisement in the active voice instead of the passive voice. An example of the active voice is: "You can reduce your golf score by ten strokes!" An example of the passive voice is: "Ten strokes can be reduced from your golf score!" The active voice makes your advertisement much stronger than the passive voice.

YOUR ADVERTISEMENT SHOULD ZERO IN ON YOUR OFFER ONLY

If you are selling information on how to lose weight, your advertisement should zero in on the merits of your information only. Do not waste any words trying to convince the potential customers that they should lose weight.

IF YOU CAN, USE A PHOTOGRAPH IN YOUR ADVERTISEMENT

I believe that using a photograph can improve advertising results. A photograph can attract the eyes of the potential customers towards your advertisement. It can also add credibility to your offer.

My Experience With Photographs

It has been my experience with photographs that when I have made my photograph work hand-in-hand with the headline of my advertisement, the result has been a very successful advertisement.

Put Captions Under Photographs

Your potential customer's eyes are naturally drawn to the photograph in your advertisement. Therefore, you should try to put one of the best points of your offer as a caption under the photograph.

ASK THE POTENTIAL CUSTOMERS TO PLACE AN ORDER

Many advertisements fail because they fail to ask for action. Asking the potential customers to place an order is typically done at the end of the advertisement. If you want to have a successful advertisement, you simply must ask the potential customers to take action—to place an order.

Ask For An Immediate Order

Asking the potential customers to place an order immediately (now) is in my opinion better than asking them simply to place an order. The idea is to encourage the potential customers to make an immediate decision rather than thinking about it for perhaps two weeks.

The longer potential customers wait to make a decision, the less likely they are to place an order. The following are a few phrases asking for immediate action: "act today," "don't wait another day," "send for your order right now" and "don't wait another minute."

The "Soft Sell" Approach

What is very interesting to note is that some of the most successful mail order advertisements simply ask for action instead of asking for immediate action. These advertisements are sometimes called "soft sell" because they are more subtle when asking for action. The "soft sell" advertisements can at times be even more effective than the ones asking for immediate action.

Look at Joe Karbo's "The Lazy Man's Way To Riches" advertisement, Figure 4.1. At the end of the advertisement he states:

> "I know you're skeptical. After all, what I'm saying is probably contrary to what you've heard from your friends, your family, your teachers and maybe everyone else you know. I can only ask you one question.
>
> How many of them are millionaires?
>
> So, it's up to you:
>
> A month from today, you can be nothing more than 30 days older—or you can be on your way to getting rich. You decide."

Note that Karbo was able to make the statement about ". . . 30 days older" because he promised not to deposit his customers' checks for 31 days.

YOU MUST ASK FOR THE ORDER

Failing to ask the potential customers to place an order is bound to cause your advertisement to fail. It is similar to the following example: a football team, down by six points, drives the length of the field to score a touchdown in the last second of the game. The game is thus tied and the extra point will of course win the game. However, for whatever reason, the coach decides not to even attempt the extra point and the game ends in a tie.

A football coach like that is a loser and an advertisement which fails to ask for an order is doomed to be a loser also. Do not be like that football coach. Do not be shy, ask the potential customers to place an order.

THE ORDER FORM OR COUPON

The order form is often referred to as the coupon, order blank or order card. Coupon is the term usually used when referring to a display (space) advertisement. The terms "order form," "order blank" and "order card" are usually used when referring to a direct mail advertisement.

The order form or coupon achieves advertising objective number five by making it easy for the potential customers to place an order. The order form or coupon is where you place the key code and it also ensures that the customer does not forget to include his or her name and address when the customer sends in his or her order.

The Order Form Or Coupon Can Bring You Additional Orders

The order form or coupon is much more than just a convenient place for your customer to fill out his or her name and address. It is a sales tool just like advertisement copy. Because it is a sales tool, the order form or coupon can bring you additional orders.

The order form or coupon should restate at least a few of the most important points made in the advertisement copy. It can also contain or restate the guarantee.

Joe Karbo's coupon in "The Lazy Man's Way To Riches" advertisement, Figure 4.1, definitely brought Karbo additional orders: "Joe, you may be full of beans, but what have I got to lose? Send me the Lazy Man's Way to Riches. But don't deposit my check or money order for 31 days after it's in the mail."

REMOVE ANY OBSTACLES FROM THE ORDER FORM OR COUPON

Remember, you must make it easy for the potential customers to place an order immediately. Your order form or coupon should not contain anything that may confuse your potential customers. Read and reread your order form or coupon. If there is anything there that might be an obstacle which could keep the potential customers from ordering, remove it.

EDITING YOUR ADVERTISEMENT

When you finish writing your advertisement, you should edit it. You can get your friends and family members to help you edit your advertisement for possible spelling and grammar mistakes. I have had family members, friends and even my typesetters edit my advertisements.

As discussed in the beginning of this chapter, before you run your advertisement you should consult a lawyer who is an expert in mail order. For more information, study very carefully "Legal Aspects To Consider Regarding Advertising" in Chapter 10, "Tax, Record Keeping and Legal Aspects."

TESTING ADVERTISEMENTS

Mail order offers you the opportunity to test your advertisement the first time you run it, thereby limiting your risk. As noted earlier in this chapter, the headline is by far the most important element of an advertisement.

Because of the importance of the headline, if you want to test elements of your advertisement, you should test two different headlines against each other. Some of the other elements you can test besides the headline include price, advertising copy and color.

Do Not Test More Than One Advertisement Element At A Time

If you want to test more elements than just the headline, make sure you do not test more than one element of the advertisement at a time. The reason is that you will not be able to determine how the different elements effected the results.

How To Test Advertisements

The most widely used method of testing display (space) advertisements is called the "split run." You run two different ads in the same issue of a publication. Half of the magazine or newspaper copies contain your ad "A" and the other half contain your ad "B." You should key the two ads differently so that you can measure the results. Note that not all newspapers and magazines can do split runs. Also, split runs cost more than regular runs.

The most widely used method of testing direct mail advertisements has been the Nth name test. To find out more specific information about testing direct mail advertisements read Chapter 11, "Direct Mail Advertising."

A Successful Test

Many mail order companies consider a test to be successful if they just break even—if the money they receive from their advertisement covers their costs. The reason is that they plan to make a lot of money on the "back end"—selling their customers other information over a period of time.

It is not unusual for a mail order company's average customer to purchase more than $200 worth of additional information after the initial sale. Let's be conservative, cut this figure in half, to $100, and let's say the initial test broke even and yielded 125 customer names. Those 125 customers, over a period of time, may buy $100 worth of additional information, for a gross profit of $12,500.

Chapter 5

The Greatest Business In The World

Based on my success, if mail order is not the greatest business in the whole wide world, I honestly do not know what is! I have made money in mail order selling information. Naturally, based on my experience, I believe information is an ideal mail order product.

The Free Enterprise System

Millions of people enjoy the benefits of the free enterprise system in the United States and all over the free world. The car you drive, the food you eat, your clothes, your television set and almost everything else in your life is a product of the free enterprise system.

MORE THAN MATERIAL POSSESSIONS

The beauty of the free enterprise system is not only the material possessions it provides. Just as important benefit of the free enterprise system is that it makes the achievement of an individual's dreams of financial independence possible.

Only in the free enterprise system can an individual start a business for himself or herself and watch it grow fulfilling all of his or hers goals. Of all the businesses a person can start in the free enterprise system, I believe the mail order business is the greatest.

Why Mail Order

There are many other reasons why I believe that mail order is the greatest business in the world besides the fact that I have made a great deal of money in it. Here is a list of just some of them.

1. The market for mail order is huge. It is a $200 billion industry and it is growing by 12% or more every year.
2. It has a big advantage over most other businesses because your customer pays you before you ship your product to him. This means you do not have to worry about not getting paid and how you will collect the money.
3. It can be done by anyone, young or old, male or female, from any walk of life.
4. It does not matter what your background is.

5. It does not even matter if you live in a big city, the smallest town or somewhere in between.
6. You can start out of your home while keeping your present job.
7. There is no need to have an office or employees.
8. You can start whenever you want by reading "My Amazing Discovery" in the morning, evening or in the afternoon of any day of the week.
9. You can sell your own information or you can sell information someone else created.
10. You can avoid incurring printing and inventory costs by having a wholesaling company mail the information directly to your customer after he or she orders. This is called drop-shipping.
11. A small mail order operator selling information can avoid competing against the big publishing companies in the bookstores.
12. You can test market your product to a specific market for free or at a relatively low cost. If your test is successful you can expand your promotion rapidly. Eventually, the whole world can be your market!

Mail Order Terminology

Most of you have heard of mail order and some of you have even heard of the following terms closely identified with mail order:

Direct mail
Direct marketing
Direct response

Let's see what all these terms mean:

Mail order—You offer a product or a service to potential customers, they order by mail and you or a drop-shipper fulfill your customers' orders by mail.

Direct mail—You send a solicitation letter, flyer or catalog to potential buyers direct by mail (direct mail) to their home or place of business. They then respond by ordering your information and you mail it to them or have it drop-shipped to them.

Direct response—You run ads, direct mail or radio or TV commercials. Your customers respond directly to you (direct response). You then mail the information to your customers or have it drop- shipped to them.

Direct marketing—You market your information directly to your potential customers (direct marketing) using mail order, telemarketing, personal sales, direct mail, or direct response. Your customers order the information from you. You can then mail the information to your customers or have it drop-shipped to them.

As you can see, direct mail, direct response and mail order can all be considered to fall under the category of direct marketing because the customers are being solicited and serviced directly. Also, direct mail, direct response and direct marketing can all involve mail order because the orders can be solicited and fulfilled by mail.

SOME OTHER TRUE MAIL ORDER SUCCESS STORIES

I am not the only person who has made a great deal of money in mail order. In fact, the mail order business has numerous other true success stories. I am writing about some of the other true mail order success stories for the same reason I included the section "My Story" in this book—to get you to start believing in yourself. To get you to start thinking "If these people could do that, so can I do that!"

Joe Karbo

The story of Joe Karbo is a classic mail order rags-to-riches story. Karbo, who never finished college, found himself $50,000 in debt with a wife and eight children to provide for. Karbo believed in himself and did not give up.

KARBO REFUSED TO DECLARE BANKRUPTCY

Karbo's attorney advised bankruptcy but Karbo had a better idea. He called his creditors and told them that although he had no money to pay them off immediately, he would pay them off over time if they agreed on a regular payment schedule. Karbo's creditors accepted his proposal.

KARBO'S EARLY MAIL ORDER SUCCESSES

A short time after Karbo made the deal with his creditors he wrote and sold through the mail a book called "The Power of Money Management." He sold over 100,000 copies of this book for $3.95 each with an advertisement headlined "Get Out of Debt in 90 Minutes without Borrowing."

He also sold more than 100,000 copies of a $10 book on horse-race handicapping and had many other successful mail order books and products before he embarked on his "The Lazy Man's Way to Riches" campaign.

"THE LAZY MAN'S WAY TO RICHES"

Karbo wrote the famous "The Lazy Man's Way to Riches" advertisement in about two hours. He sold a booklet based on his own rags-to-riches success story. The booklet was a combination of mail order marketing methods and positive thinking principles that Karbo called "Dyna Psych."

In one year alone, Karbo sold 173,000 copies of "The Lazy Man's Way to Riches." At $10 per copy, that adds up to $1.73 million in one year. "The Lazy Man's Way to Riches" has been translated into many languages and sold in countries all over the world. Over 1,250,000 copies of "The Lazy Man's Way to Riches" have been sold.

Mark Haroldsen

Mark Haroldsen was paying $135 a month rent for a run-down house in Denver, Colorado. His wife was expecting their second child and he had to borrow $300 from his father and father-in-law just to buy groceries and pay the rent. To make matters even worse, he was $7,000 in debt.

Haroldsen, who graduated with a C- average from Ames high School in Ames, Iowa, believed in himself and did not give up. He started out by investing in real estate. Then he saw a way to make even more money.

"HOW TO WAKE UP THE FINANCIAL GENIUS INSIDE YOU"

Haroldsen wrote a book called: "How to Wake Up the Financial Genius Inside You." He wrote an advertisement with the title of his book as the headline and embarked on a mail order campaign. In one year he sold over 250,000 mail order copies at $10 each. That is over $2.5 million in one year.

Haroldsen did not stop there. His book also made its way into bookstores where it made him still more money. He established a monthly magazine, the "Financial Freedom Report." He developed a personal course of instruction and ran seminars all over the country. He made a cassette tape of the course and sold it too.

Melvin Powers

Melvin Powers started in the mail order business when he wrote a book on hypnotism that no publisher would publish. Melvin Powers believed in himself and did not give up. He started with less than $100 and made millions.

He wrote a small advertisement and received 201 orders the twelfth day after the advertisement appeared. In only one day he received $1,005. Powers was on his way to a great mail order fortune.

He went on to form The Wilshire Book Company and sell millions of books, most of them by mail including well known best sellers like "Think and Grow Rich" by Napoleon Hill, "Magic of Thinking Big" by David Schwartz and "Psycho-Cybernetics" by Maxwell Maltz.

Ken Blanchard and Spencer Johnson

Many of you have heard of the "One Minute Manager" written by Ken Blanchard and Spencer Johnson. You have probably seen the book or the cassette tape for sale at your local bookstore.

But how many of you know that Blanchard and Johnson sold 20,000 copies of the book themselves at $15.95 per copy for a total of $319,000 before they sold the publishing rights to the book to Morrow & Co., a big publishing company? After Morrow & Co. purchased the publishing rights, the "One Minute Manager" sold nearly three million copies.

Sam Pitts

Sam Pitts lost his job and was left with three children to raise and support. He filed for bankruptcy. He had no formal education or even a telephone in his apartment but he had an idea.

He ran a small, $5 or $6 per week classified advertisement for 3 to 4 weeks in a local *Thrifty Nickel* (a publication similar to various local publications such as the *Greensheet, Shopper's Guide* or *Penny Savers*). He sold two typewritten pages of information about credit cards for $5 directly from his classified advertisement. This is called "The One-Step Approach" and for more information about it, see Chapter 12, "Classified Advertising."

The *Thrifty Nickel* billed him for his advertisement so he did not have to pay any up front money. He began receiving orders and filled them by making copies of two pages of information he had a friend type up. His classified advertisement business grew and he deposited $118,000 the first year.

Brainerd Mellinger

Brainerd Mellinger started his mail order business with less than $100. He imported from Germany into the United States a miniature version of the famous Black Forest cuckoo clock. The product turned out to be a huge success.

Mellinger later expanded his mail order business to include selling information by mail including an import-export training course, newsletters and seminars.

Eileen and T.J. Rohleder

Eileen Rohleder and her husband T.J. Rohleder owned a small carpet-cleaning company which barely brought in enough money to pay their bills. She read a book about mail order and decided that mail order would be a perfect at-home business.

She and her husband started their mail order business with only $300 and made over $6,500,000 in less than four years. They started with a small booklet and a small display advertisement in a magazine.

Benjamin Suarez

Benjamin Suarez (also spelled Swarez) went from working for a big company as a computer programmer to starting an astrology club by direct mail. He gave his astrology club a great name: American Astrological Association.

He went on to earn hundreds of thousands of dollars a year with numerous other successful mail order campaigns including: "Ohio Man Discovers The Secret of How to Escape The American Rat Race" and "How To Get Every Cent Uncle Sam Owes You."

David Bendah

David Bendah was in debt and barely getting by working as a waiter. Bendah believed in himself and did not give up. He put together a book on saving money at home and invested a few hundred dollars on his first advertisement. Like so many people before and after him, he found his mailbox stuffed full of orders.

This led him to form Lion Publishing Company which has sold over 500,000 books. A Lion Publishing book about unclaimed money has sold over 100,000 copies and a book about making money with your camera sold over 30,000 copies. Those two books alone brought in over $1.5 million.

Richard Thalheimer

Richard Thalheimer was selling office supplies door to door when he started his first mail order company to sell office supplies through the mail. Thalheimer put himself through law school with the profits from his first company.

He found a wristwatch chronograph, made in Asia, placed a small ad for it and made a $600 profit in one month. He then placed an ad in *Runner's World* magazine. This ad produced $90,000 in profits and led to the formation of Thalheimer's second mail order company called Sharper Image. His second company had $3 million in sales the first year.

Today, the Sharper Image catalog is one of the most prestigious mail order catalogs in the world, with over 20 million readers monthly. Sharper Image also has over 70 retail stores including stores in Japan, Switzerland and Argentina.

CUSTOMER RELATIONS

Much of Thalheimer's success is due to his excellent customer relations. All of Sharper Image products come with a risk-free 30-day guarantee. Thalheimer also offers Price Matching™ : he guarantees his customer's the best price on the products he sells. If a customer sees an advertisement with a product on sale for a lower price, Thalheimer will sell the product at that price provided the customer sends him the advertisement.

Chapter 6

Selling Information By Mail

Almost anything can be sold by mail. Just look at catalogs of some of the bigger mail order companies and you may be amazed by the variety of products and services sold through the mail. Books, jewelry, television sets, stereos, computers, golf equipment, skiing equipment, tennis equipment, furniture, multi-million dollar real estate, office equipment, etc.—almost anything can be sold by mail.

Information Is An Ideal Mail Order Product

Although almost anything can be sold by mail, I believe that information is an ideal mail order product. We live in an information age and today, more than ever before in the history of mankind, people are seeking "how to" information and specialized knowledge on a variety of subjects.

Why People Purchase Information By Mail

Have you ever wondered why so many people purchase information by mail? If you have not wondered about this in the past, you should do so now before you embark on the road to success in the mail order business. The following is a list of some of the reasons why people purchase information by mail.

1. The only way they can buy it is by mail—when people see certain information being advertised by mail and they can not find the same information elsewhere, they will usually purchase it by mail.
2. Convenience—we live in an age when in most families, both husband and wife work but they can not afford to pay anyone to clean their homes, cut their grass and shop for them. Shopping by mail is the easiest way to shop. Also, many people living in rural areas do not have access to large and wide selections of books unless they shop by mail.
3. Save money on purchases—many people compare prices and may find out that a certain book is less expensive if purchased by mail. Then they tend to make the decision to save money and buy by mail.
4. Save money on gas—for years many of us have been aware of the energy crisis and the high price of gasoline. The Gulf War against Saddam Hussein heightened that awareness and could lead to greater mail order sales.
5. Save time on parking, walking and waiting—shopping in retail shopping malls is extremely time consuming. Shopping by mail in the comfort of

your home saves time. To many people time is money so they shop by mail when they can.

6. Special interests—many people have special interests and hobbies. Information dealing with making money, health, gardening, sports, exercise and many other similar interests and hobbies is ideal for mail order marketing.
7. Avoiding contact with rude, pushy and incompetent salespersons—many people hate to shop in retail stores because many times the salespersons irritate them. In order to avoid unnecessary irritation, many people shop by mail.

The Best And Worst Months To Advertise In

Sales of certain products are very seasonal. Clothes and sports equipment are good examples. Selling information by mail is not a seasonal business but you should be aware that certain months of the year work better than other months.

My mail order experience has been in selling information to opportunity seekers. Following are the best and worst months to advertise in (best on top, worst on bottom) based on that experience.

SUMMARY

You can see from Figure 6.1 that the best months of the year are early in the year and the fall. May, June and July are three of the worst months because the weather is warm and many potential customers are outside enjoying the sun and not at home reading advertisements.

SIX BEST MONTHS:

1. January—Best month of the year.
2. February—Second best month of the year.
3. March—Small decline from February.
4. April—Small decline from March.
5. October—Almost as good as March.
6. September—Almost as good as October.

GOOD TO AVERAGE MONTHS:

7. August—Medium increase from July.
8. November—Small decline from October.

FOUR WORST MONTHS:

9. May—Medium decline from April.
10. July—Medium increase from June.
11. December—Sharp decline from November.
12. June—Worst month of the year.

Figure 6.1 The best and worst months to advertise in.

December is one of the worst months for opportunity type offers because many potential customers are not at home to read advertisements during Christmas holidays.

Average Daily Mail Order Response Rates

United States Postal Service delivers mail six days a week, Monday through Saturday. My experience has shown me that statistically speaking, more mail is delivered on some days of the week than on others. Following are average daily mail order response rates based on my experience.

SUMMARY

You can see from Figure 6.2 that more mail is delivered on Monday than on any other day of the week. This may be a result of the fact that mail is not delivered on Sunday, so that on Monday the United States Postal Service must deliver mail for Sunday and Monday.

Projecting Mail Order Results

Projecting mail order results is different than predicting mail order results. Predicting is looking into a crystal ball before any results are in and guessing what the results might be in the end. Projecting is looking at one to three weeks of results and making an intelligent estimate what the results might be in the end.

Accurately projecting mail order results is important because it allows you to make decisions regarding your next advertisement or mailing more quickly and correctly which can translate into greater profits.

Projecting mail order results is easy for me, because I have a lot of mail order experience and I have kept good records. To get the benefit of my experience, see Chapter 7, "Display Advertising" and Chapter 11, "Direct Mail Advertising" for specific information on projecting results based on my experience.

Day	% of the weekly response
Monday	29%
Tuesday	7%
Wednesday	13%
Thursday	15%
Friday	17%
Saturday	19%

Figure 6.2 Average daily mail response rates.

Price

The price you charge for the information you sell is important. Economists tell us that as we lower the price, the consumers buy more of whatever we are selling. However, in real life, economists are not always right. In real life, under the right circumstances (such as a unique offer or product), a higher price may generate more sales than a lower price.

To me, price is largely a function of what my competitors charge for similar information. You can always run a test of two different prices if you are uncertain about the price you want to charge. See "Testing Advertisements" in Chapter 4, "How To Write A Successful Advertisement."

Options For Selling Information By Mail

You have three options for selling information by mail:

1. Obtain information already written.
2. Write your own information.
3. Have someone write the information for you.

HOW TO OBTAIN INFORMATION ALREADY WRITTEN

You do not have to write your own information or have a ghostwriter write the information for you in order to sell information by mail. You can obtain information already written. By doing this you can instantly sell information by mail.

Drop-Shipping

One way you can obtain and sell information already written is by using the drop-shipping method. A number of wholesaling companies have information you can sell using the drop-shipping method.

Drop-shipping allows you to get started without incurring printing and storing costs of the information you will sell. When you drop-ship, you sell ready-made information and a drop-shipper fills your customers' orders.

A drop-shipper prints the information and also mails the information directly to your customers. David Bendah, the owner of Lion Publishing Co., in his book "Making $500,000 A Year In Mail Order" notes that he started out with drop-shipping and that since then he has published and stored all of his books.

HOW DROP-SHIPPING WORKS

The way this works is you send to the drop-shipper your customers' names and addresses and his share of the money your customers have paid you. Typically, the drop-shipper's share is from 30% to 70% of the price of the information.

WIN/WIN/WIN SCENARIO

A drop-shipping arrangement is good for all three parties involved in the transaction. In a word, it is a win/win/win scenario.

The drop-shipper wins because he or she gets about 30% to 70% of the price of the information without having to sell it to anyone. Your customer wins because he or she gets the information he or she wants. You win because you can sell the information without having to print and store it.

NAMES AND ADDRESSES OF SOME DROP-SHIPPERS

Wilshire Book Company
12015 Sherman Road
North Hollywood, CA 91605

Profit Ideas
305 East Main
Goessel, KS 67053

Mascor Publishing Co.
PO Box 8308
Silver Spring, MD 20907

Reprint Rights

Another way you can obtain and sell information already written is by purchasing reprint rights. One of my most successful mail order projects involved information I had purchased the reprint rights to. Purchasing reprint rights means that you purchase a book along with the right to have your printer reprint (reproduce) it for you.

Of course, when you purchase reprint rights you will have to mail the book to your customers. Most printers have very quick turn-around, so you can make sales before printing the books.

NAMES AND ADDRESSES OF SOME COMPANIES SELLING REPRINT RIGHTS

JLM Printers
Box 56
Lakeville, OH 44638

Lelli Printing & Advertising
2650 Cr. 175
Loudonville, OH 44842

Wholesale Books

Another way you can obtain and sell information already written is by purchasing wholesale books. Following are some companies which sell books at wholesale prices.

SpeediBooks
PO Box 482
Richfield, OH 44286

Allen Publishing Co.
PO Box 1889
Reseda, CA 91335

Premier Publishing Co.
PO Box 330309
Fort Worth, TX 76163

D & L Bramble
111 Downey Road
Brockton, MA 02402

DLM
1 DLM Park
Allen, TX 75002

Random House Inc./Outlet
Book Company
400 Hahn Road
Westminster, MD 21157

Sunnyside Publishers
PO Box 29
Lynn, MA 01903

Remainder/Bargain Books

Remainder books are books which usually did not sell well when they were originally published and consequently the publisher is trying to get rid of them. That is why they are a bargain. They can often be purchased for less than the cost of printing them.

Some remainder books may be good books which were poorly promoted by the original publisher. You can purchase remainder books for up to 90% off their original price.

The best way to analyze if a remainder book deal is good for you is to ask yourself two questions. First, can the book be profitably promoted? Second, can you purchase the book for less than it would cost you to print it? If the answer to both questions is "yes," you may have found a bargain you can make money with.

NAMES AND ADDRESSES OF SOME COMPANIES SELLING REMAINDER BOOKS

Book Sales
110 Enterprise Ave.
Secaucus, NJ 07094

Bookthrift
45 W. 36th St.
New York, NY 10018

Outlet Book Co., Inc.
400 Hahn Road
Westminster, MD 21157

The Texas Bookman
2703 W. Mockingbird Lane
Dallas, TX 75235

Crown Publishers
225 Park Avenue South
New York, NY 10003

YOU CAN FIND OTHER DROP-SHIPPERS, COMPANIES SELLING REPRINT RIGHTS, REMAINDER BOOKS AND WHOLESALE BOOKS

New drop-shippers, companies selling reprint rights, companies selling wholesale books and remainder/bargain book companies are being started all the time.

You can find their advertisements with their offers and addresses in publications listed in Chapter 7, "Display Advertising" and in other publications you can find at your local bookstores and libraries.

WRITING INFORMATION

Besides obtaining information already written, you have two other options for selling information by mail. You can write your own information or have a ghostwriter write the information for you.

You Can Write Your Own Information

Writing your own information is not as difficult as it might seem. Almost everyone at one time or another gets an idea and a desire to write a book, a booklet or a pamphlet. Very few people follow through on this idea. That is unfortunate for three reasons.

First, most people have the ability to write, especially if their idea concerns information instead of fiction. Second, writing gives you an incredible feeling of accomplishment. You will feel elated and very proud seeing your ideas and thoughts in print. Third, writing can be very financially rewarding as well.

IT IS EASY TO WRITE INFORMATION

Fiction can be very difficult to write. Information, or non-fiction as it is often referred to, usually involves a "how to" subject. This type of writing is easy to write because you do not have to be a famous writer like Stephen King to be successful.

Writing "how to" information does not require a special writing or literary style as does writing fiction. The reason for this is that "how to" information is judged by its content and not by the style of writing.

Almost anyone can write non-fiction, "how to" information. I can not show you how to become a fiction writer the caliber of a Stephen King, but I can show you how to write "how to" information.

YOUR WRITING DOES NOT HAVE TO BE PERFECT

Do not worry about making your writing perfect. You do not need to create a literary masterpiece to be successful because you will be writing information and not a work of fiction. As a result, your readers will be primarily interested in the content of your information, not the style it is written in.

Your first writing project can be small, just a short pamphlet for example. Later, as you gain experience, you can write booklets and even full-length books. You can improve your pamphlet, booklet or book and add information to it even after you start selling it. The more useful information it contains, the more value it has for the reader and the more money you can charge for it.

I will show you how you can put together a successful book, booklet or pamphlet. I will share with you a simple formula which many successful writers use to write information. If you follow the formula, you too can have a best seller on your hands.

THE EASIEST WRITING PROJECT

A directory is the easiest writing project you can undertake. One of my first mail order projects was a directory. A reason a directory is the easiest writing project is that once you do the research, the work is almost done.

A directory usually consists of compiled names and addresses and perhaps telephone numbers. You simply write an introduction and arrange the directory information you have researched in a logical order.

The Formula For Writing Information

There is a very simple formula for writing information or non-fiction. The formula is to break down a big job of writing into a number of smaller, easily manageable jobs.

When you write non-fiction, "how to" information, the first step is to choose a topic (subject) you want to write about. The second step is research. The third step is to create an outline. The fourth step is to actually write. The fifth step is editing and proofreading. You also have to choose a title, and this step can be first or last, that is up to you.

Choose A Topic

Do not put limits on yourself when choosing a topic or subject you will write about. Keep in mind that you can write about a topic you are familiar with or a topic you are not familiar with because doing research will familiarize you with your topic.

An important factor in choosing a topic is not that you are already familiar with the topic but that you are genuinely interested in it. If you are interested in it, you will enjoy doing the research, learning more about your topic. Choosing a topic you are interested in will also make writing about it much easier.

CONSIDER WHAT MOTIVATES PEOPLE TO PURCHASE INFORMATION

Before you choose your topic it is important to know what motivates people to purchase information. A reason for this is that ideally you should look at the market first, and then choose what type of information to offer to the market. I will make this easy for you by giving you a variety of reasons why people purchase information.

1. To make more money.
2. To make a dream, a goal or a desire come true.
3. Security—to protect their own or their family's future.
4. To be healthy.
5. To have more leisure time.
6. To have personal power.
7. To be their own boss.
8. Pleasure—to be able to enjoy life more.
9. To get people to like, love or admire them more.
10. To have a business of their own.
11. To be more attractive to the opposite sex.

12. To protect what they already own.
13. To own valuable things.
14. To win at gambling or horse races.
15. To make any type of work easier.

Your Job May Provide You With A Topic

Perhaps your job gives you access to information and ideas people may be interested in. This may hold true if you have a white collar or a blue collar job. Let me give you some examples.

If you work at a bank, you may be able to show people the advantages and disadvantages of the numerous types of accounts banks and savings and loans are offering to the consumers. Your readers could benefit because you would show them how they could earn more money from their bank investments and how they could save money on banking services.

If you work for an insurance company, you may be able to show people the advantages and disadvantages of the various types of insurance policies available. Your readers could benefit by obtaining better insurance coverage at lower cost.

If you work as an auto mechanic, you may be able to show people a better way to purchase a used car. You may also be able to show them how to maintain their cars in order to prevent costly break-downs from occurring down the road. Your readers could benefit by saving money in the short term and the long term.

Your Hobby May Also Provide You With A Topic

Perhaps your hobby gives you access to information and ideas people may be interested in. If you are an avid fisherman, you may be able to show people how to clean and cook their catch. If you are an avid collector of stamps, you may be able to show people which stamps to buy, which stamps not to buy, how long to hold on to them, how much to pay for them and where to buy them.

DO NOT BE AFRAID TO CHOOSE A TOPIC ALREADY COVERED

Choose your topic carefully and if you discover that it has already been covered, do not be afraid to stick to your decision because this only means that others saw the potential you see. If you discover that the topic has actually been covered numerous times, this only means that there is a lot of money in it.

How many times have topics like making more money, health, fitness, sex, relationships and hobbies been covered? They have been covered many times before and and they will be covered many more times in the future. Why? Because people are interested in those topics.

TWO CATEGORIES OF TOPICS

There are two categories of topics you can write about: general interest and special interest.

General Interest Topics

Topics of general interest appeal to a large audience and include fitness and health, moneymaking opportunities, career opportunities, child rearing, human relationships, personal finance, etc.

Special Interest Topics

Topics of special interest appeal to a narrow audience and include topics such as sailing, parachuting, canoeing, various ethnic cooking methods, flying, handwriting analysis, skiing, etc.

Research

Research is a close, careful study of a particular topic. It involves reading, taking notes and rearranging information. You can do your research at the local libraries. You can use one or more of the libraries in your area—public, city, college and university libraries.

Start at the library closest to you and you can be fairly sure to find many books on your topic. Look through the subject index file in the library for titles of books dealing with your subject. Ask the librarians to help you with your research. Most of them will be glad to do so.

BOWKER'S *BOOKS IN PRINT*

If you are not satisfied with the number of books you find in the index file, ask the reference librarian for Bowker's *Books in Print*—it lists all books still in print by subject, author and title. In the event you find books which are not located in the library where you start your research you can perhaps find those books at the other libraries in your area. If even this proves impossible, you can find them in your local bookstores or order them from the publisher.

READER'S GUIDE TO PERIODICAL LITERATURE

Magazines often provide the up-to-date information on many topics so you may also want to look through *Reader's Guide to Periodical Literature* which lists magazine articles on many topics. Reading magazine articles may lead you to the names of experts who in turn may lead you to more information if you call or write them.

ORGANIZE THE RESEARCH INFORMATION YOU COLLECT

Keep the research information you collect organized in a logical manner. You can use file folders, rubber bands, paperclips—anything to keep related items together and separate from unrelated items. Doing this will also be the groundwork for your next step: creating an outline.

Collect as much information as you can while doing your research. You may not use all of the information you collect but it will be far easier and less time consuming for you to throw out excess information than to go back and do more research once you finish outlining and start writing.

RESEARCH, DO NOT COPY

You should do research, but do not copy the research material because it is illegal to copy copyrighted material. A copyright covers the order of printed words, not ideas or thoughts expressed.

Expressing someone else's ideas in your own words is part of the research process but copying word after word, sentence after sentence, paragraph after paragraph is plagiarism. A good rule of thumb to follow is never copy from someone else's work more than three words in a row.

PERMISSION TO USE COPYRIGHTED MATERIAL

You may find material that you prefer to use exactly as it is instead of for research purposes. You may only want to quote a few words, a sentence or a few sentences from the material. This is called an excerpt, or a passage extracted from a book or an article and quoted in a new book. The author or publisher of the new book must obtain written permission to do this from the author, publisher or news syndicate of the original work.

You may want to reprint an entire article from a magazine or a newspaper or an entire chapter from a book. As was the case with an excerpt, you must obtain written permission before you can do this.

HOW PERMISSION WAS OBTAINED FOR AN ARTICLE USED IN THIS BOOK

While editing this book I came across an article about ghostwriters in the *Austin American Statesman,* a local newspaper. See Chapter 6, Figure 6.5. I found the article very interesting and thought that the readers of this book might feel the same. I decided to obtain permission to use the article.

I made a few phone calls starting with the local newspaper. I was referred to a very professional lady at the New York office of the syndicate which sold the local newspaper the article. She told me that the permission would cost $150 and that she could send me an invoice for the bill the same day. I agreed. See Figure 6.3 for a copy of the invoice.

You do not have to make the contact to obtain permission over the phone like I did. You can write the author, publisher or syndicate for permission and the entire matter can be settled by mail. See Figure 6.4 for an example of a letter you can use to obtain permission to reprint material.

COPYRIGHT YOUR OWN WRITING

You should always copyright your writing. It is valuable property or could become valuable property one day soon. For more information about copyrights see "Copyright Protection" in Chapter 10, "Tax, Record Keeping And Legal Aspects."

Create An Outline

Once you have done your research, you have an idea of what you want to write. Now you should put what you want to write in a logical order. The best and easiest way to do this is to create an outline, a table of contents. Look at the table of contents in the beginning of this book.

THE OUTLINE FOR THIS BOOK

When writing this book, I first decided what the major parts of the text would be. Then I put chapter titles below each major part. My objective was to make my book flow, from the first chapter to the last. After I had the chapter titles, I further organized the research information I had already gathered.

```
DATE:      4-22-92

INVOICE NO:    0492-118                  TERMS: NET CASH

----------------------------------------------------------------
           LOS ANGELES TIMES SYNDICATE INTERNATIONAL
----------------------------------------------------------------

PURCHASE:      Beta Books
               Attn: Walter Honek
               7101 Highway 71 West
               A-9,  Suite 245
               Austin, TX 78735-8328

----------------------------------------------------------------

PURCHASE:      Text: Well-known Ghostwriter Haunt Book Jackets by
               Anemona Hartocollis from Newsday


Usage:                                   $ 150.00


PAYMENT DUE THIS INVOICE:                $ 150.00

----------------------------------------------------------------
MAKE CHECK PAYABLE TO:  LATS-INTERNATIONAL
                        ATTN: Frank Chu, Accounting Manager
                        218 South Spring St.
                        Los Angeles, CA 90012

PAYMENT should be in US Dollars in form of an Int'l Postal Money
Order or International Draft with a U.S. Correspondent Bank
printed on draft.
----------------------------------------------------------------
```

Figure 6.3 A copy of the invoice for permission to use the article in Figure 6.5

The table of contents in the beginning of this book includes only parts and chapters, but my actual outline included much more than that. In my actual outline I wrote some but not all of the headings and subheadings I would later write about in each chapter.

YOUR OWN OUTLINE

One way to approach your outline is to take your research information and your notes and place them in logical piles on the floor. Go through the piles and reorganize them until each pile becomes a chapter in your outline.

At this point you can go back to the individual piles and organize the material and your notes until you have headings and subheadings for the individual chapters. If you find duplication, eliminate it.

Dear ______________________:

I am writing a book about ______________________ titled __________ ______________ I would like your written permission to include the excerpt below in my book.

In exchange for your permission I will acknowledge the source of the excerpt immediately preceding or following the excerpt. I will also send you a copy of my book.

Sincerely,

Material to be reprinted:

____

____

____

____

____

Title and author: ______________________________

Copyright date and holder: ______________________

Page: _____, Line _____ To Page _____, Line _____

Permission granted by: __________________________

Figure 6.4 An example of a letter you can use to obtain permission to reprint material.

Outlines Can Be Modified

Outlines are never set in concrete, so do not worry if you end up changing your outline along the way, even after you begin writing. If you write your outline by hand, you do not have to rewrite it even if you decide to make major revisions. Simply use scissors and tape or glue to add, subtract or rearrange your outline.

How Detailed Should Your Outline Be?

How detailed you make your outline is up to you. There is no right or wrong way, but keep in mind that creating a more detailed outline is likely to make the writing process easier.

Writing

Go to your outline and choose where you want to start writing. One of the advantages of writing non-fiction is that you can easily start anywhere you wish. You do not have to start at page one and proceed page by page, chapter by chapter.

I always prefer to start with the chapter that I know will be the easiest for me to write. That way, before I know it, I have already made quick progress. The important thing in writing is to get started. Once you have established momentum, it will help considerably to carry you through to the completion.

USE SIMPLE LANGUAGE

Try to use short, simple words when writing. Do not try to impress your readers with long, confusing words. Your objective is to communicate your ideas to your readers, not to impress them. The best way to achieve this objective is to write the way you speak.

ALWAYS BE PREPARED FOR CREATIVE THOUGHTS

Once you start writing you will find that your creative juices will work at the strangest times so you should always be prepared for your creative thoughts. I am not sure why, but solo activities such as jogging or driving are particularly effective in causing creative juices to flow.

Always carry a pen and paper or index cards with you regardless of where you are going or what you are doing. If you do not write down your thoughts when they occur to you, you run the risk of losing them forever. Add these thoughts to the pertinent chapter piles.

Tape Recorders

Some people prefer to carry small tape recorders, especially tiny microcassette recorders instead of pen and paper or index cards. I have two problems with this approach. First, it is far easier for me to carry an index card and a pen. Second, I hate the thought of having to transcribe what is on tape onto paper. That is an extra step I would prefer to avoid.

However, the idea of keeping a microcassette recorder in my car does have an appeal because it would allow me to record thoughts immediately instead of waiting until a red light or a stop sign. Perhaps if I lose a great thought because traffic does not allow me to stop and write it down when it comes to me, I will break down and start keeping a microcassette recorder in my car.

WRITE QUICKLY AND EDIT AND PROOFREAD LATER

Do not make the mistake of worrying about your spelling, punctuation and grammar while writing, especially during your particularly inspired sessions. The important thing is to get your ideas and thoughts on paper, not that the spelling and the grammar are perfect. You can always edit and proofread later or have other people do it. For more on this subject, see "Editing" later in this chapter.

What About Writer's Block?

Writer's block occurs when a writer looks at a blank piece of paper and for a period of time has no idea how to proceed. He or she just can not get started. Although this is a common problem when writing fiction, it should not occur when writing information especially if the writer follows the formula for writing information and breaks down a big job of writing into a number of smaller, easily manageable jobs.

In other words, if you get writer's block at any point of writing, remember that you are writing information, not fiction so your writing does not have to be perfect, only informative. Just go through the pile of information on the chapter you are working on again. Find a good starting point and start writing. It really is that simple.

SECTIONS OF THE BOOK

There are always exceptions, but most books, including this one, are divided into three main sections. The first pages are called the "front matter," followed by the text and the "back matter."

THE FRONT MATTER

The front matter consists of the material placed in the beginning of the book up to Chapter One.

Book Reviews or Testimonials

Book reviews or testimonials can be found on the first page of some books. For more information see "Reviews" in Chapter 13, "Free Publicity" and "Testimonials," in Chapter 4, "How To Write A Successful Advertisement."

The Title Page

The title page lists the title and the subtitle (if there is one) of the book. It is on an odd numbered page—on the right-hand side. It may also list the name of the author, the publisher and the location of the publisher. The title page may consist of two pages when the name of the author is listed on the preceding page.

The Copyright Page

The copyright page follows the title page and lists the name and address of the publisher, the edition of the book, the disclaimer, the copyright notice, the Library of Congress Cataloging in Publication data, the International Standard Book Number (ISBN) and "printed and bound in the United States of America."

For information about the Library of Congress Cataloging in Publication data, write to The Library of Congress, Cataloging in Publication Division, Washington D.C., 20540.

The International Standard Book Number is a unique number issued by R.R. Bowker which identifies the edition and publisher of a book. For information about obtaining an International Standard Book Number for your book, write to R.R. Bowker, 121 Chanlon Rd., New Providence, NJ 07974.

Disclaimers

Disclaimers are often found on the copyright page. They are a form of legal protection for the author and the publisher regarding the use, content or subject matter of the material in the book.

The Dedication Page

The dedication page usually consists of a short statement of praise by the author for a family member, spouse, a friend or some other third party.

Table Of Contents

The table of contents should start on an odd numbered page—on the right-hand side. It will include the number of each chapter, the title of each chapter and the beginning page number of each chapter.

The Foreword

The foreword is written by someone other than the author and it is on an odd numbered page—on the right hand side. It is in fact a pitch for the book and the name of the person making the pitch appears at the end of the foreword.

The Introduction

The introduction is where the author tells the reader why he or she wrote the information. It can come before Chapter One in which case it is part of the front matter. Or, it can be Chapter One as it is in this book, in which case it is part of the text.

Your information should start with your best foot forward. Make your introduction, especially the first couple of paragraphs as interesting as possible to capture the attention of your readers. Show them the benefits of reading your information. If your readers are bored with your introduction, or if it fails to show them the benefits of reading your information, they may not read past the introduction.

After you write it, read and reread your introduction a number of times. Put yourself in the place of the readers of your information. Ask yourself the following question: "If I was a reader, would the introduction help persuade me to keep reading?"

Ask your family members or friends for their opinion as you should do with your advertisement. See "Ask Your Family Or Friends For Their Opinion" in Chapter 4, "How To Write A Successful Advertisement."

The Acknowledgements

This is where the author thanks everyone who assisted in the preparation of the book.

The Preface

The preface was covered in the discussion of the introduction.

THE TEXT

The text consists of the main portion of the book. It starts with Chapter One and ends with the last chapter. The majority of the information is in the text.

Chapter Titles

Chapter titles should reveal the topic of each chapter. They make it easy for the reader to find what he or she wants. This is particularly true after the reader has read the book once and is referring back to something he or she has already read.

Subheads

Subheads are short lines of print usually set apart from the rest of the text. They can be made to stand out even more by using bold print, larger type size and/or using all capital letters. In writing, you can think of them as secondary chapter titles.

Footnotes

Footnotes are needed only in technical publications. Their purpose is to allow the readers doing research to follow up on the material. They can be placed on the bottom of the page, at the end of the chapter or in the appendix.

The Postscript Or Afterword

The postscript is a personal message from the author to the reader, often wishing the best of luck. Usually it is the last chapter of the text, prior to the back matter. See Chapter 14, "Postscript," in this book.

THE BACK MATTER

The back matter consists of the reference material placed at the end of the book, after the last chapter. It often contains the appendixes, the bibliography, the glossary, the index and resources.

The Appendix

The appendix contains important lists, graphs and charts and may be divided into several sections for easy reference. Books with a large appendix often are used as a valuable reference tool.

The Bibliography

The bibliography lists the research material used in writing the book.

The Glossary

The glossary is an alphabetically arranged list of words with definitions peculiar to the subject of the book.

The Index

An alphabetically arranged list of words giving the page numbers on which each item is mentioned.

Editing And Proofreading

After you have finished writing, you can start to edit and proofread. Editing is adding to, deleting from and polishing the book. Proofreading is proofing your book for spelling, punctuation and grammar. I usually get friends and family members to help me edit and proofread.

ADDITIONAL HELP

If you want to, you can get additional help for editing and proofreading. You can hire an English or Journalism major at a college or university nearest you. You can place an advertisement in the college newspaper or simply find a bulletin board in the English or Journalism department and tack on a note with your phone number on it.

You will not have to pay a student much for editing your manuscript. Most students are eager to earn a little extra money. After the editing and proofreading is completed, type or word process the final version or have someone else do it.

Choosing A Title

As noted earlier, this step can be first or last, that is up to you. A good title can definitely help sell more copies. A good advertisement headline can usually be a good title for the information offered for sale.

The title should be short, catchy and descriptive. Use simple language in your title, make sure it is easy to read and understand. Ask your family or friends about their opinion of the title.

Some examples of short, catchy and descriptive titles which became best sellers in the information field are: "Creating Wealth," "See You At The Top," "Mastering The Art Of Selling," "Nothing Down" and "The Magic Of Thinking Big."

Some titles have been so catchy and descriptive that they have even become standard phrases in the English language: "The One Minute Manager," "Your Erroneous Zones" and "I'm OK, You're OK."

HAVE A GHOSTWRITER WRITE THE INFORMATION

You do not have to write your own information, you can have a writer write the information for you. A writer who would do this is called a ghostwriter.

Ghostwriters

Just because you decide you do not want to write the information yourself does not mean that you should simply tell the ghostwriter the subject and turn him or her loose. You should help the ghostwriter put together the outline and perhaps gather some or all of the research material. If you are an expert on the topic, talk to the ghostwriter about what you know and about your experiences.

Stay on top of the ghostwriter's work. Monitor the progress to make sure the ghostwriter is following the outline and that he or she has not veered off in the wrong direction. You should do all these things because the book will still be yours and because you have the greatest stake in its success.

Read The Ghostwriter's Previous Work

Before you hire a ghostwriter, read some of his or hers previous work. If your information is "How To Make Your Own Kite" and your target market is young kids, do not hire a ghostwriter who prefers to use long and difficult words. You should definitely give this some thought because that could be the difference between success and failure.

How To Find A Ghostwriter

To find a ghostwriter you can use the same techniques I described for finding an editor. You can also contact Research Associates International, 340 E. 52nd St., New York, NY 10022 for a list of ghostwriters.

You can pay your ghostwriter a flat fee or you can offer him or her a share of the profits. If you are just starting out you may want to offer the ghostwriter a share of the profits. If you already have one or more successful marketing campaigns behind you, you may want to offer the ghostwriter a flat fee.

Ghostwriter's Have Sold Millions Of Books

Joe Karbo sold over 1,250,000 copies of "The Lazy Man's Way To Riches" and although only his name was listed as the author of his book, he did not write it. He simply gathered his own material and hired a ghostwriter to put it together on paper. See Chapter 5, "The Greatest Business In The World," for more information about Joe Karbo's success story.

Numerous other successful books have been ghostwritten. See the newspaper article in Figure 6.5.

ART

Art or artwork consists of photographs, graphs and line drawings. Art can greatly enhance the appearance of a book, booklet or pamphlet. It also serves the purpose of breaking up large chunks of printed type.

F4 Austin American-Statesman Sunday, April 12, 1992 This section is recyclable

Well-known ghostwriters haunt the book jackets of celebrities

By Anemona Hartocollis
Los Angeles Times Service

Trump

Cosby

Truman

Kennedy

Ivana Trump, who is currently promoting her new novel, *For Love Alone*, is hardly the first celebrity to put her name on a work of fiction that she didn't write, at least not alone.

Bill Cosby's best-selling books on fatherhood, which straddle a line between fiction and non-fiction, are actually written by Ralph Schoenstein, known to his friends as a funny, extremely nice man who also wrote his own tribute to parenthood, called *My Darling Daughters*. In a brief, jittery interview, Schoenstein insisted that Cosby is a full collaborator: "He dictates, spins it out, and I help put it into print." However, only Cosby's name appears on the book jackets.

One of the most notorious open secrets in the publishing industry is that the series of best-selling Washington murder mysteries ostensibly written by Margaret Truman Daniel, daughter of the late president, are cowritten by Don Bain, a professional ghostwriter living on New York's Long Island. Bain said that he had written 65 books — all but 15 of them under other names. He was willing to talk cheerfully about some projects, like a series of "adult" Westerns, published by Playboy Press, under the pen-name J.D. Hardin, or his greatest triumph as a ghostwriter — *Coffee, Tea or Me?* — a best-selling 1967 book that made the title phrase part of popular culture, which was supposedly written by two airline stewardesses, who toured to promote it.

But his name does not appear on the Truman mysteries, and he said it was "absolutely untrue" that he had anything to do with them.

Yet one journalist recalls Bain bragging at a cocktail party that he wrote the Truman books. And within the publishing industry, the Bain-Truman connection is legendary — as persistent as the never conclusively proven belief that *Profiles in Courage*, for which President Kennedy won a Pulitzer Prize, was actually written by Kennedy speech writer Ted Sorensen, or that *To Kill a Mockingbird* was written not by Harper Lee but by her cousin, Truman Capote.

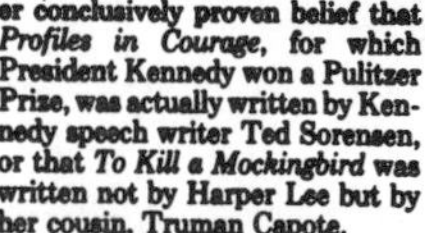

"(Margaret) Truman hasn't written any of those books. She never did," says ghostwriter Lucianne Goldberg, who has served as a speech writer in the Johnson White House and as Kitty Kelly's literary agent. "But unless she steps forward and says yes, you'll never know."

She adds: "A lot of people inside the industry think that to write one or two novels with a ghost is OK. But to let a career go for nine or ten books is sort of obscene."

"The Truman books are known to be ghosted," says Evan Marshall, a New York literary agent. "I know from a number of sources that he (Bain) wrote those books. He probably signed something on pain of death," prohibiting him from talking about it.

Even second lady Marilyn Quayle, who has just published a thriller, *Embrace the Serpent*, with her sister, Nancy Northcott, had heard the rumors about Truman. Asked in a recent interview if she had read the Truman mysteries, Quayle leaned forward and crisply volunteered: "Yes — she has a ghost."

Figure 6.5 Newspaper article about ghostwriters.

Photographs

Photographs are rarely used in fiction but often used in information or non-fiction. Photographs are the cheapest art you can use unless you can produce your own graphs or are a good enough artist to produce your own line drawings.

If you have a 35mm camera you may want to take the photographs yourself. If you have a friend who is a good photographer you can have him or her take the photographs for you. As a last resort, you can hire a professional photographer, but make sure that you shop around for the best price.

Use black and white film instead of color unless you are creating information specifically about art. The photographs you use must be converted to halftones. You and your printer will have to decide how many dots per line you need. The types of photographs that work the best are large, glossy with a lot of contrast.

Line Drawings

A line drawing or line work is a black and white drawing without any shading. If you are a good artist, you may want to produce your own line drawings. If not, and you want original line drawings in your book, you can hire a commercial artist to do them for you. Your local printers or typesetters can refer you to some. As was the case with a professional photographer, make sure that you shop around for the best price.

Clip Art

If you want to use line drawings but do not want to spend the money on a commercial artist, there is an inexpensive alternative. It is called clip art.

Clip art are ready-made commercial line drawings on a large variety of subjects which you can use without permission of the artists. They can be cut out and pasted up. You can purchase clip art at your local art store or use the clip art available at your local printers or typesetters.

Free Art

There is also free art available because any art more than 50 years old is usually in the public domain which means that the copyright has expired. When this happens no one has the rights to it and anyone can use it for free. You can find old art books containing art in the public domain at your local library.

PRODUCING AND PRINTING INFORMATION

Once your information is finished, including the art, you are ready for the production stage. The following information is meant to help you with production and assist you in your dealings with printers.

Typefaces

A typeface is a distinctive style of a set of characters. Numerous and varied typefaces are available. Family is the group name of a typeface which identifies the typeface's distinctive style or shape.

Typeface families are often named after their designers such as "Garamond" and "Goudy." Typeface families can also suggest how a typeface may be used: "Bookman" and "Century Schoolbook."

Many printers and typesetters refer to typefaces as "fonts." The two terms are often used interchangeably, especially in the desktop publishing industry. Although the distinction is not usually critical, a font is a typeface in a particular point size.

TYPES OF CHARACTERS

There are three types of characters: serif, sans serif and decorative.

Serif—A character with small lines or "tails" that project from the ends of the strokes. The text in this book is set in serif type. The headers at the top of the pages are set in an sans serif type.

Sans Serif—A character without serifs. From the French "sans," meaning "without."

Decorative—A character intended for a headline or other special use.

Layout

The layout of your information is important because non-fiction is by nature somewhat dry and relatively difficult for the average reader to read. Fiction does not have to face the same problem because it is by nature imaginative, fun and easy to read.

Have you ever looked at a non-fiction book full of page after page of type with no subheads, photographs, graphs, line drawings, exhibits (in this book they are called "figures"), tables or space for notes? That type of a layout can scare off many readers. You want the layout of your information to interest your readers, to make the information less formidable to read.

Look at some books and study their layouts. Follow the layouts of the most attractively designed books when laying out your information. Note where the page numbers are and what other information is repeated on top or bottom of each page.

LAYOUT VARIABLES

Type size and spacing affect the appearance and the length of your information. If your information will be in a large, notebook sized format, you can double space instead of single space.

Regardless of the format, you can leave extra blank space between paragraphs and before and after subheads. The more blank space there is on an average page, the less threatening and boring it appears to the reader.

Book Measurements

By far the most popular size of books, booklets and pamphlets is 5 1/2" by 8 1/2". Nevertheless, a lot of larger size books, including 8 1/2" by 11" are successfully sold through the mail and in bookstores.

I think that a book of one hundred 5 1/2" by 8 1/2" pages looks better than a book of fifty 8 1/2" by 11" pages, but that is my opinion only. The larger format definitely makes more sense if you have too much material (over 500 pages) for a 5 1/2" by 8 1/2" book.

TRIM SIZE

After the books are printed, they are bound and trimmed. Trim size of books vary depending on the printer and the equipment used. For example, a 5 1/2" by 8 1/2" book may be trimmed to 5 1/4" by 8 1/4".

SHIPPING

The size of your book, booklet or pamphlet will determine the size of your shipping envelopes, padded bags and cartons. Most 5 1/2" by 8 1/2" books can be shipped in 6" by 9" or larger envelopes or padded bags. 8 1/2" by 11" books should be shipped in bags or cartons measuring 9" by 12" or larger depending on the number of pages.

NUMBER OF PAGES

The length of your information is up to you. What is important to remember is that you should strive to give your customers value for their money. Make it your goal to sell valuable information at a fair price.

Since you will be selling information, the value is not just the length but also the quality of the information. Generally, the more specialized the information, the more value it has.

If you want to mail your information by "fourth-class book rate," you must have at least eight pages. If you want to get a Library of Congress Catalog Card Number, you need at least fifty pages.

Cover Design

The book cover should include the title, subtitle if there is one and the name of the author. You can also include a photograph or a line drawing. Make sure the cover is easy to read at a glance.

You may want to spend the extra money to have at least two colors. You should pick two bright and strongly contrasting colors. Ideally, the cover should stand out, it should be eye-catching.

The cover will make the first impression on your customers when they receive your information. Try to make sure the first impression is a good one.

Cover Material

The material for the cover of softcover books can be the same paper as the inside pages of the book (in case of a pamphlet), 70# vellum, leatherette cover stock, antique cover stock or kromecote (glossy).

The cover should be sealed with a lacquer coating or a laminate coating. Coating protects the cover against scuffing during shipment and provides a shiny look. Laminate is a thin plastic film that is rolled off a roll and applied with heat. Lacquer coating is applied like an ink. Durosheen is a lacquer or UV coating. It is a coating which is dried with ultraviolet light and does not crack like a varnish coating might.

Your printer can supply you with different cover stocks and coating samples. As an example, the cover of this book is 12 point C1S (coated on one side) with film lamination.

The Back Cover

There are a number of possibilities of what can go on the back cover.

1. You can have a paragraph or two entitled: "About The Author." Here you would state the background of the author.
2. You can print the table of contents on the back cover.
3. You can use the back cover as sales copy for your information by stating the benefits your customer will gain by reading it.
4. You can print testimonials and book reviews on the back cover. See the back cover of this book.
5. You can print the logo of your company if you have one. See the bottom left-hand corner of the back cover of this book.
6. You can print the bar code with the International Standard Book Number. The bar code consists of black vertical lines and some numbers and it identifies the ISBN, which in turn identifies the publisher, title, author and edition of the book. See the bottom right-hand corner of the back cover of this book.

The Spine

The spine is the part of the book which connects the front cover to the back cover. It usually contains the title, the name of the author and a logo of the publishing company.

Camera-Ready

Camera-ready is the complete copy, artwork or mechanical which is ready for printing. It is black ink on white paper ready for your printer.

Light blue color is invisible to the printer's camera so you can use it to write or mark on your camera-ready. You can buy this type of a pencil, pen or marker at your local art store or your typesetter or printer may give you a light blue pencil for free.

Never use an eraser on your camera-ready. You can use liquid paper to cover anything on your camera-ready that you do not want to show on the printed page. Once your book is camera-ready, keep it clean. Put it away in a safe place where no one is likely to spill something on it or otherwise damage it.

CAMERA-READY PAGE LAYOUT

The exact page layout of your camera-ready depends on your printer and what type of binding you will be using. A typical page layout for a 5 1/2" by

8 1/2" book consists of two camera-ready pages placed side-by-side on an 8 1/2" by 11" sheet.

Before you or your printer make the page layout of your camera-ready, one of you should make a dummy to be sure you are placing the correct pages together.

DUMMY

The dummy is the preliminary "mock-up" of the book, booklet, pamphlet or any printed piece folded to the exact size of the finished job. It is used to verify its correct appearance and size. Use a copy of your camera-ready and not the original when making a dummy.

THE PROCESS FOR MAKING A DUMMY FOR A SADDLE STITCHED PAMPHLET OR BOOKLET

To show how to make a dummy, I am going to take you through the process for making a dummy for an eight page saddle stitched 5 1/2" by 8 1/2" pamphlet. Follow the directions and make your own eight page dummy. If you do that you will learn the process for making a dummy for any length saddle stitched pamphlet or booklet.

The Directions

Take four 8 1/2" by 11" sheets of paper and cut them exactly in half to produce eight 5 1/2" by 8 1/2" pages. Number the eight 5 1/2" by 8 1/2" pages of paper 1 through 8. Write the word "cover" on page number 1 and the words "back cover" on page number 8.

Take the cover (page number 1) and tape it side-by-side to the back cover (page number 8), with the cover on the right. Take page number 2 and tape it side-by-side to page number 7, with page number 7 on the right.

Take page number 3 and tape it side-by-side to page number 6, with page number 3 on the right. Take page number 4 and tape it side-by-side to page number 5, with page number 5 on the right. You now have four 8 1/2" by 11" sheets of paper.

A Pattern

You probably notice a pattern. You taped the lowest numbered pages side-by-side to the highest numbered pages, with the odd numbered pages always on the right.

The Directions Continued

Now take the 8 1/2" by 11" sheet of paper with page numbers 8 and 1 and lay it face down so that page number 1 is on the left. Take the sheet with page numbers 2 and 7 and lay it face up on top of the one with page numbers 8 and 1 so that page number 2 is on the left and page number 7 is on the right.

Take the sheet with page numbers 6 and 3 and lay it face down on top of the one with page numbers 2 and 7 so that number 3 is on the left. Take the sheet with page numbers 4 and 5 and lay it face up on top of the one with page numbers 6 and 3 so that page number 4 is on the left and page number 5 is on the right.

Now fold the sheets to the right and you should see page number 1 (the cover) on top. Flip page number 1 over like you are reading a book and you will see two blank pages with no numbers on them. Did we make a mistake? No, we are simply not finished making the dummy.

Flip the next page over and you should see page numbers 2 and 3. Tape the three outside edges of page number 2 to the three outside edges of page number 1. Tape page number 3 to page number 2 along the middle, where the two pages meet. Flip page number 3 over and you should again see two blank pages. Flip the next page over and you should see pages 4 and 5.

Tape the three outside edges of page 4 to the three outside edges of page 3. Flip page 5 over and you should again see two blank pages. Tape these two blank pages together along the middle, where they meet. Flip the next page over and you should see pages 6 and 7. Tape the three outside edges of page number 6 to the three outside edges of page number 5.

Flip page 7 over and you should again see two blank pages. Tape these two blank pages together along the middle, where they meet. Flip the next page over and you should see page number 8 (the back cover). Tape the three outside edges of page number 8 to the three outside edges of page number 7.

Check The Dummy

You are done. You have finished making a dummy of an 8 page pamphlet. Now check the dummy. Flip it over so that page number 1 (the cover) is on top. Flip page 1 over and you should see pages 2 and 3. Flip page 3 over and you should see pages 4 and 5. Flip page 5 over and you should see pages 6 and 7. Flip page 7 over and you should see page 8 (the back cover).

Do not worry if the pages of your dummy are not exactly even. The objective is not that the dummy should look good but that the pages are put together correctly.

Now you know that your original set up of pages 1 and 8, 2 and 7, 3 and 6 and 4 and 5 side-by-side with the odd numbered pages on the right was the correct page layout and you are ready to put together the page layout of your camera-ready.

Keep The Dummy

Do not throw away the dummy because your printer will need to see it before he or she prints your book. If you have trouble putting together your dummy, you can always have your printer do it for you.

After you have your first books printed, you should always keep one of them to use as a dummy for your next printing even if you use the same printer. Never give your camera-ready to a printer without a dummy unless he or she will make it for you.

Cutting And Pasting

If you use photographs or line drawings you will have to do some cutting and pasting unless your typesetter does it for you. Let's say you have a photograph which you have already converted into a halftone and now you just need to cut it to the correct size and paste it in the appropriate place on your camera-ready.

You need a knife to cut the photograph to the correct size. The best knife to use is an exacto knife, an inexpensive knife used for artwork and found in art stores. Then you need a substance to stick the cut photograph to your camera-ready.

You can use rubber cement or Lectro stick wax. Both of these substances will allow you to reposition your photograph if you are not satisfied with how well you set it the first time.

You can use a light table or a T-square and a light blue pencil to mark where you want to cut and place the photograph before you cut it and properly align it. Some local printers or quick copy shops in your area may have light tables or T-squares you can use in their store for a small hourly fee.

Typewriter

The easiest and least expensive way to produce the camera-ready of your information is to type it. Once the information is typewritten on typing paper the way you want it to look when it is printed, you can take it to your printer. In other words, your typewritten material is your camera-ready.

The disadvantage of using a typewriter to produce your camera-ready is that it produces the lowest quality of output. The right-hand margins are uneven or ragged because a typewriter does not do true typesetting.

If you decide to use a typewriter, you should consider using the 8 1/2" by 11" format because the ragged right margin is much less of a factor in the eyes of the reader when each page is that large.

If you do not know how to type you can learn how very easily. Go to your local library and pick out a book on teaching yourself how to type. If you do not own a typewriter, call the local printers or quick copy shops because some of them may let you use theirs for a small hourly fee. While you have them on the phone, ask them if they also have a desktop publishing system including a laser printer you could use.

Laser Printing

Desktop Publishing is an inexpensive method of producing high quality (resolution of 300 to 1,000 dot per inch or dpi) in-house laser typesetting using a computer, word processing or page layout software and a laser printer. It is easy to learn, especially since most of the software has become quite user friendly. If your local printer has desktop publishing equipment, they can also assist you in learning how to use it.

COMPUTER SYSTEMS

If your local printers offer you a choice of computer system to learn, I would recommend Apple Macintosh over IBM Personal Computers or one of the many IBM PC clones. A reason is that a Macintosh is by far the easiest to learn and to use. You do not even have to learn any commands to run it.

Linotronic Printing

Linotronic printing is higher than 1250 dots per inch printing produced by a machine which uses a light-beam laser to expose the copy onto a special RC paper. It is much more expensive than laser printing. In the unlikely event that you want your camera-ready to have a higher resolution than 300 dots per inch, you can have your information typeset using linotronic printing.

Binding

There are a number of different methods of binding books. Before the books can be bound, the pages must be collated—assembled in a proper numerical or logical sequence.

SADDLE STITCHING

Saddle stitching is a method of binding softcover books using staples. This is one of the least expensive binding methods and many printers and quick copy shops are set up for it. It is also referred to as wire stitching.

Saddle stitching is done by laying out the book with the cover and the pages of the book collated, then stapling (usually in two places) and folding over to make a book. Because paper is "lost" when wrapped around the spine, saddle stitching can only be used for books around 80 pages or less, depending upon the thickness of the paper.

Face Trimming

If the book is more than just a few pages, the inside pages will stick out farther than the outside pages. (A greater amount of outside than inside pages is "lost" when wrapped around the spine). This does not look attractive and you should request that the face of the booklet be trimmed. This means cutting the uneven edges off to produce a smooth and even right edge.

SIDE STITCHING

Side stitching is another inexpensive method of binding books using staples. It is done by laying out the book with the cover and the pages of the book collated, then stapling (usually in two places) from the front to the back cover without folding the pages over as in saddle stitching.

Since paper is not "lost" by wrapping around the spine as in saddle stitching, side stitching can be used to bind books of even a couple of hundred pages. The disadvantage of side stitching is that the books will not open to lay flat.

PERFECT BINDING

Perfect binding is done by stacking the pages, folding the cover around the pages and gluing the pages and the cover at the spine. It is inexpensive and produces very attractive, professional results. Almost all books sold in bookstores are bound using this method.

Perfect binding produces a squared-off spine on which you can print the title and the name of the author. It can only be used for books of at least 50 pages. If your information is not longer than that you may have to use a heavy weight of paper in order to have the thickness required to produce a squared-off spine.

If you are having large quantities of books printed and your information is long enough, perfect binding is the ideal binding method to use.

SPIRAL WIRE BINDING

Spiral wire binding is a coil of wire wound through the holes on the back edge of the book. It is inexpensive but looks cheap, like a notebook. Spiral wire books do not sell well at bookstores.

They do have an advantage over side stitched books because when opened, the book and the pages lay flat for easier reading. Also, you can purchase a relatively inexpensive binding machine at an office supply store and bind your books yourself.

PLASTIC COMB BINDING

Plastic comb binding is similar to spiral wire binding except that plastic instead of wire is used to bind the book. It is relatively expensive, yet looks cheap, like a notebook.

VELO-BINDING

Velo-binding is two hard plastic strips applied at the spine of the book. It is similar to side stitching except it uses melted plastic rivets. Although inexpensive, velo-binding is strong and looks very professional. As was the case with spiral wire binding, you can purchase a relatively inexpensive binding machine at an office supply store and bind your books yourself.

UNI-BINDING

Uni-binding uses a process similar to perfect binding to produce clear plastic covers with black or white spines. The book is placed inside a Uni-bind cover and the spine is then heated and compressed by a machine which glues the pages to the spine. Uni-binding is best for printing small quantities of books. It is inexpensive and produces attractive, professional results.

CLOTH BINDINGS

Cloth binding is a method used for binding hard cover books. It consists of Smyth sewing the stacked pages together and gluing them between two hard paper boards.

Printing Methods

There are basically two printing methods which you can use to print your information. They are called offset printing and photocopying.

OFFSET PRINTING

The printing method which dominates book printing today is called offset printing. Offset printing is a method of printing where the image or the impression from the offset plate is transferred to a blanket and then to the paper. It is also known as photo offset.

PHOTOCOPYING

If the first printing of your information is very small, less than 250 copies, photocopying should be less expensive than offset printing. But do not rush to the local library to photocopy your information. They usually have old copiers which are not of high enough quality for this kind of a job.

High Quality Copiers

Many local printers and quick copy shops have modern, high quality copiers such as the Xerox 8200 and 9500 which copy on both sides of the paper and also collate. They are capable of producing nearly perfect copies without the dots and streaks associated with regular, old copy machines.

Copiers such as the Xerox 8200 and 9500 can produce copies of about the same quality as offset printing. These copiers are large and are usually not set up in the front like the self service machines. They are typically in the back, behind the counter, to be operated only by the employees of the printer or quick copy shop.

Use The Original Camera-Ready Or A First Generation Copy

According to a local quick copy shop I have used, a first generation copy produced on a top quality copier like the Xerox 8200 or 9500 often reproduces better than the original camera-ready. You should talk to your printer before making a decision which one to use.

However, never use a copy of your first generation copy as the camera-ready because the print quality will probably not be as good. Always use either the original camera-ready or a first generation copy every time you have your information photocopied.

Accept Only Quality Work

Before you ask a local printer or quick copy shop for a quote, ask them to make a two sided photocopy of two pages of your camera-ready so you can see what type of quality their copier produces. If they give you copies with dots and streaks, tell them the quality is not acceptable to you and ask them if they can do something to improve the quality. Perhaps simply cleaning the copier glass with a glass cleaner and a paper towel or replacing the toner will solve the problem.

If they again give you copies with dots and streaks, do not listen to excuses. They may try to convince you that every copier will do that, which is not true. Simply repeat the procedure with another local printer or quick copy shop until you are satisfied with the copy quality.

Paper Selection

If you end up photocopying your information, you can use the standard 20 pound bond copy paper for the inside pages. If you have your information offset printed, you have several choices.

Uncoated book stock—The most common are 50-pound or 60-pound. It is used in most books.

Newsprint—Less expensive than uncoated book cover but it looks cheap.

Textured paper stock—Expensive and may make printing more difficult.

Coated book stock—Usually coated with gloss or matte. It looks good but is expensive.

I recommend you use 50-pound paper or 20-pound white bond. The 50-pound paper is commonly referred to by printers as "50# white offset book."

Selecting A Printer

Select a printer for your information very carefully. Solicit at least four and even better, five or more quotes before selecting a printer.

LOCAL PRINTERS AND QUICK COPY SHOPS

Local printers and quick copy shops can print and bind your book. Call or visit a few of the local printers or quick copy shops, tell them the length of your information, the type of cover, binding and paper you are interested in using and ask them for quotes.

Also ask for samples of their previous jobs. It is not unusual for some quotes to be three times higher than others, so do not rely only on your local printers and quick copy shops for quotes.

OUT OF TOWN PRINTERS

Contact at least one of the short-run printers and at least one of the longer-run printers listed at the end of this chapter. Short-run printers specialize in offset printing of 250 to several thousand copies and they can sometimes even be competitive on longer runs.

Send the printers you decide to contact a short letter stating the length of your information, the type of cover, binding and paper you are interested in using. Ask them for a quote including shipping, for samples of their previous jobs and for any general information they may have about pricing.

Also ask how long it will take to have the books printed and delivered. Usually they will send you not only a quote but also a pricing pamphlet to help you estimate costs.

Study And Compare The Quotes And Pricing Pamphlets

When you receive the quotes and pricing pamphlets, study them carefully and compare them. Make sure that the printers you wrote to included the price of shipping.

OUT OF TOWN PRINTERS MAY GIVE YOU MUCH LOWER QUOTES

You may find that the out of town printers quotes are much lower than the local printers even with the shipping costs included. If that is the case, you will probably select the out of town printer with the lowest quote.

GIVE YOUR LOCAL PRINTERS AND COPY SHOPS ONE MORE CHANCE

Before you give the low quote out of town printer the job, call your local printers and copy shops and tell them about the low quote you received from the out of town printer. It may be possible for them to lower their quote enough to be competitive and still make a profit on your job.

COMPARING QUALITY: OUT OF TOWN PRINTERS VERSUS LOCAL PRINTERS

The local printers and copy shops may tell you that they can not even come close to matching the out of town quotes but that they would produce a higher quality product. You should always compare the sample you received from the out of town printer with the local printer's sample, but I would be skeptical of that claim because I have had just the opposite happen. An out of town printer whose quote was less than half of the local printer's quote produced a higher quality book than the local printer.

QUOTES COULD BE SIMILAR

On the other hand, you may find that the out of town printers quotes are about the same as the local printers and quick copy shops quotes. If that is the case, you may decide to select a local printer or a quick copy shop.

GET EVERYTHING IN WRITING

Ask for quotes in writing not only because it makes it easier to compare various quotes but also because you want the printers to commit to what they will do. If there are changes in your job after you receive the quote, get the printer to give you a new quote. It is always best to have everything in writing, just to be safe. That way there should be no surprises when the bill arrives.

Count the books when they are delivered to you by an out of town printer or when you pick them up from a local printer. Anyone can make a mistake and it is possible that the printer will print half the books he or she was supposed to. It is also possible that half of the out of town printer's shipment gets lost in the mail or that some of the books arrive damaged.

Keep Your Camera-Ready

Make sure the printer returns your camera-ready. You may not use the same printer the next time and you may make changes in the camera-ready. Keep your camera-ready in a safe place such as a file folder or a large envelope.

PRINTERS

The following are some information and book printers. You can also compare prices and services with your local printers and quick copy shops.

Short-Run Printers

As noted earlier, short-run printers specialize in offset printing of 250 to several thousand copies and they can sometimes even be competitive on longer runs.

Lelli Printing & Advertising
2650 Cr. 175
Loudonville, OH 44842
419-994-5302

Di's Graphics & Printing
10104 Westminister Avenue
Garden Grove, CA 92643

Speedy Books
P.O. Box 482
Richfield, OH 44286

Longer-Run Printers

Longer-run printers usually specialize in offset printing of 1,000 or more copies.

Eerdam's Printing Co.
231 Jefferson Ave., SE
Grand Rapids, MI 49503
616-459-4591

BookMasters
638 Jefferson St.,
P.O. Box 159
Ashland, OH 44805
313-475-9145

McNaughton & Gunn
P.O. Box 10
Saline, MI 48176
313-429-5411

Adams Press
500 North Michigan Avenue
Chicago, IL 60611
312-236-3838

Omni Press
P.O. Box 7214
Madison, WI 53707-7214
1-800-828-0305

Harlo Printing Company
50 Victor
Highland Park, MI 48203
313-883-3600

Arcadia Graphics
P.O. Box 711
Kingsport, TN 37662
615-378-1000

Braum-Brumfield, Inc.
100 North Stabler Road
P.O. Box 1203
Ann Arbor, MI 48106
313-662-3291

R.R. Donnelly & Sons
2223 S. Martin Luther King Dr.
Chicago, IL 60616
312-326-8000

Mitchell-Shear
713 West Ellsworth Road
Ann Arbor, MI 48108

Thompson-Shore, Inc.
7300 W. Joy Road
Dexter, MI 48130
313-426-3939

Maverick Publications
63324 Nels Anderson Road
Bend, OR 97701
503-382-6978

Dinner & Klein
600 S. Spokane Street
Seattle, WA 98134
206-682-2494

Rose Printing
P.O. Box 5078
Tallahassee, FL 32301
904-576-4151

Spillman Printing
1801 9th Street
Sacramento, CA 95814
916-448-3511

Cushing-Malloy
P.O. Box 8632
Ann Arbor, MI 48107
313-663-8554

Book-Mart Press, Inc.
2001 Forty Second St.
N. Bergen, NJ 07047
201-684-1129

Book Press
Putney Road
Brattleboro, VT 05301
802-257-7701

Kimberly Press
5390-P Overpass Rd.
Santa Barbara, CA 93111
805-964-6469

Offset Paperback
P.O. Box N
Route 309
Dallas, PA 18612
717-675-5261

Viking Press
7000 Washington Avenue S.
Eden Prairie, MN 55344
800-328-7327

Publishers Press
1900-P West 2300 South
Salt Lake City, UT 84119
801-972-6600

Graham Printing
17475 Gale Avenue
Rowland Heights, CA 91748
818-964-7354

Griffin Printing
544 West Colorado Street
Glendale, CA 91204
818-244-2127

Chapter 7

Display Advertising

Display advertising is also called space advertising. For the purpose of this book, a display advertisement is the advertisement in a publication such as a newspaper or a magazine. Advertising space is the actual space the display advertisement occupies in a publication.

The first step to successful advertising, including display advertising, is to write a successful advertisement. For more on this, read Chapter 4, "How To Write A Successful Advertisement." The second step to successful display advertising is to target your potential customers by using the right publications to sell your information.

Target Your Potential Customers

There are literally thousands of publications you can run your advertisements in. In order to target your potential customers, you need to find publications which are read by your potential customers especially if your information deals with a special interest topic.

STANDARD RATE AND DATA SERVICE

One way you can do this is looking through the *Standard Rate and Data Service*. Your public or nearby college library should have a copy or you may want to subscribe. Write to *Standard Rate and Data Service*, 3002 Glenview Rd., Wilmette, Illinois 60091.

Standard Rate and Data Service catalogs magazines by different categories in a monthly publication called *Consumer Magazine and Farm Publication Rates and Data*. Decide which category your information falls under and look up the magazines in that category. *Standard Rate and Data Service* also publishes a book dealing with newspapers: *Newspaper Rates and Data*. This is also a monthly publication.

YOUR OWN RESEARCH

Another way you can find publications which are read by your potential customers is by doing your own research. Go to your local bookstores, libraries and newsstands. They also place publications by categories. As was the case with *Standard Rate and Data Service* publications, decide which category your information falls under and look up the magazines in that category.

Look through the publications to see if your successful competitors are advertising there. If they are, you are on the right track. Write to the publications stating you are a potential advertiser and ask them to send you, for free, their latest media kit and some back issues of the publications. You will thus start building your own very important file of publications and information.

The Media Kit

The media kit, also known as the media package, contains valuable information about the publication including circulation, which is the number of copies of the publication sold and distributed. This figure usually includes newsstand sales, subscribers and samples.

The media kit also includes a detailed demographic description of the publication's readers. This information includes the average age, income and education of the readers.

In addition, the media kit includes other important information such as the percentage of men versus women readers, readership claims, the advertisement space sizes available, closing dates and rates. Some publications may send you a rate card instead of their media kit. The rate card is the magazine or newspaper card which lists the rate per agate line for advertising in that publication. Most publications usually include the rate card with their media kit.

How To Find Successful Competitors

How can you find out which competitors are successful? Simply by looking at the back issues of the publications they advertise in. Libraries often have back issues of publications and you should receive some back issues from the publications you write to. If your competitor's advertisements are there month after month, they are successful.

The best criterion you can use to decide where to place your display advertisements is to advertise where your successful competition advertises.

Circulation

The classic way of comparing advertising rates is to compare them to their circulation figures. The idea is to come up with a rate of X dollars per 1,000 circulation, or cost per one thousand circulation.

BEWARE OF "READERSHIP" CLAIMS

One problem with this is that some publications try to muddy the water by making "readership" claims in addition to their circulation figures. They want you to believe that up to five or six different people read every copy of every issue of their publication. This type of claim is overly optimistic, in my opinion. So, when figuring out the cost per one thousand circulation, always stick to the actual circulation figures, never use the inflated "readership" figures.

SUBSCRIBERS VERSUS NEWSSTAND BUYERS

Another problem with using circulation figures to compare advertising rates is that all circulation rates are not created equal. Let's say publications "A" and "B" have circulations of 100,000 each.

The circulation of Publication "A" consists of 80,000 mailed copies (subscribers and samples) and 20,000 copies sold at the newsstands. The circulation of publication "B" consists of 90,000 mailed copies and 10,000 copies sold at the newsstands.

My Opinion

In my opinion, potential customers who receive their publication by mail are more likely to become mail order buyers than potential customers who buy their publication at the newsstands. Therefore, I believe that a display advertisement in publication "B" should receive more orders than a display advertisement in publication "A."

Another Opinion

Some other mail order experts have an opinion regarding this issue which is opposite of mine: that a display advertisement in publication "A" should receive more orders than a display advertisement in publication "B." Here are some reasons why:

The first reason is that the people who buy a publication from a newsstand are buying it because they are interested in the publication and are therefore more likely to read it than the subscribers.

Second, the subscribers may lose interest in the publication before their subscription runs out or they may simply receive so many publications every month that they do not have the time to read all of them. Third, an advertiser is more likely to reach new potential customers in publication "A" because it has a greater newsstand circulation and newsstand buyers are new potential customers.

WE DO AGREE ON ONE POINT

However, despite the difference of opinion regarding the value of the newsstand reader versus the subscriber, mail order experts agree on one point: some potential customers need to see a display advertisement two to three times before they will place an order.

These potential customers feel an advertiser could be a "fly-by-night" operator until they see his or her advertisement more than once. After they see the advertisement a few times, the advertiser gains credibility in their eyes and they are no longer reluctant to place an order.

CONCLUSION ABOUT CIRCULATION

You should compare cost per one thousand circulation before placing your display advertisements. But remember that the best criterion you can use to decide where to place your display advertisements it is to advertise where your successful competition advertises.

Display Advertisement Space

Publications have many different advertisement space sizes which can range from two inch advertisements to full page advertisements. In between they have 1/6, 1/3, 1/2 or 2/3 of a page advertisement space. A 2/3 of a page advertisement is called a junior page.

For more specific information about advertisement space, study the media kits you received after writing to various publications. See Figure 7.1 for examples of display advertisements of different sizes.

Newspaper Advertising

One advantage of newspaper advertising is that it can bring fast results. If you run a newspaper advertisement, you can receive one-half of your total

Figure 7.1 Display advertisements of different sizes.

orders within three days of receiving your first order. This is just one reason why newspapers are used for selling information by mail.

Another reason is that there are literally thousands of newspapers in the United States which makes direct competition less likely. Also, it is easier to run an advertisement on credit if you run it in a local newspaper than if you run it in a national publication whose headquarters may be far away.

WHAT DAY IS BEST FOR NEWSPAPER ADVERTISING?

Sundays are generally considered to be better than any other day of the week. One reason for this is that some people only subscribe to or only buy the Sunday newspaper. This may be because they do not have time to read the newspaper on other days of the week or because the main reason they buy the Sunday newspaper is that it has a lot of advertisements.

Another reason Sunday is considered better than any other day of the week is that people tend to keep the Sunday newspaper the longest. Perhaps they do this in order to hold on to the advertisements a few days longer.

A few experts disagree that Sunday is better than any other day of the week. They point out that Sunday advertising rates are often higher than the rates for the other days of the week. They also point out that there is more competition on Sunday than the other days of the week. These experts prefer the smallest issue of the week, usually Monday or Tuesday.

MORNING OR AFTERNOON NEWSPAPER EDITIONS?

It is generally agreed that the afternoon newspaper editions are better than the morning editions for advertising purposes. This may be because people are too busy getting ready for work to carefully read the newspaper in the morning.

We live in such a fast changing world that by the time people get home from work their morning edition is already old news so perhaps many of them forget about their morning newspaper and simply watch TV or listen to the radio to get the latest news.

WHICH SECTION OF THE NEWSPAPER TO USE

The best place for display advertisements is the front of a section of the newspaper. The second best place for display advertisements is in the back of a section.

How do you decide which section of the newspaper you want your display advertisement to go in? This depends on the type of information you are selling. If your information is a business opportunity you should try the business section, the financial section or the sports section. If your information is a travel guide you should try the travel section or the lifestyle section.

WHICH NEWSPAPERS TO USE

If you decide to use newspapers, you should start with local ones and expand from there. See Appendix A for a listing of some of the newspapers in the United States.

Other Local Publications

There are other local publications besides newspapers you can advertise in. As is the case with local newspapers, it is easier to run an advertisement on credit if you run it in a local publication than if you run it in a national publication.

Local publications such as *Thrifty Nickel, Greensheet, Shopper's Guide* and *Penny Savers* are usually found on newsstands in front of grocery or drug stores. There are over ninety *Thrifty Nickel* publications across the United States, perhaps in your area.

Sam Pitts started his business with a classified advertisement in a local *Thrifty Nickel* and went on to deposit $118,000 his first year in business. He ran his advertisement for 3 to 4 weeks without paying any up front money because the *Thrifty Nickel* billed him. See Chapter 5, "The Greatest Business In The World," for more information about Sam Pitts' success story.

Magazine Advertising

Unlike newspapers and other local publications, magazines are distributed nationwide. They also reach a specific consumer. As mentioned earlier, *Standard Rate and Data Service* catalogs magazines by categories.

Magazines are kept longer and reread more often than newspapers. This means there is more of a chance that a typical reader will see and read your advertisement and perhaps place an order. Magazines are also passed along to friends and relatives more often than newspapers. This means that magazines have a greater readership than newspapers.

The following magazines appeal to opportunity seekers and purchasers of other types of information by mail.

American Opportunities
2650 CR 175
Loudonville, OH 44842

Income Opportunities
380 Lexington Ave.
New York, NY 10168-0035

Winning
15115 S. 76th E. Avenue
Bixby, OK 74008

Small Business Opportunities
1115 Broadway
New York, NY 10010

Income Plus
73 Spring Street, Suite 303
New York, NY 10012

Money Making Opportunities
11071 Ventura Blvd.
Studio City, CA 91604

New Business Opportunities
2392 Morse Avenue
Irvine, CA 92714

Entrepreneur
2392 Morse Avenue
Irvine, CA 92714

Jackpot, National
Shopper Monthly
PO Box 6547
Jacksonville, FL 32236

MC Publications
Income Magazine
2002 London Rd., RM 101
Duluth, MN 55812

Business Opportunities Digest
301 Plymouth Drive N.E.
Dalton, GA 30721-9983

Official Detective Stories
235 Park Ave.
New York, NY 10003

Money
1271 Ave. of the Americas
New York, NY 10020

Popular Science
1000 Town Center, Suite 1830
Southfield, MI 48075

Star
600 S.E. Coast Avenue
Lantana, FL 33464

Globe
535 5th Avenue
New York, NY 10017

Entrepreneurial Woman
P.O. Box 570
Clearwater, FL 34617-0570

Prevention
33 East Minor Street
Emmaus, PA 18098

Popular Mechanics
224 West 57th Street
New York, NY 10019

50 Plus
P.O. Box 1510
Clearwater, FL 33517

INC Magazine
38 Commercial Wharf
Boston, MA 02110-3883

Workbench
4251 Pennsylvania Avenue
Kansas City, MO 64111

American Legion Magazine
700 N. Penn Street
Indianapolis, IN 46206

Projecting Display Advertising Results

Projecting display advertising results involves looking at one to three weeks of results and making an intelligent estimate what the results may be in the end. I always keep accurate records of all of my display advertising results for at least ten weeks. You should keep accurate daily and weekly records of your orders. Figure 7.2 is based on the results from some of my display advertisements.

Figure 7.2 has two columns. The first column indicates time—the days and weeks of receiving orders. The second column shows the percentage of the total cumulative orders received through the days or weeks in the first column.

When making your own projections, keep in mind that due to various variables your experience will probably slightly differ from mine.

Display Advertisement Positioning

The position of your display advertisement in a publication is important. The more visible your advertisement, the better results you will get. Do not be disheartened if you do not end up getting a forward position. Although overall my advertising results have been better when I had a forward position, some of my best results were achieved when I had a back position.

ALWAYS ASK FOR THE POSITION YOU WANT

Nevertheless, you should always ask for a forward position. You many not get what you ask for, but chances are that if you do not ask, another advertiser who does ask will get the position you want.

Newspaper And Tabloid Positioning

If you plan to run your display advertisement in newspapers or tabloids, you should specify that you want your advertisement positioned in the "upper half" or "above the fold." This is because advertisements running along the bottom are not very visible.

Time	% of total cumulative orders
Day 1	.1%
Day 2	2%
Day 3	4%
Day 4	8%
Day 5	12%
Day 6	16%
Day 7	20%
Day 8	22%
Day 9	25%
Day 10	27%
Day 11	29%
Day 12	31%
3 Weeks	48%
4 Weeks	59%
5 Weeks	68%
6 Weeks	76%
7 Weeks	81%
8 Weeks	84%
9 Weeks	87%
10 Weeks	90%

Figure 7.2 Ten weeks of cumulative display advertising results.

Right Hand Page

If you are running a full page advertisement, it is vital that you get a right hand page. Do not run a full page advertisement if the publication will not guarantee a right hand page.

Potential customers notice right hand pages more than left hand pages. Also, a right hand page makes it easier for potential customers to place an order since the coupon is usually at the bottom right corner of the display advertisement and it is easier to cut it out on a right hand page.

Remember, often you can not control the exact position of your display advertisement. However, it never hurts to ask for the best position possible.

Key Codes

Use a different key code for every display advertisement you run in every publication you run it in. For example, in January you may run advertisement A in publications Q and T and in February in publications Q, T and Z.

You can use three digit key codes printed after your address inside the coupon for your display advertising, like I do. So, you may use the key codes Dept. 101 and Dept. 102 for January publications Q and T and key codes Dept. 201, Dept. 202 and Dept. 203 for February publications Q, T and Z.

Placing The Advertisement

After you do your research and receive the media kits you requested you can make a decision where to place your advertisement. To place the advertisement, you must have an actual "stat" or "velox" or "mechanical" ready unless you start with a newspaper advertisement.

The "stat" or "velox" is the camera ready version of your advertisement which a local typesetter can prepare for you. In a word, you give the typesetter your hand-written or typed advertisement and they set the type for you. If you start with a newspaper advertisement, the newspaper may prepare the "stat" or camera ready for you.

I use a local typesetter. In the past I also used an out-of-state typesetter. They did good work, but I have learned since then that it is better to use a local typesetter because you can talk to them face to face.

As discussed earlier in Chapter 4, before you run your advertisement you should consult a lawyer who is an expert in mail order. For more information, study very carefully "Legal Aspects To Consider Regarding Advertising" in Chapter 10, "Tax, Record Keeping and Legal Aspects."

Remnant Space Advertising

You can contact publications and let them know you are interested in remnant space advertising. Almost every month many magazines are left with a few unsold pages of advertising. Sometimes the pages were actually sold but one or more advertisers cancelled. These unsold pages are called remnant or standby pages.

REMNANT SPACE IS A PROBLEM FOR MAGAZINES

When this happens, and it happens often, the magazines have a problem. They must sell the remnant space because their printers can not print a magazine with an odd number of pages. As a matter of fact, saddle stitched (pages are stapled, not glued) magazines must be printed with the total page numbers, including the cover, in multiples of four: 4, 8, 12, 16 . . . 88 . . . 100.

If in the last minute the magazine publisher finds himself with 97 pages and his magazine is saddle stitched, he must find a way to sell three pages of advertising quickly. The alternative is to come up with editorial articles or public service announcements which will not make him any money.

YOU CAN SAVE 20% TO 80%

The publisher will then usually have his account executives (advertising sales people) contact advertisers who have previously expressed an interest in remnant space advertising. In this way you can save from 20% to 80% of regular cost of advertising, depending on the deal you work out.

Per-Inquiry Deals

Per-inquiry deals are also known as PI deals or commission deals. A per-inquiry deal is a deal you make with a publication. You do not pay anything for the advertisement, only for actual inquiries or orders your advertisement generates. Exactly how this is handled depends on the publication.

Some publications insist that the inquiries or orders come to them. Other publications allow you to have the inquiries or orders come directly to you. Obviously, you must key code all advertisements, especially per-inquiry advertisements.

NEGOTIATE THE BEST DEAL

Per-inquiry deals can vary dramatically. They can range from 50 cents per inquiry to 50% commission per order. It is up to you to negotiate the best deal you can.

If the inquiries or orders come directly to you, you send the publication its share once a week or once a month, according to the deal. If the inquiries or orders come to the publication, they send you your share according to the deal.

ASK FOR PER-INQUIRY DEALS

Finding per-inquiry deals is not easy because most publications do not reveal in their media kits that they offer per-inquiry deals. This is because they do not want all their advertisers to know that they can make these types of deals. As is the case with so many things in life, you have to ask for a per-inquiry deal in order to get it.

Melvin Powers, whose success story is in Chapter 5, "The Greatest Business In The World," has stated that he has a number of per-inquiry deals which result in thousands of orders a week. He has asked for per-inquiry deals and is reaping the rewards for asking.

Obtain Lower Advertising Rates

You do not have to get remnant space advertising or per-inquiry deals in order to save money on advertising. You can obtain lower advertising rates from publications you place your advertising with. However, you must ask for the lower rates first. I have been able to get discounts simply by asking for them. I have also been able to get free color simply by asking for it.

Another trick I learned involved an interesting negotiation technique. I simply put off making decisions whether to run advertisements in various publications until the last possible minute.

As their deadlines approach, publications become much more likely to make deals. Many advertising executives work on commission. The more advertising space they sell, the more money they make. Also, they are under pressure from management to sell advertising space. Many times, as their deadlines approached they have called me offering excellent deals.

For more information on placing your advertisement, see Chapter 9, "How I Save Up To 17% Of Display Advertising Costs." For information on how you can get free advertising, see Chapter 13, "Free Publicity."

Part II

WHAT I HAVE LEARNED SINCE I GOT STARTED

Chapter 8

How To Start A Mail Order Business

Mail order is an easy business to start because it does not require elaborate equipment, expensive machinery or office space. You can start your business out of your home and continue to run it from there even after you make a lot of money.

TYPES OF BUSINESS STRUCTURE

Your new mail order business can be in the form of one of the following three types of business structures (organizations): a sole proprietorship, a partnership or a corporation. Each has advantages and disadvantages.

Sole Proprietorship

Sole proprietorship is the simplest and most common form of business structure or organization. It means the business is a one person operation which is not incorporated. You call all the shots, you alone collect all the profits and you are responsible for all the debts or losses.

YOU ARE IN THE DRIVER SEAT

You call all the shots because you do not have to satisfy any partners, stockholders or a board of directors. You can of course listen to the advice of others, but in the end you are in the driver's seat. Many successful businessmen spend their business lives as sole proprietors, never taking on one or more partners and never incorporating.

NO CONTRACTS ARE REQUIRED

A sole proprietorship allows you to run your business under your own name. Unlike the other forms of business structure, a sole proprietorship does not require any contracts to be drawn up.

TAX ADVANTAGE

As a sole proprietor, you enjoy a major tax break: the government considers you and your business as one. This means your profits are taxed only once, as part of your personal income. In other words, you pay no income tax on the net income of your business as such.

Corporations, with the exception of a Subchapter S corporation, are taxed twice. A sole proprietorship must file Schedule C, Profit or Loss From Business, each year for the Internal Revenue Service. For more tax information, contact your local Internal Revenue Service office.

PERSONAL LIABILITY

The major disadvantage of a sole proprietorship is personal liability. As a sole proprietor, you are personally liable for any losses, debts and obligations incurred by your business—you have unlimited personal liability. This means even your personal assets you own outside of your business can be sold to meet the debts of your business.

OTHER FACTS TO CONSIDER

The importance of the drawback of a sole proprietorship, personal liability, is reduced when you look at the alternatives more closely. This is because personal liability in a partnership is compounded by the fact that you are liable for the actions and commitments of your partners even if you did not participate in the decisions which led to a liability.

Also, even forming a corporation can not save you from personal liability as has been proven in numerous cases in which customers and creditors have successfully "pierced the corporate veil."

Partnership

A partnership is a non-incorporated business in which there is a sharing of profits along with dividing work of managing the business. My business is now a partnership. The partnership is less complicated than the corporation but more complicated than the sole proprietorship. Let's discuss the advantages of partnerships first.

"TWO HEADS ARE BETTER THAN ONE"

The main advantage of having a partner is that he or she may supply what you lack. The old saying "two heads are better than one" is generally true. Partners should be able to do better as a team than they could do separately provided they get along personally and provided they also complement each others talents and abilities. Partners can share the work load, give each other moral support and can work together to make vacation planning easier than in a sole proprietorship.

TAX ADVANTAGE

Partnerships, like sole proprietorships have an advantage over corporations because each partner's share of the partnership's profits is taxed only once, as part of each partner's personal income.

MORE PAPERWORK

Although the paperwork you must file with a partnership is a great deal less than the paperwork a corporation must file, it is nevertheless greater and more complicated than the paperwork you must file as a sole proprietor. A partnership must file Form 1065, United States Partnership Return of Income, each year for the Internal Revenue Service. For more tax information, contact your local Internal Revenue Service office.

This does not mean that you pay more income taxes because you are involved in a partnership versus being a sole proprietor. Form 1065 is only an "information return," identifying each partner and showing how much income should be reported by each partner on his own personal income tax return. Each partner must attach a copy of the partnership's tax return to his own personal return.

THE DISADVANTAGES

Now, let's look at the disadvantages of partnerships. A major disadvantage of a partnership is that although the old saying "two heads are better than one," is generally true, it is not always true in business partnerships. Some partnerships are formed on the basis of the fact that the partners are casual friends on a personal basis with no regard given to their business compatibility.

Before anything else, partners must decide how decisions will be made and who has the final say. Partners must also decide who will be responsible for which tasks. Consequently, before starting a partnership, a written agreement should be drawn up by an attorney.

Another disadvantage of a partnership involves personal liability. As discussed earlier, you are liable for the actions and commitments of your partners even if you did not participate in the decisions which led to a liability.

Corporation

The third and most complicated form of business structure is the corporation. The corporation is a form of business organization created by the state solely through legislation as state laws allow existing businesses (sole proprietorships and partnerships) as well as new businesses to incorporate.

The corporation's name must include the words "Inc." or "Corp." or "Ltd." to let people know they are doing business with a corporation. The word "Company" or "Co." in the corporate name is not enough in most states.

Corporate law is so complicated and the disadvantages, including incomplete control of your own company and double taxation are so great that many mail order companies shy away from it.

THE ADVANTAGES

The problem of personal liability inherent in sole proprietorships and partnerships is considered the main advantage of the corporate business structure. However, as mentioned earlier, the "piercing of the corporate veil" has become common enough to seriously damage this advantage.

Most business books cite lower income taxes as another advantage of corporations. However, while it is true that corporate income tax rates are lower than personal income tax rates, there is one big problem. This problem is called double taxation.

THE DISADVANTAGES

Unlike sole proprietorships and partnerships, corporations, with the exception of Subchapter S corporations, are taxed twice. First, the corporation is taxed on its profits. Second, the business owner is taxed on the dividends, salary and benefits the corporation pays him. The business owner can thus pay almost twice as much in income taxes if he or she uses the corporate business structure.

HEADACHES

Another disadvantage of the corporation is that incorporating your business can bring you many headaches. The federal, state, city and county government officials are known to pounce on newly formed corporations.

You will be told to fill out various corporate forms and pay for various corporate licenses, costing you valuable time and money. The amount of paperwork the government expects from corporations is immense and takes time and money that the business owner could otherwise invest in building his or her business.

A corporation must have a board of directors and hold stockholder's meetings. A corporation must also publish minutes of the stockholder's meetings and pay an annual registration fee.

CONCLUSION

In conclusion, the easiest business structure for a person starting a mail order business to choose is the sole proprietorship.

My advice to anyone considering the partnership or corporate form of business structure for their newly started mail order business is to think before you leap into something you may not like later. Postpone forming a partnership or incorporating until you have some experience as a sole proprietor in the mail order business.

COMPANY NAME

You can use your own name for your new mail order business. If you use your own name, you generally do not have to register it with your local city or county clerk. Joe Karbo used his own name to sell his "The Lazy Man's Way To Riches" and he earned millions of dollars in the process.

Karbo's advertisement used a laid back, soft sell approach and using his own name fit that approach. Obviously, this worked for Karbo.

Fictitious Name

You may have in mind a name for your new mail order business that is not your own. Most states require you to register a fictitious name. This is very easily done. You simply register your company name as a "D.B.A." (doing business as) for a modest fee.

Before registering the name, check first to make sure no one is already using the name you plan to use. A clerk at the city or county clerk's office can give you instructions on how to do this.

YOUR MAILING ADDRESS

Choosing a mailing address worries many people starting a mail order business. Fortunately, there are a number of choices available.

As mentioned earlier, you can start and run your business from your home. You do not have to rent expensive office space. However, if you plan to start your business from home, you may not want to use your home address as your mailing address for privacy reasons.

Home Or Post Office Box Address?

When I first thought about starting my own business, I read that using a post office box number for my address could harm my new business. The author stated that a post office box address would make my potential customers believe that I was a fly-by-night operator—someone who would take their money and then disappear into the night without ever sending them the information I advertised.

I had no intention of doing that but I also could not afford to take the chance on a post office box address. At the same time, I did not want to use my apartment address for family privacy reasons.

I was literally caught between the rock and the hard place. I ended up using my home address. Later, after I had already made a lot of money, I discovered an alternative to using my home address or a post office box address.

Private Mail Box Centers

I found out that I could rent a box from a private mail box center, like Mail Boxes Etc., and in effect, rent their street address. My box number became a suite number.

Today

Today I am renting an office instead of having my office in my home. So, I am having my business mail come directly to my office.

Listed below are examples of mailing addresses: a home address, a post office box address and a private mail box center suite address.

Your Name
3005 Thompson Street
Your City, State, Zip Code

Your Name
P.O. Box 1155
Your City, State, Zip Code

Your Name
5563 Woodraw Ln., Suite 258
Your City, State, Zip Code

EIGHT METHODS YOU CAN USE TO START A MAIL ORDER BUSINESS

There are at least eight methods you can use to start a mail order business. How you chose to start your business is totally up to you.

Free Publicity

You can use free publicity to start your mail order business. For more information on free publicity, read Chapter 13, "Free Publicity."

Write An Advertisement And Sell It

You can simply write an advertisement (see Chapter 4, "How To Write A Successful Advertisement") and sell it. You can sell it to someone already in the mail order business, a friend, a family member or anyone else interested in buying it.

You can sell your advertisement outright, for an up-front fee or for a share of future profits. You can make a deal and sell only the direct mail rights to the advertisement and keep the display advertisement rights for yourself or vice versa.

If you decide to sell your advertisement, you should advise the person who buys your advertisement that he or she should consult a lawyer who is an expert in mail order before he or she runs the advertisement. This is what I have advised you to do before you run your advertisement. For more information, see "Legal Aspects To Consider Regarding Advertising" in Chapter 10, "Tax, Record Keeping And Legal Aspects."

Write Information And Sell It

You can simply write information (see Chapter 6, "Selling Information By Mail") and sell it. You can sell it to someone already in the mail order business, a friend, a family member or anyone else interested in buying it.

You can sell your information outright, for an up-front fee or for a share of future profits. You can make a deal and sell only the rights to sell the information using direct mail and keep the rights to sell the information using display advertising for yourself or vice versa.

If you decide to sell the information to someone, you should advise the person who buys your information that he or she should consult a lawyer who is an expert in mail order before he or she runs an advertisement selling the information. For more information, see "Legal Aspects To Consider Regarding Advertising" in Chapter 10, "Tax, Record Keeping And Legal Aspects."

SELL YOUR INFORMATION TO A PUBLISHER

In addition, you can go to your local library or bookstore and find books containing information similar to yours. The name and address of the book publisher is usually listed on one of the first few pages of each book.

You can contact the publishers to find out if they are interested in purchasing your information. You can make a deal and sell the publisher only the rights to sell the information in bookstores and keep the rights to sell the information by mail.

Royalties

The publisher will pay you a royalty, or a share of the proceeds resulting from the sale of your book. The royalty is usually around 10% of the price of each hard cover book sold. If your book sells well, you could make millions of dollars.

You could even negotiate a graduated royalty which could work something like this: 10% of the price for the first 5,000 hard cover books sold, 12% on the next 5,000 and 15% on sales above 10,000.

Beware Of Net Profit Offers

If a publisher offers you 10% of the net profit of your books sold, do not take it. It is too easy for a publisher to pad his expenses and thus not show a profit even if your book sells well. Getting paid a percentage of the price of each book sold (a percentage of the gross sales) is a much better and safer deal for the author.

Soft Cover And Paperback Royalties

In addition, after a book is published in a hard cover version, it is later released in a soft cover or paperback version. This means still more royalties for you. In terms of percentages, royalties on soft cover and paperback books are usually lower than royalties on hard cover books.

Soft cover royalties usually range from 7% to 10% and mass market paperback publishers usually pay between 4% and 7.5% royalties. In terms of dollars, the royalties on soft cover and paperback books can be even more lucrative for the author than hard cover royalties because many more versions of soft cover and paperback books are usually sold.

Subsidiary Rights

Do not forget subsidiary rights when negotiating your royalty. These rights include movies, TV, book clubs, etc. Sometimes subsidiary rights could make you more money than the royalty for the sales of the books.

Door-To-Door Sales

You can start your mail order business with door-to-door sales. This direct marketing method allows you to start your business without marketing or advertising costs. Be prepared to present the benefits of your product by using your product, advertisement and any testimonials you have. As much as possible, relate the benefits in terms of dollars. Always ask for the order. Remember the old saying: "Ask and you shall receive."

You can start by marketing your product to your friends, relatives and people in your neighborhood. Then, you can expand your market geographically. You can also hire other people to make door-to-door sales for you and pay them strictly on a commission basis.

Telephone Sales

You can start your mail order business with telephone sales. This is another direct marketing method. If you start by making only local phone calls, you can avoid any marketing or advertising costs. Calling your friends, relatives and neighbors is the easiest way to get started. In addition, you can call potential customers from the local telephone directory and/or other local sources. Then, you can expand your market geographically. You can also hire other people to make the telephone calls for you and pay them strictly on a commission basis.

Create a telephone sales script presenting the benefits of your product by using your product, advertisement and any testimonials you have. As much as possible, relate the benefits in terms of dollars. Always ask for the order.

Classified Advertising

You can start your mail order business by using classified advertising. For more information, read Chapter 12, "Classified Advertising."

Display Advertising

You can start your mail order business as I did, with display advertising. For more information about display advertising, read Chapter 7, "Display Advertising."

Direct Mail Advertising

Direct mail advertising is another way you can start your mail order business. For more information, read Chapter 11, "Direct Mail Advertising."

Chapter 9

How I Save Up To 17% Of Display Advertising Costs

One of the mistakes I made when I first started my mail order business was having an advertising agency place my first advertisement. Since then I have learned my lesson and have consistently saved between 15% and 17% off regular rates on all display advertising I placed.

How do I do it? It is really very simple. I established my own advertising agency. Many businesses, from small ones to huge mail order operations set up their own in-house agencies to place their advertising.

Why do businesses do this? Because by submitting their advertising on their own agency's "Insertion Order Form" they are allowed to deduct 15% from the advertising display rate. To figure out my 15% discount, I simply multiply the advertising rate by .15. To figure out the cost of my advertisement after my 15% discount, I subtract my discount from the advertising rate.

How I take another 2% discount:

I take another 2% discount for sending my check with my advertising order. Most publications offer a 2% "cash" discount because they prefer to be paid up front instead of having to send out bills. To figure out my cash discount, I take out my 15% advertising agency discount, then multiply the new rate by .02.

To figure out the net amount I will pay for the advertising space, I subtract my 15% advertising agency discount and my 2% cash discount from the regular display advertising rate.

Yet Another 15% Discount Is Possible!

Some publications offer yet another 15% discount in addition to the 15% advertising agency discount and the 2% cash discount. This additional 15% discount is for mail order display advertising. This discount can be calculated in the same manner as the 15% advertising agency discount: multiply the advertising rate by .15.

How I Set Up My Own, In-House Advertising Agency

Setting up my own, in-house advertising agency was easy. The first thing I did was come up with a name that was different from my mail order company's name. Then I went to the County Clerk's Office to register the name.

Before I registered the name I checked first to make sure no one was already using my advertising agency company name. A clerk at the County Clerk's Office gave me excellent instructions on how to do this.

Then I created an "Insertion Order Form." To see a version of the insertion order form I have used, look at Figure 9.1. You can type in or typeset your own advertising agency's name and make copies of Figure 9.1 if you want.

Once I created the "Insertion Order Form," I had my own advertising agency. All I have done since then is simply submit my advertisement, my "Insertion Order Form" and the check for the advertisement space minus the 15% advertising agency discount and the cash discount.

How To Fill Out The Insertion Order Form

I am including a version of the insertion order form I have used, Figure 9.1. I will give you instructions on how to fill it out. You can either type or write on your insertion order form.

INSTRUCTIONS

1. The name of your advertising agency goes on top, above "MEDIA INSERTION ORDER." You should also include your address and telephone number.
2. "Date:"—fill out the date.
3. "To Publisher of:"—the name of the publication.
4. "Advertiser:"—your name, or if you are using a company name, the assumed name.
5. "For (product):"—the headline of your advertisement or the title of your information.
6. "Space"—fill out the size of your advertisement. Example: "1/3 page" or "1/2 page" or "full page."
7. "Times"—fill out the number of consecutive times you want your advertisement to run.
8. "Dates of Insertion"—fill out the issues of the publication you want your advertisement to run in. Example: "February 1992 issue."
9. "Position:"—fill out your preference for the position of your advertisement in the publication. "As far forward as possible" is a common preference. If you are running a full page advertisement, you should fill out "Right hand page, as far forward as possible."
10. "Key:"—the key code you want to appear on your advertisement. The publication will put your key code on your advertisement free of charge.
11. "Rate:"—the regular display advertising rate.
12. "Agency Commission (%):"—fill out 15 in the parenthesis for the 15% advertising agency discount and the dollar amount of the discount to the right.
13. "Discount (%)"—fill out the appropriate cash discount percentage figure in the parenthesis and the dollar amount of the cash discount to the right if you will take the cash discount.
14. "NET:"—the net dollar amount of the advertisement.

15. "ADDITIONAL INSTRUCTIONS:"—here you can remind the publication of your position request and the key code you want plus any additional instructions you may want to give the publication.
16. "Order issued by:"—sign your name.

MEDIA INSERTION ORDER

Date: ______________________

To Publisher of: ______________________

Advertiser: ______________________

For (product): ______________________

Space: ______________________

Times: ______________________

Dates of Insertion: ______________________

Position: ______________________

Key: ______________________

Rate: ______________

Agency Commission (   ): ______________

Discount (   ): ______________

NET: ______________

ADDITIONAL INSTRUCTIONS:

____

____

____

PLEASE ACKNOWLEDGE

After publication, please send one complete copy of this issue and two tear sheets

Order issued by: ______________________

Figure 9.1 Media insertion order form.

Chapter 10

Tax, Record Keeping And Legal Aspects

Local and state governments, as well as the federal government have various regulations you must follow. Tax, record keeping and legal aspects are important in any business, including selling information by mail.

TAX ASPECTS

There are several types of taxes you should be aware of. The first type is income taxes. Many states and of course, the federal government require you to pay income taxes. The second and third types of taxes you should be aware of are the sales tax and the use tax.

Internal Revenue Service

Perhaps the most feared federal government entity is the IRS (Internal Revenue Service). Almost everyone has heard horror stories about the IRS. The best thing you can do to remain on good terms with the IRS is to be well informed yourself and/or to have a competent accountant or CPA (certified public accountant) help you.

The IRS's own *Your Federal Income Tax* (Publication 17) and *Tax Guide For Small Business* (Publication 334) contain excellent information. You can pick up copies of each at your local IRS office.

SMALL BUSINESS TAX EDUCATION PROGRAM

The IRS has a program called the Small Business Tax Education Program (STEP). It is a cooperative effort with local organizations to provide business tax education to the small business owner.

The STEP instructors teach small business owners how to fill out business or employment tax forms, which taxes they are responsible for and which they are not, what records to keep and how to keep them, the role of the IRS and how to deal effectively with various offices in the IRS, what other help is available from the IRS and other federal, state or local agencies and how to get it when you need it plus various other topics of interest to small business owners.

The costs for the program vary. Some of the courses offered by STEP are free as a community service. Courses offered through an educational facility may include costs for course materials in addition to tuition.

If you are interested in the IRS Small Business Education Program, contact the IRS Taxpayer Education Coordinator in your area. Their addresses and telephone numbers are listed in Appendix B.

Sales Tax

Most states in the United States collect a sizable sales tax in addition to taxing income. You must collect the required sales tax from customers who live in your state and report and give that money to your state once a year or four times a year. For more information about sales taxes contact your state's sales tax department.

Use Tax

The use tax can be a confusing and a complicated matter. The use tax is contingent upon the location of your "place of business." What makes the use tax confusing and complicated is that mail order businesses go across state lines and that states have a different idea of what "place of business" means.

In 1967 the United States Supreme Court banned states from imposing tax-collection obligations on businesses that have no "physical presence" within their borders. The 1967 ruling said that imposing such obligations would violate due-process rights and interfere unduly with interstate commerce.

However, in October of 1991 the United States Supreme Court agreed to reconsider its 24-year-old curb on sales tax collections from out-of-state firms. The court agreed to settle a North Dakota dispute over a state's authority to force out-of-state catalog companies to collect the sales and use taxes its residents owe on mail-order purchases after the North Dakota Supreme Court ruled last May that the 1967 United States Supreme Court ruling is an "obsolescent precedent" that need not be followed.

In May of 1992 the Supreme Court declined to overrule its 1967 ruling by a vote of 8-1. However, the Supreme Court said that Congress has the power to decide whether states may impose sales taxes on items sold by mail by out-of-state firms. This could affect most of the nation's mail order businesses and the Direct Marketing Association is planning a lobbying campaign to block any new tax. Contact your state's sales tax department for more information about the use tax.

RECORD KEEPING ASPECTS

Always keep good records for two reasons. The first reason is that this is a good business practice. For example, by keeping good records of the orders you receive you will know which publications or mailing lists work best for you. This knowledge is important for your success.

The second reason for keeping good records is for tax purposes. Keep good records of the money you receive from your business—income, and the money you spend on your business—expenses. You can do this by using a simple bookkeeping system or by hiring a bookkeeper, accountant or a CPA.

Keeping Records Of Orders

Keeping good records of orders begins when you receive the orders. You should have a good system for handling your incoming mail. I will share with you the system I use. It works well for me but it is possible you may find ways to improve it.

Incoming Mail

The United States Postal Service delivers mail six days a week, Monday through Saturday, except on holidays. I usually work on my incoming mail every day it is delivered, including Saturdays. You may want to take your weekends off and open your Saturday mail on Monday.

STEP 1—OPEN THE MAIL

The first step is to open each piece of the incoming mail and see what is in it. If it is an order, I check to see if the customer's name and address on the coupon or order form is legible. If it is not 100% legible, I check the return address on the outside of the envelope. If the name and address on the envelope is more legible I use it to fill the order.

STEP 2—SORT THE MAIL

The second step is to sort the mail into different piles. Let's say I open a letter and it contains an order. I place checks, cashier's checks and money orders together but I sort them by dollar amounts.

For example, all checks, cashier's checks and money orders for $49 go in the same pile. Other piles may be for $52, $53 or $56. I use the same system for cash—one dollar bills on one pile, $5 bills on another pile, etc. Using this simple system makes it easier to prepare bank deposit slips.

After having sorted the money I sort the coupons or the order forms. Each display advertisement coupon has a key code which tells me which publication the customer ordered from. I sort all display advertisement coupons by key codes.

Each direct mail advertisement order form also has a key code which tells me which quarter of which mailing list the customer's name came from. I sort all direct mail advertisement order forms by key codes.

I Do Not Wait For Checks To Clear

Please note that I only separate the coupons and order forms by key codes and not by the method of payment. Many mail order operators separate coupons and order forms which were paid for by regular checks because they are afraid that the checks might bounce. They wait for the checks to clear before shipping the information to the customers who paid by check.

I have found that only about two to three percent of all regular checks bounce. I do not believe it is fair to the other 97% or 98% of the customers whose checks will clear to hold their orders hostage. Therefore I do not wait for the checks to clear before I ship the information to the customers who paid by check.

In a word, I treat all orders the same, regardless of the method of payment. I would rather take a chance of sending books to people whose checks will bounce than making the honest 97% to 98% majority wait an extra two to three weeks to receive what they paid for.

Mail Which Does Not Contain Orders

Not all incoming mail contains orders. I also receive other types of mail including inquiries, bills, advertising, questions, comments and complaints.

Inquiries usually come from potential customers who subscribe to or purchase various publications I advertise in. Bills are invoices from printers, publications I advertise in and my various suppliers.

Advertising mail consists of numerous offers I receive from other mail order companies. Questions and comments come from existing customers and potential customers. Comments also come from various book reviews.

Complaints

Complaints are usually from customers who did not receive a book. Usually what happens is that their letter of complaint and the book crossed in the mail. Sometimes it turns out that either the letter containing their order did not reach me or that the book I mailed to them did not reach them.

The main reason this happens is that every mail order transaction involves a number of human beings and regrettably, human beings do make mistakes. Here is a list of some of the mistakes that have occurred in mail order transaction I have been involved in:

1. The customer (being human) may put the wrong address or zip code on the envelope when he sends his order to me and consequently his letter may never reach me.
2. The customer may put the correct address on his letter to me but the mail carrier (being human) may deliver it to the wrong box or address.
3. The customer's letter reaches me, but I may make an error in typing the customer's address label (I am human too). Consequently, his book never reaches him.
4. The customer's letter may reach me, but his address on the coupon, order form and envelope is illegible. Consequently, despite my best efforts to decipher his address, his book never reaches him. See Appendix C.
5. The customer puts a correct address on his letter to me, I type his address label correctly, but the mail carrier (being human) may deliver the book to the wrong address.
   In the past, when I have used private postal boxes, their employees (being human) almost daily placed someone else's mail in my box. If they did that, then I can only assume that some of my mail ended up in someone else's box and never reached me.
6. The customer (being human) puts an old address on his letter to me. I type his address label correctly, but the book never reaches him.

Recently, at a suggestion of a local Postmaster, I had the phrase "address correction requested" printed on my envelopes and have found that some books have come back to me with the new, correct address printed on the envelope. I then mail the book for the second time, using the new, hopefully correct address and the book usually reaches the customer.

7. The customer puts a correct address on his letter to me, I type his address label correctly, but the Postal Service destroys the address label on the envelope containing his book.
   The Postal Service has returned to me numerous books I have mailed to my customers with the words "damaged in Postal Service handling" stamped on the envelopes.

Conclusion About Complaints

I am giving you this list of some of the mistakes that have occurred in my mail order transactions in order to help you understand how mistakes happen. Hopefully, knowing this will make you a more tolerant mail order business person when dealing with the inevitable customer complaints.

Your attitude should be that regardless of who made a mistake, your customer deserves to have his complaint taken care of quickly and fairly. With that in mind, you should try to take care of your complaints the day you receive them.

STEP 3—RECORD THE ORDERS

After I have opened and sorted the orders, the next step is to count and record the orders.

Order Sheet For Display Advertisements

I use a separate order sheet for each display advertisement I run. On top of the order sheet I write the name of the publication, the issue, the key code and the name of the product I advertised. See Figure 10.1.

Below and on the far left is "Days"—the number of days column, starting with number 1. Next to it is "Date"—a column with blank spaces in which I write the actual dates of the orders (Dec. 12, 1991 for example). The next columns are "DT" (daily number of orders) and "CT" (the total or cumulative number of orders).

Order Sheet For Direct Mail Advertising

I use a separate order sheet for each mailing list I use. On top of the order sheet I write the date of mailing, the name of the mailing list used, the number of mailing pieces sent, the key code for the mailing list used and the name of the product I advertised. See Figure 10.2.

Below and on the far left is "Days"—the number of days column, starting with number 1. Next to it is "Date"—a column with blank spaces in which I write the actual dates of the orders (Dec. 12, 1991 for example). The next columns are "DT" (daily number of orders) and "CT" (the total or cumulative number of orders).

STEP 4—SHIP THE ORDERS

After I have opened, sorted the mail and recorded the orders, the next step is to ship the orders. As discussed earlier, I ship all orders at the same time, regardless of how the individual customers paid for their orders.

Ship The Orders Quickly

Try not to fall behind on your incoming mail. Your goal should be to ship the orders as soon as possible, preferably within 48 hours after receiving them.

Order Sheet For Display Advertisements

Publication ____________ Issue ____________

Key Code ________ Product ____________

Days	Date	D.T.	C.T.	Days	Date	D.T.	C.T.
1				31			
2				32			
3				33			
4				34			
5				35			
6				36			
7				37			
8				38			
9				39			
10				40			
11				41			
12				42			
13				43			
14				44			
15				45			
16				46			
17				47			
18				48			
19				49			
20				50			
21				51			
22				52			
23				53			
24				54			
25				55			
26				56			
27				57			
28				58			
29				59			
30				60			

Figure 10.1 Order sheet for display advertisements.

The law requires that all orders must be shipped within 30 days after receiving them or the customers must be sent an explanation as to when the orders will be mailed. Also, the law requires that the customer must be given an option to get a full refund if he or she does not want to wait any longer than 30 days. More about this and other legal matters later in this chapter.

One thing you can do that will help you in shipping the orders is to prepackage the orders. That way the orders will be ready for postage and labeling and quick shipment. Shipping the orders quickly is a good as well as ethical and legal way of doing business. Fast service encourages repeat business.

Order Sheet For Direct Mail Advertising

Date of Mailing ______________ Mailing List ______________

No. of Pieces______ Key Code ______ Product ______________

Days	Date	D.T.	C.T.	Days	Date	D.T.	C.T.
1				31			
2				32			
3				33			
4				34			
5				35			
6				36			
7				37			
8				38			
9				39			
10				40			
11				41			
12				42			
13				43			
14				44			
15				45			
16				46			
17				47			
18				48			
19				49			
20				50			
21				51			
22				52			
23				53			
24				54			
25				55			
26				56			
27				57			
28				58			
29				59			
30				60			

Figure 10.2 Order sheet for direct mail advertising.

Outgoing Mail

Your outgoing mail is all the mail you send out including the orders you ship. There are different ways you can save money on your outgoing mail.

HOW TO SAVE MONEY ON YOUR OUTGOING MAIL

You can ship your orders first class, at special fourth-class book rate or bulk rate. Orders shipped first class reach the customers more quickly than orders shipped at special fourth-class book rate and bulk rate and that is why I ship my orders first class. You can save money on the orders you ship at special fourth-class book rate or bulk rate.

Special Fourth-Class Book Rate

The United States Postal Service offers a special fourth-class book rate which is less expensive than first class. You must stamp "special fourth-class book rate" on each package. Special fourth-class book rate does not have to meet various requirements of bulk rate.

For example, you do not have to sort your mail into ZIP-code sequence and you do not have to mail more than 200 pieces at one time. Orders shipped at fourth-class book rate should reach your customers about as quickly as orders shipped bulk rate.

Bulk Rate

I use bulk rate to ship my direct mail advertising because it saves me a lot of money on postage over first class. Bulk mail can be stamped, postage metered or sent with the bulk rate permit printed on the outside envelope. For information regarding my experience in testing stamped and postage metered bulk rate outside envelopes, see Chapter 11, "Direct Mail Advertising."

Mail shipped at bulk rate must meet various requirements. There must be at least 200 identical pieces in each mailing or the mailing must weigh at least 50 pounds.

You must sort all mail into ZIP-code sequence and must meet specific mailing requirements regarding bundling, labeling and sacking. Contact your local post office for the most up-to-date information regarding the bulk rate requirements.

A bulk rate mailing permit is required before you can use bulk rate. You can contact your local post office for more information on how to obtain a bulk rate mailing permit or you can do what I do. I have mailing service companies mail my direct mail advertising for me using their bulk mailing permits. For more information regarding mailing service companies see Chapter 11, "Direct Mail Advertising."

Obtain Up-To-Date Information

Postal rates and regulations change often so you should contact your local post office for the most up-to-date information available regarding first class, fourth-class book rate and bulk rate. You can also order the *Domestic Mail*

Manual from the Superintendent of Documents, U.S. Government Printing Office, Washington, D.C. 20402.

Bookkeeping

Look at Schedule C, Profit or Loss From Business, (Sole Proprietorship) in the IRS's own *Tax Guide For Small Business* (Publication 334) mentioned earlier. You can use Schedule C as a guide for recording, separating and filing your income and expense receipts and records.

GENERAL TIPS

I am not a bookkeeper, accountant or a CPA so I can give you only some general tips:

1. File and record all of your deposit receipts. Keep copies of all your business income bank deposit slips.
2. File all of your expense receipts. Keep all copies of all your business expense receipts regardless of how you pay for them: by cash, check or credit card. Never throw away receipts because you expect to receive the cancelled check back from your bank or a detailed statement from your credit card issuing bank. It is better to have duplicate copies of your business expenses than to have no copies or proof of the business expense at all.
3. Record your business expenses in chronological order. Simply list your business expenses on a sheet of paper in chronological order. Write the date of each expenditure, whom you paid, item or service purchased (what you paid for), the check number if you paid by check (if you paid by cash or credit card note that information here) and the amount you paid. See Figure 10.3.
4. Record your business expenses by category. You can use the categories listed in the Schedule C, Profit or Loss From Business, (Sole Proprietorship) in the IRS's own *Tax Guide For Small Business* (Publication 334).

You or your bookkeeper, accountant or CPA can do this weekly or monthly based on the record of your business expenses in chronological order. See Figure 10.4.

LEGAL ASPECTS

Legal aspects are as important when selling information by mail as they are in any other business.

Registering Your Business

In some areas you may need to obtain a business license for a modest fee. If that is the case, you will also need to fill out a simple application. In other areas you may not need a business license. Call your local city or county clerk to see if you need to register your mail order business.

The Mail Order Merchandise Rule

As mentioned previously, you must ship all orders within 30 days after receiving them. This is known as the Federal Trade Commission's Mail Order Merchandise Rule. If you are unable to ship your customers' orders within the 30 day period, you must send your customers an "option notice."

Chronological Record Of Expenses

Date	Whom Paid	Item Purchased	Check #	Amount

Figure 10.3 Chronological record of expenses.

This notice gives the customer a new shipping date and also gives him the option of either cancelling the order and getting a full refund or agreeing to the new shipping date. You must include instructions on how to cancel the order in the "option notice." You must also provide your customer with a free method to reply to you (a self-addressed and stamped envelope).

Record of business expenses by category

Week Beginning ____________ Week Ending ______________

Business Expenses	Week Total	Total Prior	Total To Date
Advertising			
Bank charges			
Car expenses			
Commissions			
Dues and publications			
Freight			
Insurance			
Interest			
Inventory			
Laundry & cleaning			
Legal & Prof. services			
Office supplies			
Pension & profit sharing			
Postage			
Printing			
Rent			
Repairs			
Taxes			
Telephone			
Travel & entertainment			
Utilities			
Wages			

Figure 10.4 Record of business expenses by category.

If your customer agrees to the delay date given in the first notice, but you can not meet the new shipping date, you must send a second "option notice." The order is considered automatically cancelled and you must issue a full refund if your customer does not sign his consent on the second "option notice."

REFUNDS

If a prepaid order is cancelled, you must mail your customer a refund within seven business days. If your customer orders with a credit card, you must adjust his account within one billing cycle.

EXCEPTIONS TO THE MAIL ORDER MERCHANDISE RULE

There are some exceptions to the Mail Order Merchandise Rule. The rule does not apply to mail order photo-finishing; magazine subscriptions and other serial deliveries (except for initial shipment); seeds and plants; COD (cash-on-delivery) orders; or credit orders where your customer's account is not charged before the merchandise is mailed.

Pay Refunds

In the mail order business you can not satisfy all the people all of the time. Everyone in the mail order business receives refund requests. That's part of business. You have to pay refunds and pay them promptly. My goal is to pay all refunds within 24 hours. I have a number of letters on file from customers thanking me for a prompt refund.

Copyright Protection

Copyright is a form of protection provided by the laws of the United States to the authors of "original works of authorship" including literary, dramatic, musical, artistic and certain other intellectual works. Copyright is the right of an author to control the reproduction of his work and it protects the author's original and creative works from unauthorized reproduction by others.

In other words, the author has a complete monopoly over the work he or she has copyrighted. A copyrighted work may not be printed, published, dramatized, translated, adapted, broadcasted or reproduced in any other way without the consent of the author. Both published and unpublished works are protected.

HOW TO SECURE A COPYRIGHT

The way in which copyright protection is secured under the present law is frequently misunderstood. No publication or registration or other action in the Copyright Office is required to secure a copyright. In a word, copyright is secured automatically when the work is created. To put it even more simply, your work is copyrighted as soon as you write it.

Copyright Registration

In general, copyright registration is a legal formality intended to make a public record of the basic facts of a particular copyright. Registration is not necessary, it is not a condition of copyright protection. It may be made at any time within the life of the copyright.

However, there are certain definite advantages to registration. For example, registration establishes a public record of the copyright claim and is often necessary before any infringement suits may be filed in court.

Notice Of Copyright

When a work is published under the authority of the copyright owner, a notice of copyright should be placed on all publicly distributed copies. The notice is required even on works published outside of the United States.

Failure to comply with the notice requirement can result in the loss of certain additional rights otherwise available to the copyright owner. The use of the copyright notice is the responsibility of the copyright owner and does not require advance permission from, or registration with, the Copyright Office.

Form Of Notice

The copyright notice should contain all of the following three elements:

1. The symbol © (the letter C in a circle), or the word "copyright," or the abbreviation "Copr."; and
2. The year of first publication of the work. In the case of compilations or derivative works incorporating previously published material, the year date of first publication of the compilation or derivative work is sufficient; and
3. The name of the owner of the copyright (probably your name) or an abbreviation by which the name can be recognized, or a generally known alternative designation of the owner. Example: © 1991 John Doe.

Registration Procedures

In general, to register your work, send the following three elements in the same envelope or package to the register of Copyrights, Copyright Office, Library of Congress, Washington, D.C. 20559.

1. A properly completed application form.
2. A nonrefundable filing fee of $20 for each application. Do not send cash. Use a check or a money order payable to the Register of Copyrights.
3. A nonreturnable deposit of the work being registered (a copy of your work). The deposit requirements vary in particular situations. The general requirements are as follows:

- If the work is unpublished, one complete copy.
- If the work was first published in the United States on or after January 1, 1978, two complete copies of the best edition.
- If the work was first published in the United States before January 1, 1978, two complete copies of the work as first published.
- If the work was first published outside the United States, whenever published, one complete copy of the work as first published.

As you can see, registering a copyright is easy and it costs only $20. For the correct application forms and other printed information put out by the

Copyright Office, write to the Register of Copyrights, Copyright Office, Library of Congress, Washington, D.C. 20559. Complete the original 8 1/2 inch by 11 inch application forms the Copyright Office sends you using ink pen or typewriter.

Form TX is for published and unpublished non-dramatic literary works. It is generally used for a written document in a book form. See Figure 10.5 for a reduced version of Form TX and Figure 10.6 for line-by-line instructions for filling out Form TX.

HOW LONG COPYRIGHT PROTECTION ENDURES

Works Originally Copyrighted On Or After January 1, 1978

A work that is created (fixed in tangible form for the first time) on or after January 1, 1978, is automatically protected from the moment of its creation, and is ordinarily given a term enduring for the author's life, plus an additional 50 years after the author's death. In the case of "a joint work prepared by two or more authors who did not work for hire," the term lasts for 50 years after the last surviving author's death. For works made for hire, and for anonymous and pseudonymous works (unless the author's identity is revealed in Copyright Office records), the duration of copyright will be 75 years from publication or 100 years from creation, whichever is shorter.

Works that were created before the present law came into effect, but had neither been published nor registered for copyright before January 1, 1978, have been automatically brought under the statute and are now given Federal copyright protection. The duration of copyright in these works will generally be computed in the same way as for works created on or after January 1, 1978: the life-plus-50 or 75/100-year terms will apply to them as well. However, all works in this category are guaranteed at least 25 years of statutory protection.

Works Copyrighted Before January 1, 1978

Under the law in effect before 1978, copyright was secured either on the date a work was published, or on the date of registration if the work was registered in unpublished form. In either case, the copyright endured for a first term of 28 years from the date it was secured. During the last (28th) year of the first term, the copyright was eligible for renewal. The new copyright law has extended the renewal term from 28 to 47 years for copyrights that were subsisting on January 1, 1978, making these works eligible for a total term of protection of 75 years. However, the copyright must be timely renewed to receive the 47-year period of added protection.

For more detailed information on the copyright term, write to the Copyright Office and request Circulars 15a and 15t. For information on how to search the Copyright Office records concerning the copyright status of a work, ask for Circular 22.

Legal Aspects To Consider Regarding Advertising

Before you write and run your advertisement, study very carefully "A MISTAKE I MADE" following.

A MISTAKE I MADE

As I discussed earlier in this book, the last money making offer I purchased before I discovered my amazing discovery was about mail order. I received a booklet a few pages long.

The author of the booklet gave me a little advice on how to write an advertisement. However, the author let me down by neglecting to advise me that before I run my advertisement I should consult a lawyer who is an expert in mail order so that he or she could review my advertisement and the information I was selling to make sure that they are not in violation of various federal provisions regarding advertising. Please note that I wrote ". . .consult a lawyer who is an expert in mail order. . . ." because from my experience, a lawyer whose specialty is not mail order does not have the expertise necessary to review the advertisement and information being sold by mail.

Because the author let me down by neglecting to advise me that I should consult a lawyer who is a real expert in mail order, I did not do it, and that was a mistake I made. As a result, I unknowingly violated various federal provisions regarding advertising which resulted in postal authorities stopping my mail and seizing part of my assets from two and a half years of business. It took me time and money to work out a civil settlement with the government. All of this could have been avoided if I had known how important it is to consult a lawyer who is an expert in mail order before running my advertisements. It took me two and a half years to find lawyers whose specialty is mail order and who therefore have the expertise necessary to review my advertisements and the information I am selling by mail. In fact, no information about mail order I have ever read advises the reader to consult a lawyer who is an expert in mail order and provides names and addresses of such lawyers who could review the reader's advertisement and the information the reader is selling to make sure that they are not in violation of various federal provisions regarding advertising. Read the following paragraph perhaps ten times to find out exactly what to do so that you do not have to repeat the mistake I made.

I can not give you legal advice, because I am not a lawyer, but I can state the following: to the best of my knowledge, the following lawyers are experts in mail order. To make sure that I do not have to repeat the mistake I made, I consult one of them before I run an advertisement. To make sure that you do not have to repeat the mistake I made, you should consult one of them or any other lawyer who is an expert in mail order before you run an advertisement. In addition, before you write and run your advertisement study very carefully the United States Postal Service, 39 U.S. Code 3005, Figure 10.7.

Charles F. Abbott
Attorney At Law
3737 Foothill Drive
Provo, Utah 84604

Sheldon S. Lustigman
Attorney At Law
60th Floor
Empire State Building
New York, NY 10118

Gronek & Armstrong
Attorneys At Law
227 West Monroe Street
Chicago, IL 60606

Lamet, Kanwit & Associates
Attorneys At Law
600 S. Federal Street, Suite 201
Chicago, IL 60605

FORM TX
UNITED STATES COPYRIGHT OFFICE

REGISTRATION NUMBER

TX TXU

EFFECTIVE DATE OF REGISTRATION

Month Day Year

DO NOT WRITE ABOVE THIS LINE. IF YOU NEED MORE SPACE, USE A SEPARATE CONTINUATION SHEET.

1

TITLE OF THIS WORK ▼

PREVIOUS OR ALTERNATIVE TITLES ▼

PUBLICATION AS A CONTRIBUTION If this work was published as a contribution to a periodical, serial, or collection, give information about the collective work in which the contribution appeared. Title of Collective Work ▼

If published in a periodical or serial give: Volume ▼ Number ▼ Issue Date ▼ On Pages ▼

2

a NAME OF AUTHOR ▼ DATES OF BIRTH AND DEATH Year Born ▼ Year Died ▼

Was this contribution to the work a "work made for hire"? ☐ Yes ☐ No

AUTHOR'S NATIONALITY OR DOMICILE Name of Country OR { Citizen of ▶ Domiciled in ▶

WAS THIS AUTHOR'S CONTRIBUTION TO THE WORK Anonymous? ☐ Yes ☐ No Pseudonymous? ☐ Yes ☐ No If the answer to either of these questions is "Yes," see detailed instructions.

NATURE OF AUTHORSHIP Briefly describe nature of the material created by this author in which copyright is claimed ▼

b NAME OF AUTHOR ▼ DATES OF BIRTH AND DEATH Year Born ▼ Year Died ▼

Was this contribution to the work a "work made for hire"? ☐ Yes ☐ No

AUTHOR'S NATIONALITY OR DOMICILE Name of country OR { Citizen of ▶ Domiciled in ▶

WAS THIS AUTHOR'S CONTRIBUTION TO THE WORK Anonymous? ☐ Yes ☐ No Pseudonymous? ☐ Yes ☐ No If the answer to either of these questions is "Yes," see detailed instructions.

NATURE OF AUTHORSHIP Briefly describe nature of the material created by this author in which copyright is claimed ▼

c NAME OF AUTHOR ▼ DATES OF BIRTH AND DEATH Year Born ▼ Year Died ▼

Was this contribution to the work a "work made for hire"? ☐ Yes ☐ No

AUTHOR'S NATIONALITY OR DOMICILE Name of Country OR { Citizen of ▶ Domiciled in ▶

WAS THIS AUTHOR'S CONTRIBUTION TO THE WORK Anonymous? ☐ Yes ☐ No Pseudonymous? ☐ Yes ☐ No If the answer to either of these questions is "Yes," see detailed instructions.

NATURE OF AUTHORSHIP Briefly describe nature of the material created by this author in which copyright is claimed ▼

NOTE

Under the law, the "author" of a "work made for hire" is generally the employer, not the employee (see instructions). For any part of this work that was "made for hire" check "Yes" in the space provided, give the employer (or other person for whom the work was prepared) as "Author" of that part, and leave the space for dates of birth and death blank.

3

a YEAR IN WHICH CREATION OF THIS WORK WAS COMPLETED This information must be given in all cases. ◀ Year

b DATE AND NATION OF FIRST PUBLICATION OF THIS PARTICULAR WORK Complete this information ONLY if this work has been published. Month ▶ Day ▶ Year ▶ ◀ Nation

4

COPYRIGHT CLAIMANT(S) Name and address must be given even if the claimant is the same as the author given in space 2 ▼

See instructions before completing this space

TRANSFER If the claimant(s) named here in space 4 are different from the author(s) named in space 2, give a brief statement of how the claimant(s) obtained ownership of the copyright. ▼

DO NOT WRITE HERE OFFICE USE ONLY

APPLICATION RECEIVED

ONE DEPOSIT RECEIVED

TWO DEPOSITS RECEIVED

REMITTANCE NUMBER AND DATE

MORE ON BACK ▶ • Complete all applicable spaces (numbers 5-11) on the reverse side of this page. • See detailed instructions. • Sign the form at line 10.

DO NOT WRITE HERE

Page 1 of ______ pages

Figure 10.5 Form TX

EXAMINED BY

FORM TX

CHECKED BY

CORRESPONDENCE
Yes

FOR COPYRIGHT OFFICE USE ONLY

DO NOT WRITE ABOVE THIS LINE. IF YOU NEED MORE SPACE, USE A SEPARATE CONTINUATION SHEET.

5

PREVIOUS REGISTRATION Has registration for this work, or for an earlier version of this work, already been made in the Copyright Office?
☐ **Yes** ☐ **No** If your answer is "Yes," why is another registration being sought? (Check appropriate box) ▼
☐ This is the first published edition of a work previously registered in unpublished form
☐ This is the first application submitted by this author as copyright claimant
☐ This is a changed version of the work, as shown by space 6 on this application
If your answer is "Yes," give **Previous Registration Number** ▼ **Year of Registration** ▼

6

DERIVATIVE WORK OR COMPILATION Complete both space 6a & 6b for a derivative work; complete only 6b for a compilation.
a. Preexisting Material Identify any preexisting work or works that this work is based on or incorporates. ▼

b. Material Added to This Work Give a brief, general statement of the material that has been added to this work and in which copyright is claimed. ▼

See instructions before completing this space.

7

—space deleted—

8

REPRODUCTION FOR USE OF BLIND OR PHYSICALLY HANDICAPPED INDIVIDUALS A signature on this form at space 10, and a check in one of the boxes here in space 8, constitutes a non-exclusive grant of permission to the Library of Congress to reproduce and distribute solely for the blind and physically handicapped and under the conditions and limitations prescribed by the regulations of the Copyright Office: (1) copies of the work identified in space 1 of this application in Braille (or similar tactile symbols); or (2) phonorecords embodying a fixation of a reading of that work; or (3) both.
a ☐ Copies and Phonorecords b [ ] Copies Only c [ ] Phonorecords Only

See instructions.

9

DEPOSIT ACCOUNT If the registration fee is to be charged to a Deposit Account established in the Copyright Office, give name and number of Account.
Name ▼ **Account Number** ▼

CORRESPONDENCE Give name and address to which correspondence about this application should be sent. Name/Address/Apt/City/State/Zip ▼

Area Code & Telephone Number ▶

Be sure to give your daytime phone ◀ number

10

CERTIFICATION* I, the undersigned, hereby certify that I am the
Check one ▶
[ ] author
[ ] other copyright claimant
[ ] owner of exclusive right(s)
[ ] authorized agent of
Name of author or other copyright claimant, or owner of exclusive right(s) ▲
of the work identified in this application and that the statements made by me in this application are correct to the best of my knowledge.

Typed or printed name and date ▼ If this application gives a date of publication in space 3, do not sign and submit it before that date.

date ▶

Handwritten signature (X) ▼

11

MAIL CERTIFICATE TO

Certificate will be mailed in window envelope

Name ▼

Number/Street/Apartment Number ▼

City/State/ZIP ▼

- Complete all necessary spaces
- Sign your application in space 10

1. Application form
2. Non-refundable $10 filing fee in check or money order payable to Register of Copyrights
3. Deposit material

Register of Copyrights
Library of Congress
Washington, D.C. 20559

* 17 U.S.C. § 506(e): Any person who knowingly makes a false representation of a material fact in the application for copyright registration provided for by section 409, or in any written statement filed in connection with the application, shall be fined not more than $2,500.

February 1990—200,000

U.S. GOVERNMENT PRINTING OFFICE 1990 262-308/11

Figure 10.5 (Continued)

Filling Out Application Form TX

Detach and read these instructions before completing this form. Make sure all applicable spaces have been filled in before you return this form.

BASIC INFORMATION

When to Use This Form: Use Form TX for registration of published or unpublished non-dramatic literary works, excluding periodicals or serial issues. This class includes a wide variety of works: fiction, non-fiction, poetry, textbooks, reference works, directories, catalogs, advertising copy, compilations of information, and computer programs. For periodicals and serials, use Form SE.

Deposit to Accompany Application: An application for copyright registration must be accompanied by a deposit consisting of copies or phonorecords representing the entire work for which registration is to be made. The following are the general deposit requirements as set forth in the statute.

Unpublished Work: Deposit one complete copy (or phonorecord).

Published Work: Deposit two complete copies (or phonorecords) of the best edition.

Work First Published Outside the United States: Deposit one complete copy (or phonorecord) of the first foreign edition.

Contribution to a Collective Work: Deposit one complete copy (or phonorecord) of the best edition of the collective work.

The Copyright Notice: For works first published on or after March 1, 1989, the law provides that a copyright notice in a specified form "may be placed on all publicly distributed copies from which the work can be visually perceived." Use of the copyright notice is the responsibility of the copyright owner and does not require advance permission from the Copyright Office. The required form of the notice for copies generally consists of three elements: (1) the symbol "©", or the word "Copyright," or the abbreviation "Copr."; (2) the year of first publication; and (3) the name of the owner of copyright. For example: "© 1989 Jane Cole." The notice is to be affixed to the copies "in such manner and location as to give reasonable notice of the claim of copyright." Works first published prior to March 1, 1989, **must** carry the notice or risk loss of copyright protection.

For information about notice requirements for works published before March 1, 1989, or other copyright information, write: Information Section, LM-401, Copyright Office, Library of Congress, Washington, D.C. 20559.

PRIVACY ACT ADVISORY STATEMENT Required by the Privacy Act of 1974 (Public Law 93-579)

AUTHORITY FOR REQUESTING THIS INFORMATION
- Title 17, U.S.C., Secs. 409 and 410

FURNISHING THE REQUESTED INFORMATION IS
- Voluntary

BUT IF THE INFORMATION IS NOT FURNISHED
- It may be necessary to delay or refuse registration
- You may not be entitled to certain relief, remedies, and benefits provided in chapters 4 and 5 of title 17, U.S.C.

PRINCIPAL USES OF REQUESTED INFORMATION
- Establishment and maintenance of a public record
- Examination of the application for compliance with legal requirements

OTHER ROUTINE USES
- Public inspection and copying
- Preparation of public indexes
- Preparation of public catalogs of copyright registrations
- Preparation of search reports upon request

NOTE
- No other advisory statement will be given you in connection with this application
- Please keep this statement and refer to it if we communicate with you regarding this application

LINE-BY-LINE INSTRUCTIONS

1 SPACE 1: Title

Title of This Work: Every work submitted for copyright registration must be given a title to identify that particular work. If the copies or phonorecords of the work bear a title (or an identifying phrase that could serve as a title), transcribe that wording *completely* and *exactly* on the application. Indexing of the registration and future identification of the work will depend on the information you give here.

Previous or Alternative Titles: Complete this space if there are any additional titles for the work under which someone searching for the registration might be likely to look, or under which a document pertaining to the work might be recorded.

Publication as a Contribution: If the work being registered is a contribution to a periodical, serial, or collection, give the title of the contribution in the "Title of this Work" space. Then, in the line headed "Publication as a Contribution," give information about the collective work in which the contribution appeared.

2 SPACE 2: Author(s)

General Instructions: After reading these instructions, decide who are the "authors" of this work for copyright purposes. Then, unless the work is a "collective work," give the requested information about every "author" who contributed any appreciable amount of copyrightable matter to this version of the work. If you need further space, request additional Continuation sheets. In the case of a collective work, such as an anthology, collection of essays, or encyclopedia, give information about the author of the collective work as a whole.

Name of Author: The fullest form of the author's name should be given. Unless the work was "made for hire," the individual who actually created the work is its "author." In the case of a work made for hire, the statute provides that "the employer or other person for whom the work was prepared is considered the author."

What is a "Work Made for Hire"? A "work made for hire" is defined as (1) "a work prepared by an employee within the scope of his or her employment"; or (2) "a work specially ordered or commissioned for use as a contribution to a collective work, as a part of a motion picture or other audiovisual work, as a translation, as a supplementary work, as a compilation, as an instructional text, as a test, as answer material for a test, or as an atlas, if the parties expressly agree in a written instrument signed by them that the work shall be considered a work made for hire." If you have checked "Yes" to indicate that the work was "made for hire," you must give the full legal name of the employer (or other person for whom the work was prepared). You may also include the name of the employee along with the name of the employer (for example "Elster Publishing Co., employer for hire of John Ferguson").

"Anonymous" or "Pseudonymous" Work: An author's contribution to a work is "anonymous" if that author is not identified on the copies or phonorecords of the work. An author's contribution to a work is "pseudonymous" if that author is identified on the copies or phonorecords under a fictitious name. If the work is "anonymous" you may: (1) leave the line blank; or (2) state "anonymous" on the line; or (3) reveal the author's identity. If the work is "pseudonymous" you may: (1) leave the line blank; or (2) give the pseudonym and identify it as such (for example: "Huntley Haverstock, pseudonym"); or (3) reveal the author's name, making clear which is the real name and which is the pseudonym (for example "Judith Barton, whose pseudonym is Madeline Elster"). However, the citizenship or domicile of the author **must** be given in all cases.

Dates of Birth and Death: If the author is dead, the statute requires that the year of death be included in the application unless the work is anonymous or pseudonymous. The author's birth date is optional, but is useful as a form of identification. Leave this space blank if the author's contribution was a "work made for hire."

Figure 10.6 Line-by-line instructions for filling out Form TX.

Author's Nationality or Domicile: Give the country of which the author is a citizen, or the country in which the author is domiciled. Nationality or domicile **must** be given in all cases.

Nature of Authorship: After the words "Nature of Authorship" give a brief general statement of the nature of this particular author's contribution to the work. Examples: "Entire text"; "Coauthor of entire text"; "Chapters 11-14"; "Editorial revisions"; "Compilation and English translation"; "New text."

3 SPACE 3: Creation and Publication

General Instructions: Do not confuse "creation" with "publication." Every application for copyright registration must state "the year in which creation of the work was completed." Give the date and nation of first publication only if the work has been published.

Creation: Under the statute, a work is "created" when it is fixed in a copy or phonorecord for the first time. Where a work has been prepared over a period of time, the part of the work existing in fixed form on a particular date constitutes the created work on that date. The date you give here should be the year in which the author completed the particular version for which registration is now being sought, even if other versions exist or if further changes or additions are planned.

Publication: The statute defines "publication" as "the distribution of copies or phonorecords of a work to the public by sale or other transfer of ownership, or by rental, lease, or lending"; a work is also "published" if there has been an "offering to distribute copies or phonorecords to a group of persons for purposes of further distribution, public performance, or public display." Give the full date (month, day, year) when, and the country where, publication first occurred. If first publication took place simultaneously in the United States and other countries, it is sufficient to state "U.S.A."

4 SPACE 4: Claimant(s)

Name(s) and Address(es) of Copyright Claimant(s): Give the name(s) and address(es) of the copyright claimant(s) in this work even if the claimant is the same as the author. Copyright in a work belongs initially to the author of the work (including, in the case of a work made for hire, the employer or other person for whom the work was prepared). The copyright claimant is either the author of the work or a person or organization to whom the copyright initially belonging to the author has been transferred.

Transfer: The statute provides that, if the copyright claimant is not the author, the application for registration must contain "a brief statement of how the claimant obtained ownership of the copyright." If any copyright claimant named in space 4 is not an author named in space 2, give a brief, general statement summarizing the means by which that claimant obtained ownership of the copyright. Examples: "By written contract"; "Transfer of all rights by author"; "Assignment"; "By will." Do not attach transfer documents or other attachments or riders.

5 SPACE 5: Previous Registration

General Instructions: The questions in space 5 are intended to find out whether an earlier registration has been made for this work and, if so, whether there is any basis for a new registration. As a general rule, only one basic copyright registration can be made for the same version of a particular work.

Same Version: If this version is substantially the same as the work covered by a previous registration, a second registration is not generally possible unless: (1) the work has been registered in unpublished form and a second registration is now being sought to cover this first published edition, or (2) someone other than the author is identified as copyright claimant in the earlier registration, and the author is now seeking registration in his or her own name. If either of these two exceptions apply, check the appropriate box and give the earlier registration number and date. Otherwise, do not submit Form TX; instead, write the Copyright Office for information about supplementary registration or recordation of transfers of copyright ownership.

Changed Version: If the work has been changed, and you are now seeking registration to cover the additions or revisions, check the last box in space 5, give the earlier registration number and date, and complete both parts of space 6 in accordance with the instructions below.

Previous Registration Number and Date: If more than one previous registration has been made for the work, give the number and date of the latest registration.

6 SPACE 6: Derivative Work or Compilation

General Instructions: Complete space 6 if this work is a "changed version," "compilation," or "derivative work," and if it incorporates one or more earlier works that have already been published or registered for copyright, or that have fallen into the public domain. A "compilation" is defined as "a work formed by the collection and assembling of preexisting materials or of data that are selected, coordinated, or arranged in such a way that the resulting work as a whole constitutes an original work of authorship." A "derivative work" is "a work based on one or more preexisting works." Examples of derivative works include translations, fictionalizations, abridgments, condensations, or "any other form in which a work may be recast, transformed, or adapted." Derivative works also include works "consisting of editorial revisions, annotations, or other modifications" if these changes, as a whole, represent an original work of authorship.

Preexisting Material (space 6a): For derivative works, complete this space and space 6b. In space 6a identify the preexisting work that has been recast, transformed, or adapted. An example of preexisting material might be: "Russian version of Goncharov's 'Oblomov'." Do not complete space 6a for compilations.

Material Added to This Work (space 6b): Give a brief, general statement of the new material covered by the copyright claim for which registration is sought. Derivative work examples include: "Foreword, editing, critical annotations"; "Translation"; "Chapters 11-17." If the work is a **compilation**, describe both the compilation itself and the material that has been compiled. Example: "Compilation of certain 1917 Speeches by Woodrow Wilson." A work may be both a derivative work and compilation, in which case a sample statement might be: "Compilation and additional new material."

7 SPACE 7: Manufacturing Provisions

Due to the expiration of the Manufacturing Clause of the copyright law on June 30, 1986, this space has been deleted.

8 SPACE 8: Reproduction for Use of Blind or Physically Handicapped Individuals

General Instructions: One of the major programs of the Library of Congress is to provide Braille editions and special recordings of works for the exclusive use of the blind and physically handicapped. In an effort to simplify and speed up the copyright licensing procedures that are a necessary part of this program, section 710 of the copyright statute provides for the establishment of a voluntary licensing system to be tied in with copyright registration. Copyright Office regulations provide that you may grant a license for such reproduction and distribution solely for the use of persons who are certified by competent authority as unable to read normal printed material as a result of physical limitations. The license is entirely voluntary, nonexclusive, and may be terminated upon 90 days notice.

How to Grant the License: If you wish to grant it, check one of the three boxes in space 8. Your check in one of these boxes, together with your signature in space 10, will mean that the Library of Congress can proceed to reproduce and distribute under the license without further paperwork. For further information, write for Circular R63.

9,10,11 SPACE 9, 10, 11: Fee, Correspondence, Certification, Return Address

Deposit Account: If you maintain a Deposit Account in the Copyright Office, identify it in space 9. Otherwise leave the space blank and send the fee of $10 with your application and deposit.

Correspondence (space 9): This space should contain the name, address, area code, and telephone number of the person to be consulted if correspondence about this application becomes necessary.

Certification (space 10): The application can not be accepted unless it bears the date and the **handwritten signature** of the author or other copyright claimant, or of the owner of exclusive right(s), or of the duly authorized agent of author, claimant, or owner of exclusive right(s).

Address for Return of Certificate (space 11): The address box must be completed legibly since the certificate will be returned in a window envelope.

Figure 10.6 (Continued)

JUDICIAL OFFICER
Washington, DC 20260-6100

39 U.S. Code 3005

False representations; lotteries

(a) Upon evidence satisfactory to the Postal Service that any person is engaged in conducting a scheme or device for obtaining money or property through the mail by means of false representations, including the mailing of matter which is nonmailable under section 3001(d) of this title, or is engaged in conducting a lottery, gift enterprise, or scheme for the distribution of money or of real or personal property, by lottery, chance, or drawing of any kind, the Postal Service may issue an order which--

(1) directs the postmaster of the post office at which mail arrives, addressed to such a person or to his representative, to return such mail to the sender appropriately marked as in violation of this section, if the person, or his representative, is first notified and given reasonable opportunity to be present at the receiving post office to survey the mail before the postmaster returns the mail to the sender;

(2) forbids the payment by a postmaster to the person or his representative of any money order or postal note drawn to the order of either and provides for the return to the remitter of the sum named in the money order or postal note; and

(3) requires the person or his representative to cease and desist from engaging in any such scheme, device, lottery, or gift enterprise.

For purposes of the preceding sentence, the mailing of matter which is nonmailable under such section 3001(d) by any person shall constitute prima facie evidence that such person is engaged in conducting a scheme or device for obtaining money or property through the mail by false representations.

Figure 10.7 United States Postal Service, 39 U.S. Code 3005.

2

(b) The public advertisement by a person engaged in activities covered by subsection (a) of this section, that remittances may be made by mail to a person named in the advertisement, is prima facie evidence that the latter is the agent or representative of the advertiser for the receipt of remittances on behalf of the advertiser. The Postal Service may ascertain the existence of the agency in any other legal way satisfactory to it.

(c) As used in this section and section 3006 of this title, the term "representative" includes an agent or representative acting as an individual or as a firm, bank, corporation, or association of any kind.

(d) Nothing in this section shall prohibit the mailing of (1) a newspaper of general circulation containing advertisements, lists of prizes, or information concerning a lottery conducted by a State acting under authority of State law, published in that State, or in an adjacent State which conducts such a lottery, (2) tickets or other materials concerning such a lottery within that State to addresses within that State. For the purposes of this subsection, "State" means a State of the United States, the District of Columbia, the Commonwealth of Puerto Rico, and any territory or possession of the United States, or (3) an advertisement promoting the sale of a book or other publication, or a solicitation to purchase, or a purchase order for any such publication, if (A) such advertisement, solicitation, or purchase order is not materially false or misleading in its description of the publication; (B) such advertisement, solicitation, or purchase order contains no material misrepresentation of fact provided, however, that no statement quoted or derived from the publication shall constitute misrepresentation of fact as long as such statement complies with the requirements of subparagraphs (A) and (C); and (C) the advertisement, solicitation, or purchase order accurately discloses the source of any statements quoted or derived from the publication. Paragraph (3) shall not be applicable to any publication, advertisement, solicitation, or purchase order which is used to sell some other product in which the publisher or author has a financial interest as part of a commercial scheme.

(e) (1) In conducting an investigation to determine if a person is engaged in any of the activities covered by subsection (a) of this section, the Postmaster General (or any duly authorized agent of the Postmaster General) may tender, at any reasonable time and by any reasonable means, the price advertised or otherwise requested for any article or service that such person has offered to provide through the mails.

Figure 10.7 (Continued)

3

(2) A failure to provide the article or service offered after the Postmaster General or his agent has tendered the price advertised or otherwise requested in the manner described in paragraph (1) of this subsection, and any reasons for such failure, may be considered in a proceeding held under section 3007 of this title to determine if there is probable cause to believe that a violation of this section has occurred.

(3) The Postmaster General shall prescribe regulations under which any individual seeking to make a purchase on behalf of the Postal Service under this subsection from any person shall--

(A) identify himself as a employee or authorized agent of the Postal Service, as the case may be;

(B) state the nature of the conduct under investigation; and

(C) inform such person that the failure to complete the transaction may be considered in a proceeding under section 3007 of this title to determine probable cause, in accordance with paragraph (2) of this subsection.

Figure 10.7 (Continued)

Chapter 11

Direct Mail Advertising

Direct mail advertising involves sending your sales material directly to your potential customers. It can be done in one of two ways: renting names of potential customers from others or by using your own list of customers. Direct mail advertising is a multi-billion-dollar method of doing business in the United States. One out of every four books are sold through direct mail advertising.

As was the case with display advertising, the first and most important step to successful direct mail advertising is to write a successful advertisement. For more on this, read Chapter 4, "How To Write A Successful Advertisement."

ADVANTAGES OF DIRECT MAIL ADVERTISING

Direct mail advertising has four major advantages over other mail order advertising.

1. Ability to specifically target your market.
2. Ability to make your advertising personal.
3. Makes it possible to give the potential customer more advertising material than display and classified advertising.
4. Makes it harder for your competition to keep track of your operation.

Direct Mail Advertising Targets Your Market

As was the case with display and classified advertising, the second step to successful direct mail advertising is to target your potential customers. Direct mail advertising offers the best approach for specifically targeting your market. It is the rifle approach while display and classified advertising can often, but not always be compared to the shotgun approach.

For example, let's say you have some information to sell to women gardeners. Using display and classified advertising in various publications you can easily reach many gardeners, but probably not exclusively women gardeners. Using direct mail advertising, you can send your sales material directly to your target—women gardeners.

RIFLE APPROACH

This is the rifle approach because direct mail advertising allows you to target your market precisely. Direct mail advertising's ability to precisely target the market is a reason why a number of mail order firms do almost all of their marketing by direct mail.

Direct Mail Advertising Makes Your Advertising Personal

Another advantage of direct mail advertising is that it gives you the ability to make your advertising personal. With direct mail advertising, you are dealing with your potential customer on a one-on-one basis.

In other words, direct mail advertising makes it possible for you to speak to your potential customer directly. Direct mail accomplishes this by coming to your potential customer by itself—it is not somewhere inside a publication like display or classified advertisements.

More Advertising Copy Can Lead To Greater Success

Direct mail advertising makes it possible to give the potential customer more advertising copy than display and classified advertising. The idea is that the more words you use in the advertising copy, the more potential customers will place an order. Classified advertisement copy is typically only a few words in length. Display advertising, especially full page advertising, allows you to use hundreds of words in the advertising copy.

However, even a full page display advertisement can not compare with a direct mail advertisement with respect to the number of words of advertising copy you can use. A direct mail advertisement is not limited to one page and consequently can use more words. Most direct mail sales letters are four pages long and many are even longer.

Also, the sales letter is not the only component of the direct mail package. The circular, the order form, the outside envelope and even the return envelope can all contain advertising copy and thus help make the sale.

Harder For Your Competition To Keep Track Of Your Operation

Keeping your business operation as confidential as possible is important in any type of business including mail order. You ideally want your competitors to know as little about your mail order operation as possible.

Maintaining confidentiality regarding your successful mail order operation is important because you do not want your competitors to try to duplicate your success. Keeping your operation concealed from your competitors is almost impossible when you are doing display and even classified advertisements. They can easily see that you are repeating your ads.

It is not as easy for your competitors to monitor your success when you use direct mail advertising. They may have their own names on some of the mailing lists you are using but not on all of them. Your competitors will therefore see only a small fraction of your direct mail advertising campaign. It is easy to see that keeping your mail order success concealed from your competitors is much easier to accomplish when using direct mail advertising.

FIVE STEPS TO SUCCESSFUL DIRECT MAIL ADVERTISING

There are five steps to successful direct mail advertising.

1. Write a successful advertisement.
2. Prepare your direct mail package.
3. Choose the mailing lists you will use.
4. Test your direct mail package using the mailing lists of your choice.
5. Another test, continuation, rolling out, new tests and repetition.

WRITE A SUCCESSFUL ADVERTISEMENT

The first step to successful direct mail advertising is to write a successful advertisement. Consider all of the factors in step one when you prepare your direct mail package. See Chapter 4, "How To Write A Successful Advertisement" for a detailed explanation on how to do this.

PREPARE YOUR DIRECT MAIL PACKAGE

Once you have completed step one, written a successful advertisement, you are ready for step two, preparing your direct mail package.

TWO DIRECT MAIL PACKAGE GOALS

When preparing your direct mail package, keep two goals in mind. Your first goal is to encourage the potential customers to open and read your direct mail package. Your second goal is to convince the potential customers to order your information.

HOW WILL YOUR POTENTIAL CUSTOMERS REACT?

While you are preparing your direct mail package continuously ask yourself the following question: how will your potential customers react when they receive your direct mail package?

The First Direct Mail Package Goal

Since my first goal when preparing my direct mail package is to encourage the potential customers to open and read my direct mail package, I always want to make sure that I am sending my potential customers a package that is of high quality. To be perfectly honest, my direct mail package appears to be of high quality because of the impression it creates, not because I use expensive paper or expensive, custom graphics.

I do spend a little extra money by adding color, photographs and clip art. I believe that the few extra dollars I spend on those items give my direct mail packages a high quality appearance.

The reason I send a high quality direct mail package is that I believe the first impression is all important in encouraging the potential customers to open and read the package.

FLY-BY-NIGHT OPERATORS HURT EVERYONE IN MAIL ORDER BUSINESS

Many potential mail order customers are wary of purchasing by mail. Perhaps they have ordered something in the past and received nothing in return. Perhaps they sent the product back and asked for a refund and did not get a refund.

These types of customer rip-offs are typical of fly-by-night mail order operators. Fly-by-night mail order operators are hurting not only their consumers but also everyone in the mail order business.

They hurt everyone in the mail order business because their customers become leery of all mail order offers. A leery potential customer will rarely become a customer.

HONEST, HIGH QUALITY MAIL ORDER OPERATORS COME TO THE RESCUE

Fortunately for the consumers most mail order operations are not fly-by-night. Most mail order operations are run by honest people who seek to satisfy their customers.

Also, the largest and most visible mail order companies tend to be honest and high quality mail order operations. As an example, Sharper Image has a very high quality catalog and a reliable refund policy. In contrast, fly-by-night operators usually send cheap, poor quality direct mail packages.

The high quality of my package shows the potential customers that I am not a fly-by-night operator. This helps in achieving the first goal of my direct mail package: to encourage the potential customers to open and read my direct mail package.

The Second Direct Mail Package Goal

The second goal I have for my direct mail package is to convince the potential customers to order my information. In order to effectively do this, I must make my direct mail package appealing to the potential customers.

CREATE AN APPEALING DIRECT MAIL PACKAGE

There are two reasons for creating an appealing direct mail package. First, making the direct mail package appealing will help in encouraging the potential customers to open and read the direct mail package. Second, the appealing nature of the direct mail package is the key to persuading the customers to send in the order.

Each one of your potential customers can respond in two ways when he receives your direct mail package. Your potential customer may send you money or he may throw your direct mail package in the trash.

STUDY DIRECT MAIL PACKAGES

You can look in the classified sections of various magazines and newspapers to find numerous advertisements offering free details. Write to them and ask for their free details. Most of them will send you their direct mail package. Study all the components of their direct mail packages.

The Sales Letter

The most important component of a direct mail advertising package is the sales letter. The job of the sales letter is to sell your information. The sales letter is like a display advertisement, only you can make it longer and more personal. Refer to Chapter 4, "How To Write A Successful Advertisement" for ideas on how to write a successful advertisement.

THE LENGTH OF THE SALES LETTER

The sales letter can consist of one page or many pages. Note that a two, three, or four page letter usually will produce better results than a one page letter. Never worry about writing too much. The most important thing is to use as many words as you need to sell your information.

The most successful letters are four or more pages long. Some successful letters have been eight pages or longer and are usually used when selling very expensive information. If you are selling really expensive information ($100 or more), you should probably use more than a four page letter.

SALES LETTER MARGINS

There are differing opinions on how wide or narrow sales letter margins should be. I like to leave at least an inch of blank space on all four sides of every page of my sales letters. There are several reasons for this.

First, I believe it makes the sales letter look more personal. Second, it makes each individual line of copy easier to read because the eyes do not have to read as far from left to right.

DRAW ATTENTION TO IMPORTANT SENTENCES

All the important sentences should be highlighted in a manner to draw attention to them. Use a different color from the body of the letter, **bold type,** *italics,* CAPITAL LETTERS, <u>underlining</u> or you can write them out in cursive.

A MISTAKE I MADE

Be careful not to go too far with drawing attention to the important sentences. In the past I have made my most important sentences not only bold but also much larger type than the rest of the copy.

I know this was a big mistake since my response went down. I believe the response went down because the huge type placed next to regular copy made my sales letter look disjointed.

I USE SUBHEADS IN MY SALES LETTERS

Based on my experience, I believe it is a good idea to use subheads in sales letters. Refer to Chapter 4, "How To Write A Successful Advertisement," for a discussion of the benefits of using subheads.

THE TYPED SALES LETTER

Remember, one of the advantages of direct mail advertising is the ability to make it personal. When you type a letter you are aligning your left margin—the left side of the letter is even. The right margin is uneven or ragged, it is not justified.

THE JUSTIFIED MARGINS SALES LETTER

A typed sales letter without question makes the letter appear more personal. Yet many of the recent successful direct mail sales letters I have seen use "justified margins" like I do. Justified margins mean both the left and right margins are aligned. This eliminates the uneven or ragged right margin. See Figure 11.1.

The Advantage And The Disadvantage Of The Justified Margins Sales Letter

The advantage of the justified margins sales letter is that it is easier to read than a typewritten letter. The disadvantage of the justified margins sales letter is that you lose some of the personal feel of a typewritten sales letter with uneven right margins.

MY SALES LETTER

I prefer to use justified margins sales letters to produce an even right margin. I am making a compromise and thus taking a risk here. I am sacrificing some of the personal feel of a typewritten sales letter in exchange for making my sales letter easier to read.

P.S. AT THE END OF THE SALES LETTER

The best sales letters always use a P.S. at the end of the letter. You may ask yourself, do the writers of the letters really forget something? No. The P.S. is included in the best sales letters because the writers know that the potential customers read the P.S.

The P.S. should be fairly short and to the point. You can use the P.S. to make two different types of statements. First, you can use it to restate an important benefit of your information. Second, you can use it to make a statement you have not previously made.

USE A PHOTOGRAPH FOR A BETTER RESPONSE

If you can, use a photograph on your sales letter. Using a photograph should improve your response because it makes the sales letter even more personal. I

T. ROBERT GRILLI

Diversified Financing

P.O. BOX 283
LINCOLN, RHODE ISLAND 02865
TEL. OFFICE (401) 353-2180
RESIDENCE (401) 353-4171

A REALISTIC AND SUPERB WAY TO MAKE $100,000 PLUS ... EVERY YEAR!

Act within the next 30 days and receive – absolutely free – lifetime consultations with financial expert Robert Grilli, the specialist who's gathered all the information you need on "HOW TO BECOME A SUCCESSFUL MONEY-BROKER". Bob charges $150 each hour to all others – but his expertise is free to you – for life – if you sign up now. A deal that no one else in the industry makes available. Just Bob. But only if you act within the next 30 days.

Dear Friend:

My name is Bob Grilli, and I'm going to share something with you that can change your life. To begin with, it may strike you as too good to be true. But I can assure you, it isn't. It's real. With the resources I'm making available to you – and the free consultations I'm prepared to give you for life – you're about to benefit from one of the best financial opportunities I've discovered in my nearly 30 years in the financial services business.

It's Money-Brokering. A Superb way of making maximum money for the least possible work.

What's a Money-Broker? And Why Does Anyone Need One?

A money-broker is an individual who brings a lender who has money to loan together with a person who needs money for business or personal reasons. So, who needs anyone like that? Why doesn't the person needing money just walk into a bank and get it?

****

"We should close this month out with something around $170,000 net, divided between two 'hard working' individuals (not too shoddy for just being in business no longer than twelve weeks). With the greatest thanks to you and your organization".

Mitchell Ambris – Birmingham, MI.

****

There are lots of people in the world – and you know some of them – who have been turned down by banks, credit unions and other traditional money-lending sources. These are people who have a good reason for borrowing, but can't persuade one of the usual lending sources to give them a chance – or a dime. These people need money for their growing businesses, to take advantage of a once-in-a-lifetime investment opportunity, or to handle a devastating personal emergency. They need help. And they need it now! But ... the traditional lender says ... "No Way"!

Figure 11.1 T. Robert Grilli's justified margins sales letter.

believe that the old saying "a picture is worth a thousand words" holds true in advertising.

A MISTAKE I MADE: "WHAT IS THE PRICE OF YOUR INFORMATION?"

For some time I placed the price of my information on the order form only. However, I noticed I was receiving a number of letters from potential custom-

Enter the Money-Broker ... the individual who helps these people raise the money they so urgently need.

Simply put ... the Money-Broker is the go-between. The individual who connects the person who needs money with the source who lends it. As a money-broker you put up no money yourself. You risk absolutely nothing.

Your only function is to bring borrower and lender together in order to secure a loan for the borrower. And for this - you are paid a very handsome fee. It's that simple!

When You're A Money-Broker, You Make BIG MONEY, And You Make It In Two Ways

Being a financial go-between is profitable - very, very profitable. You can easily make over $100,000 a year working part-time. You'll make your big money by getting a commission on every loan that takes place as a result of your connecting the person who needs money with the source that lends it. **Here's How It Works:**

You'll make anywhere from 2% to 10% depending on the size of the loan. As the loan amount goes up, your percentage goes down. But even though the percentage goes down on larger loans ... THE MONEY YOU MAKE GOES UP. On a small loan - $30,000 say - you get 10% or $3,000. For a $100,000 loan you get - 6% or $6,000. On a $500,000 loan (and these are very common) you get **only 4%. Yet, that "only 4%" comes out to $20,000.** THAT'S A LOT OF MONEY. AND AS THE MONEY-BROKER WHO HELPED PUT THIS DEAL TOGETHER ... IT'S ALL YOURS!

You also profit by getting a **$100** application fee from all the people who sign up for your services. That's right! In this business, people pay at least $100 to even have their applications considered. And, if you get just five prospects a weeks (a very low number if you follow my directions) you'll make **$500 a week** in application fees alone for very, very part-time work. As I said, you just can't beat it. But let me stress: this is small change compared with what you'll make on your commissions. Still, it all adds up to dramatically improving your lifestyle!

****

"In one and a half months, I have made almost $90,000, which I have split with a partner. Most of the deals I am coming across are for $200,000 and up; the highest in almost two months being $10,000,000 - (10 MILLION). I wish I had started earlier"!

Phillip W. Richard - Indianapolis, IN.

****

Sounds Good! But, What's The Catch?

The "catch", if you want to call it that, is that you've got to know two things:

How to find the people who need loans ... and
How to find the lenders with the money to loan.

If you can solve these two problems, you're going to make **Big Money** as a Money-Broker. I guarantee it.

And that's where I come in. Because I have the information you need in a very handy, easy-to-follow manual. It's called HOW TO BECOME A SUCCESSFUL MONEY-BROKER. With it, you'll solve the two key problems of the money-broker business and start to get the **big money** you want ... **fast!**

Figure 11.1 (Continued)

ers who for some reason did not get the order form with their direct mail package.

Some of them then wrote to me asking for the price of my information. Of course, I sent them an extra order form and they usually then ordered, but I asked myself the following question: how many orders have I lost because the potential customers did not want to take the trouble to write asking for the

Using "HOW TO BECOME A SUCCESSFUL MONEY-BROKER" you get:

1. **124 of the most flexible lending sources** throughout the United States - names, addresses and telephone numbers. These are the sources (I call them the Prime Lending Institutions) who'll lend to your clients, the people who can't get loans from traditional sources. And you get complete details on what types of loans they make. Now you can connect your clients with sources who will lend them money - and reap a handsome commission for yourself!

2. **167 Venture Capital sources.** Sources who'll loan money to new businesses - names, addresses and telephone numbers. These are the people who are waiting to hear from your clients. The clients who come to you needing business start-up money. And when the loan goes through - you get a big commission for yourself!

3. **Samples of all the forms** your clients must complete so the loan source has all the information it needs. You don't need to create these forms. We already have. And you don't have to fill them out. Your clients do - quickly and easily.

4. **The three classified ads** you need to attract the people who need loans. We've tested these ads and they work. Run them and you'll have as much business as you can handle. And remember, you get **$100** from every application you process. And those **big commission checks** every time a loan gets approved! Why, I even give you the proven letter you can send to the people responding to your ad, the letter that gets them to sign up **FAST!**

5. **Updates.** Like any industry, this one changes. But I don't leave you out on a limb. As new information becomes available - new sources where your clients can get loans - I tell you. No one has more up-to-date information in this field than I do. And what I have I give to you. It's that simple. And guess what? There's no extra cost for the updates. You get them as part of your one-time-only investment in becoming a money-broker.

****

Remember, you make at least $100 for every application you process and up to 10% commission on every loan that's approved. These dollars add up fast till you have REALLY BIG MONEY. All yours. For whatever you like.

To make sure you get these big commissions and to answer any questions you have about money-brokering, don't forget that when you take advantage of this Special Offer you also get <u>unlimited free lifetime consultations</u> from me, Bob Grilli. Ask me any question. Let me help you make your money-brokering business a success. All for FREE. Instead of for my regular $150 per hour price. But only if you act within the next thirty days! Otherwise you'll have to pay my regular $150 per hour fee.

****

Your Complete Money-Broker Program Comes With Our Promise Of Satisfaction And A Full Money-Back Guarantee.

I know you're probably skeptical about what you're reading. I told you you'd probably think it was too good to be true. But maybe this will convince you. **If you're not absolutely satisfied with what I send you, absolutely convinced that it can help you make real money in the lucrative money-broker business, send back your manual and materials within ten days and I'll refund 100% of your money.** That's right. Read and re-read it. Benefit from what I send you. And if you're not absolutely convinced you can profit from it, return it within 10 days for a full refund. No questions asked.

Figure 11.1 (Continued)

price? To solve this problem I now place the price on the sales letter as well as on the order form.

ANOTHER MISTAKE I MADE: I DID NOT PRINT MY RETURN ADDRESS ON MY SALES LETTER

Over time I also noticed that a number of my direct mail customers sent in their orders with their own envelope instead of using the return envelope

YOU ONLY LOSE WHEN YOU DO NOTHING. Because if this is as good as I say it is, you win. And if it's not, you lose nothing. What could be fairer?

Need Money Yourself?

Do you need money for yourself, for business or personal reasons? Your manual comes complete with all the details you need so you can take advantage of the 124 Prime Lending Institutions I tell you about. **And if you have any questions - any question whatsoever about how to get a loan from these sources for your own personal reasons, call my business at (401) 353-2180.** Want to call after business hours? Fine, use my personal home number (401) 728-7644. I don't keep banker's hours and I'm ready for you when you need help or advice!

Now What?

You're probably expecting me to tell you that all this - everything you need to get established in the lucrative money-broker business with lifetime access to me as your personal consultant - will cost you several hundred dollars. If you guessed that, you'd be in the same ballpark as my accountant. He thinks my price for this service is far, far too low. So low as to make you suspicious.

The truth is, I've already made a lot of money. And, while I certainly won't just give my hard-found information away, I do want to make it as inexpensive as possible for those who can profit from it. For you. Call it corny, but I want to give something back as my way of saying "thank you" for all the breaks I've had in this business.

That's why the price of all this - everything you need to become a successful money-broker - is just $79.95 complete, shipping included. Far less than the cost of just one single hour of my consulting time alone. Far less then you'll make when even a single person fills out just one of your loan application forms.

Now, are you ready to make real money as a money-broker - knowing that if you are not 100% satisfied, I will cheerfully refund every last cent of your money?

I hope you are. Because I'm ready to help you. Just fill out the enclosed coupon now, so I can send you everything you need to become a money-broker and start making really big money right away - and know exactly what to do to get money whenever you need it for your clients or yourself.

Sincerely,

T. R. Grilli
Financial Specialist and author of HOW TO BECOME A SUCCESSFUL MONEY-BROKER

P.S. Remember, act within the next 30 days and I'll give you unlimited free consultations for life. Not at my regular rate of $150-per-hour. But FREE! Now you have a private consultant on retainer who knows this business inside out. Ready to help you when you need it. But only if you act now.

****

"This is my first year in business and at the rate I am going my income for this year will be a six digit figure. I would like to thank you for introducing me to this business."
Gregory A. Conte - Los Angeles, CA.

****

Figure 11.1 (Continued)

they should have received with their direct mail package. This led me to conclude that some of them were not receiving the return envelope just like in the previous example others did not get the order form.

I did not think more about this for a while because they were still sending in their orders using their own envelopes. They were obviously able to find my return address either on the order form or on the outside envelope I sent my direct mail package in.

Later on I received a direct mail package asking me to subscribe to a magazine. I did not have time to decide what to do at the moment I opened the direct mail package so I put it aside.

A few days later I looked at the sales letter again and decided to give the magazine a try. However, to my amazement I discovered that I had accidentally thrown away the order form, the outside envelope and the return envelope which came with the package.

I then had to reread the sales letter to find the subscription price and the mailing address of the magazine so I could place my order. If the price and the return address had not been on the sales letter, I could not have subscribed to the magazine.

This unusual incident led me to start printing my return address on my sales letter in addition to having it on the outside envelope, return envelope and the order form. Now, if one of my potential customers is ready to order but can only find my sales letter, he can do so since both the price and my return address are there.

The Circular

The circular, also known as the flier, is separate from the sales letter and either restates the most important points of the sales letter or contains additional information and often an illustration or photograph. The circular can provide very important support for a sales letter which does not have a photograph or an illustration.

The first goal of the circular is to capture the potential customer's attention. The second goal of the circular is to convince the potential customer to order your information.

If the information you are selling is high priced ($100 or more), then your circular should be professionally done. It should be multicolored and printed on glossy or unusually thick or thin paper.

The Order Form

The order form can be completely separate from the other components of a direct mail advertising package. It can also be printed on the sales letter or circular. A separate order form provides the easiest way for your customers to place an order. They do not have to cut or tear the order form. They only have to fill it out.

A perforated order form has small holes, similar to the holes between postage stamps. It is easily detachable from the sales letter or circular it is printed on. The customers simply fill out the order form and tear it along the perforation.

The order form can also be printed on a component of the direct mail advertising package such as the sales letter or circular without a perforation. The customers fill out the order form and send it in along with the direct mail advertising package component it is printed on or they cut the order form in order to separate it. I have noticed that recently even some large companies have been printing their order forms on the sales letter or circular without a perforation. A perforation adds to the cost of a direct mail advertising package and printers do not always do a very good job with them.

For a further discussion of order forms, see Chapter 4, "How To Write A Successful Advertisement."

A DETACHABLE MONEY-BACK GUARANTEE PRINTED ON A SEPARATE ORDER FORM

Using a separate order form gives you the opportunity to place a detachable money-back guarantee on the order form. Typically, the detachable money-back guarantee repeats the guarantee stated on the rest of the order form. It allows the customer to keep a record of the order. See Figure 11.2 for an example of a detachable money-back guarantee printed on a separate order form.

YET ANOTHER MISTAKE I MADE

Typically, if a mailer uses a number 10 window envelope as his outside envelope, the potential customer's name and address is printed on a label which is then pasted to the back of the order form or the back of the return envelope. The direct mail package is then stuffed into the outside envelope in such a way that the address label shows through the see-through window of the number 10 window outside envelope.

When I first started my mail order business I pasted my potential customers' names and address labels to the back of the order form. The front of the order form had blank spaces so that my customers could fill out their names and addresses.

About a year ago I became intrigued by a direct mail package I received that had the potential customer's name and address label pasted on the front of the order form. I thought this was advantageous because the potential customer did not even have to take the time to fill out his name and address on the order form. All he had to do was write a check and mail in his order.

Since I am always looking for ways to make it easier for my customers to order from me, I implemented the idea. For my next mailing I had all the potential customers' names and address labels pasted on the front of the order form. I impatiently waited to see the results.

I was surprised to learn that I had made a mistake. Fortunately, it was not a big mistake, since my response went down only slightly. Why was this a mistake? Because mailing lists are not perfect and because many people change their addresses often.

Up To 10% Address Changes

What I discovered when processing my incoming mail (the orders) was that maybe up to ten percent of the people who ordered had to change something on the name and address label. Some had to add their middle initial to the label. Others moved so they had to scratch out the old and write the new address. Still others discovered that their name was misspelled on the label.

Some of the orders even came from individuals who now lived at the address on the label instead of the potential customer whose name was on the label. These customers (new or current occupants) had to scratch out the name of the potential customer who had moved from that address and write their own name on the label.

ORDER FORM

MID-AMERICAN OPPORTUNITY RESEARCH ENTERPRISES
M.O.R.E.
The Omni Center, 250 N. Kansas
Wichita, Kansas 67214

AOP-001

Dear Eileen,
Please RUSH me my "COMPLETE BUSINESS START-UP PACKAGE" For Making Big Money With My Answering Machine Without Working Hard. I understand I have as long as I want to look it over and give it a try. If I am not happy for any reason, I may return it for a full MONEY-BACK GUARANTEE [Less $3.00 shipping & handling]. I also expect to receive your personal consultation services FREE for sending in my order within the 10 day period. On that basis, here is $29.95. All orders shipped in 48 hours.

☐ Check or Money-Order for $29.95 Enclosed:

Because of the heavy package I will be sending you, please add $3 for shipping & handling. Thank You!

Name ____________________

Address ____________________

City ____________ State ________ Zip ________

Phone (____) ______-________

Please give street adress for fast U.P.S. shipment

Retain This Portion for Your Records

The amount you sent was: ________

The date you sent your order was: ________

Type of publication ordered ....

"A Complete Business Start-Up Package, For You To Make Fantastic Money with your Answering Machine" WITHOUT WORKING HARD!

You can take as long as you like to test my program and prove to yourself that it is everything I say it is. If for any reason you wish to return it during that time, you may do so, with a full MONEY BACK GUARANTEE. [Less $3.00 shipping & handling]

Figure 11.2 A detachable money-back guarantee.

Many Potential Customers Complained

Worse, I discovered a lot of orders with angry remarks complaining that a mistake was made on their name or address. Still worse, I opened a number of letters with no check inside, only an angry note about the same problem.

These potential customers stated in their letters that they did not order because when they got ready to fill out their name and address on the order form, they saw the mistake. Of course, I suspect that for every person who took the time to write me a letter complaining about that mistake, there were probably twenty or maybe fifty or more who simply got mad and threw away the entire direct mail package.

Let The Customer Fill Out His or Her Name And Address

The lesson here is to let the customer fill out his or her name and address on the order form. Having had more time to think this through, I now believe that pasting the name and address label on the front of the order form makes the order form somehow less personal. Perhaps the name and address label reminds the customer that their name came from a mailing list.

Testimonials

It is a big plus for your direct mail package if you can include testimonials from your previous customers. For a detailed discussion of testimonials, see Chapter 4, "How To Write A Successful Advertisement."

The Money-Back Guarantee

The money-back guarantee is an important component of the direct mail package. It can be completely separate from the other components of the package. If that is the case, it should be printed on special paper with perhaps a fancy border to draw attention to it.

The money-back guarantee can also be printed on the sales letter, the circular (flier), or on the order form. I prefer to print the money-back guarantee on the order form and on the sales letter so that the potential customer can not possibly miss it. For a more detailed discussion of money-back guarantees, see Chapter 4, "How To Write A Successful Advertisement."

The Outside Envelope

The outside envelope is a critical component of a direct mail package. If the potential customer does not open the outside envelope, he will never see the offer that is inside. Therefore, you have to make sure the outside envelope is of high quality and that it is appealing.

The purpose of the outside envelope is to encourage your potential customer to open it. You can do this by using four different approaches.

THE BLANK OUTSIDE ENVELOPE

This approach relies on the curiosity of the potential customer. The outside envelope is left blank, except for the potential customer's name and address and perhaps the mailer's return address. The theory for this approach is that the potential customer will open the envelope because if he does not, he will never know who sent it or if it is important. See Figure 11.3.

THE "TEASER" OUTSIDE ENVELOPE

This approach relies on a "teaser", a phrase related to your offer inside the envelope. The "teaser" is designed to encourage your potential customer to

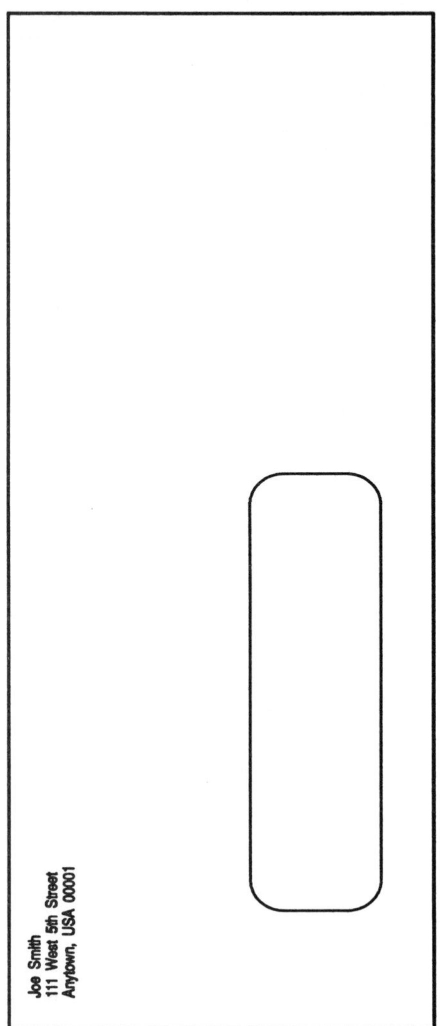

Figure 11.3 The blank outside envelope.

open the outside envelope. The "teaser" must be short because there is not enough room on the outside envelope to write a long story. Figure 11.4 is an example of a "teaser" outside envelope.

THE "OFFICIAL" OUTSIDE ENVELOPE

Some direct mail advertisers attempt to give their outside envelopes the appearance of an official letter. They try to make the potential customer believe

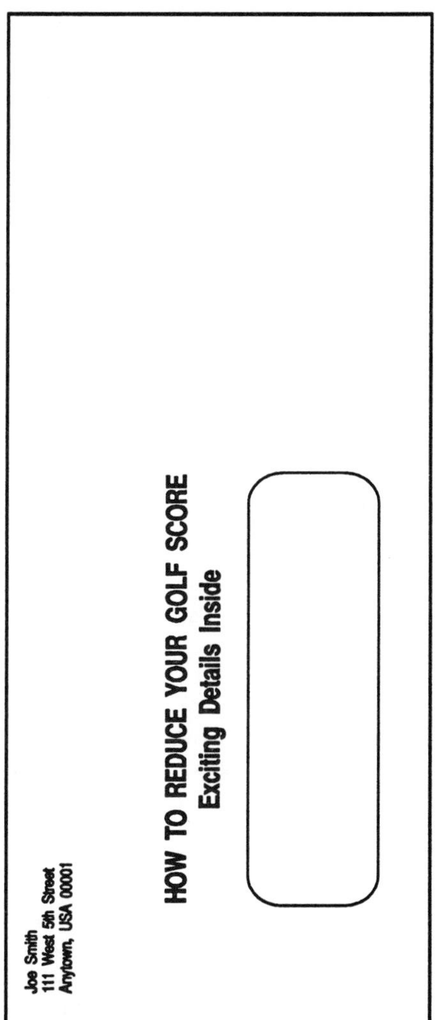

Figure 11.4 The teaser outside envelope.

the letter is coming from the United States government. The theory for this approach is that the potential customer will open the envelope believing it contains official United States government documents.

My Personal Objection To The "Official" Outside Envelope Approach

Before I go on, let me make one point perfectly clear. I have never tried this approach and do not ever intend to try it. I simply do not agree with this approach. I do not believe it is fair or ethical to trick people in such a manner. I am including it here only because it is something I have learned about since I started my business.

It is in fact a widely used approach. I have received numerous "official" direct mail packages since I started my business simply because I have placed myself on many different mailing lists so I can learn more about this business.

The "Official" Outside Envelope's Credibility Problem

Although I have never tried this approach, I do believe it serves its purpose of encouraging the potential customer to open the envelope. However, there is another problem with this approach, in addition to my strong personal objection.

The additional problem is one of credibility. The advertiser using this approach is trying to trick his potential customer into opening the envelope. However, once the potential customer opens the envelope he will realize that he has been fooled. At this point the advertiser has lost credibility, perhaps irreparably. The loss of credibility must hurt the response rate. Because of this problem, and more importantly, because of my personal objection to this approach, I recommend against anyone trying it.

THE "CONFIDENTIAL" OR "PERSONAL" OUTSIDE ENVELOPE

Some direct mail advertisers use the words "confidential" or "personal" on the outside envelope. This approach is typically used by direct mail advertisers whose target market consists of business people or executives who have secretaries screen their mail.

The secretary is usually instructed to throw away "junk mail." By using words like "confidential" or "personal" on the outside envelope the advertiser is trying to get his direct mail package through to the potential customer—the business person or executive.

There are several problems with this approach. First, this approach has been overused and as a result it has become a dead giveaway for a direct mail package. Thus, more than likely, the secretary will realize what it is despite the words on the envelope and will throw it away as instructed by her boss.

Second, if the envelope is opened by the potential customer, the advertiser will lose credibility if there is nothing confidential or personal in the envelope.

MY EXPERIENCE WITH THE BLANK, "CONFIDENTIAL" AND "TEASER" OUTSIDE ENVELOPES

As I mentioned earlier, because of my personal objection to the "official" outside envelope approach I have never tried it, nor do I intend to try it in the future. I have tried the "confidential" or "personal" outside envelope approach and was not happy with the results.

I have also tried both the blank outside envelope and the "teaser" outside envelope approaches. More importantly, I have actually tested both of these approaches one against the other to see which is more effective. For me, the "teaser" envelope worked about twenty percent better than the blank envelope.

WHAT SIZE OF OUTSIDE ENVELOPE TO USE

The standard size "Number 10" outside envelope works best for most direct mail offers. For that reason, it is the one you will see used most often. However, numerous successful offers have used larger or smaller outside envelopes.

REGULAR OR WINDOW OUTSIDE ENVELOPE?

The window outside envelope is used more often than a regular envelope. I always use the window outside envelope because I think it simply looks better than a regular envelope. To me, the window outside envelope is a high quality envelope and a regular outside envelope is a cheap envelope. The window envelope usually costs a little more than a regular envelope but I think the extra cost is well worth it.

The Self-Addressed Envelope

The self-addressed envelope is also known as the "reply" envelope or the "return" envelope. The self-addressed envelope, like the order form, makes it easy for your customer to order. See Figure 11.5.

INCLUDE A SELF-ADDRESSED ENVELOPE IN YOUR DIRECT MAIL PACKAGE

If a self-addressed envelope is included in a direct mail package, then all the potential customer has to do to order is fill out his name and address on the order form, insert the order form and his money in the self-addressed envelope and seal, stamp and mail the self-addressed envelope.

Since a self-addressed envelope definitely makes it easy for your customer to order, it should be included in your direct mail package. I always include a self-addressed envelope with my direct mail package because I believe that it increases the response more than enough to pay for itself.

THE SELF-ADDRESSED STAMPED ENVELOPE

The self-addressed stamped envelope is also known as the "postage-free" envelope or the "postage paid" envelope. If you decide to use the self-addressed stamped envelope, you should not use regular postage stamps because the potential customers who do not order will not use the envelope and that will be a waste of your money.

THE BUSINESS REPLY SELF-ADDRESSED ENVELOPE

Instead of using regular postage stamps, what you can do is get a "business reply mail" permit from the post office. This permit gives you permission to have your printer print a business reply self-addressed envelope. The post office can give you details about the permit and your printer can print this type of an envelope for you once you give him your permit number.

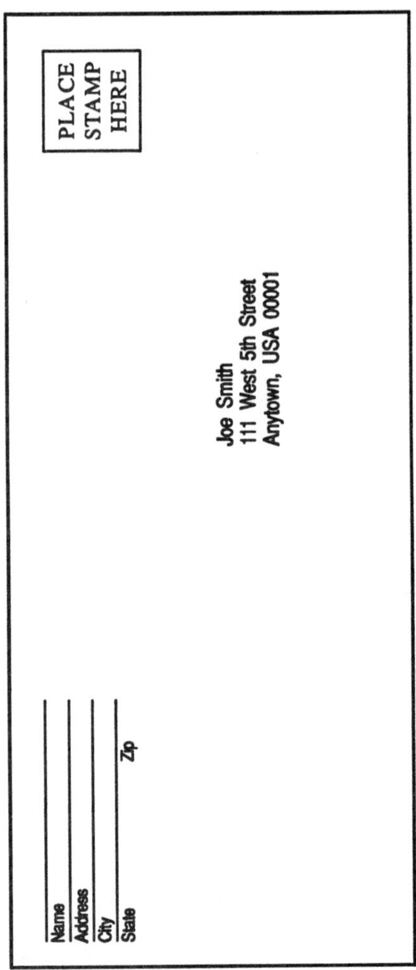

Figure 11.5 The self-addressed envelope.

The Advantage Of The Business Reply Self-Addressed Envelope

The advantage of using the business reply self-addressed envelope instead of a self-addressed stamped envelope is that you do not pay any postage for the envelopes that are not used by your potential customers. The only way a potential customer can use your business reply self-addressed envelope is if he mails it back to you either with his order or without it.

The Disadvantages Of The Business Reply Self-Addressed Envelope

There are three disadvantages of the business reply self-addressed envelope. First, you must pay the post office for the business reply mail permit. Second, because this type of an envelope requires special, extra handling by the post office, you must pay the post office not only regular first class postage but also an additional premium for every envelope that is sent back to you.

The third disadvantage of the business reply self-addressed envelope is that you must pay the post office postage for every business reply self-addressed envelope that is sent back to you. This means that even if your potential customer mails back your business reply self-addressed envelope without an order you still have to pay for the postage.

CONCLUSION

Since a self-addressed envelope definitely makes it easy for potential customers to order, I always include it in my direct mail package. I believe that the self-addressed envelope increases the response more than enough to pay for itself.

I do not recommend the use of the self-addressed stamped envelope or the business reply self-addressed envelope for the previously cited reasons.

Envelope Suppliers

Here are some envelope suppliers.

Best Envelope
2000 East Randolmill Road
Suite 610
Arlington, TX 76011
817-265-8889

Envelope Express
1020 East 18th Avenue
N. Kansas City, MO 64116
816-474-0404

Triangle Envelope Co.
P.O. Box 10127
Nashville, TN 37224
615-244-1205

West Vaco
3800 E. Woodpark Blvd.
Charlotte, NC 28203
704-596-2671

Design Distributors Inc.
45 East Industry Court
Deer Park, NY 11729
516-242-2000

Envelope Express
301 Arthur Court
Bensenville, IL 60106
708-616-9696

Gilmore Envelope Co.
540 Worth Street
Los Angeles, CA 90063
213-268-3401

Glendale Envelope Co.
801 Airway
Glendale, CA 91201
818-243-2127

Equitable Envelope & Paper Corp.
30 New Bridge Road
Bergenfield, NJ 07621
201-384-8300

Mail Well Envelope
360 West Bugatti
Salt Lake City, UT 84115
801-487-9681

Mail Well Envelope
221 North 48th Avenue
Street Phoenix, AZ 85043
602-272-2691

Ohio Envelope
5161 West 164th
Cleveland, OH 44142
216-267-2920

Direct Mail Package Printers

Here are some direct mail package printers. They can also print booklets. You can also compare prices and services with your local printers and with printing and mailing service companies listed at the end of this chapter.

SpeediBooks
P.O. Box 482
Richfield, OH 44286

Henry Birtle Co.
1143 E. Colorado Street
Glendale, CA 91205
818-241-1598

Printing Factory
199 Terry Road
Smithtown, NY 11788
516-361-9394

Creative Printing
3rd & Vernon Street
Ironton, OH 45638
614-533-2428

Equitable Envelope & Paper Corp.
30 New Bridge Road
Bergenfield, NJ 07621
201-384-8300

Web Graphics
625 North Washington
Wichita, KS 67214
316-265-0101

Trade Rotary
5301 Exchange Street
Los Angeles, CA 90039
818-247-6746

Lelli Printing & Advertising
2650 Cr. 175
Loudonville, OH 44842
419-994-5302

Budget Printing
2765 W. Jefferson, Suite H
Springfield, IL 62702
217-546-2737

VALCO
1535 Hart Place
Brooklyn, NY 11224
718-372-0100

Dinner & Klein
600 S. Spokane Street
Seattle, WA 98134
206-682-2494

CHOOSE THE MAILING LISTS YOU WILL USE

Choosing the mailing list you will use is the single most important factor in achieving direct mail success. A mailing list is a collection of names and addresses that have something in common. You "use a mailing list" by mailing your direct mail package to the names on that list. There are three categories of mailing lists. The three categories are:

1. Compiled lists
2. Mail response lists
3. Your own or "in-house" list

The Difference In Ownership

There are a number of differences between the above three categories of mailing lists. One difference is ownership.

YOU OWN YOUR OWN OR "IN-HOUSE" LIST

Your own or "in-house" mailing list is just that—your own list. It is a mailing list of people who have purchased one of your products through the mail. You can use the names on your own list as often as you like and you do not have to pay anyone a rental fee for using them.

COMPILED LISTS AND MAIL RESPONSE LISTS

Compiled lists and mail response lists are similar in that they are both owned by an outside party. To be able to use them you have to rent them. When you rent a compiled list or a response list you are renting it for a one-time only use.

This means if you want to use the same mailing list again later, you have to rent it again. You are not allowed to copy a mailing list you rent.

"SEEDING" OF MAILING LISTS

Mailing list owners and mailing list managers "seed" their mailing lists. Seeding means putting a few random "dummy" or "decoy" names on the list. It is done to prevent unauthorized use of the list. This is something you should do with your own mailing list before you put it up for rent.

To "seed" their mailing lists, list owners and mailing list managers add their own names and addresses and names and addresses of some of their friends and relatives to their mailing lists. This way, if you rent one of their mailing lists, and use it twice, your direct mail package will go to the decoy names twice.

IT DOES NOT PAY TO VIOLATE MAILING LIST RENTAL AGREEMENTS

The second time the list owners and mailing list managers receive your direct mail package, they will know that you used their list for the second time without paying for it. At that point they will bill you for the second, unauthorized use of their mailing list and they may even sue you.

THE BUYERS BECOME YOUR NAMES

When you rent a compiled or a mail response list and some of the names on those lists order from you, the names and addresses of those who ordered become yours—you can add them to your own or "in-house" list. Obviously, since those names are now yours you do not have to pay anyone when you use them again.

Your Own Mailing List

Your own or in-house mailing list is a list of the names and addresses of all the people who have ordered from you. Regardless of how you get started in the mail order business, your own list can mean big money to you because of follow-up business. By follow-up business I mean using your own mailing list to sell to your previous buyers some different information in the future. Let me show you some examples of how this can work.

YOU CAN USE YOUR OWN NAMES AS OFTEN AS YOU LIKE

A big advantage your own mailing list has over all other lists is that you can use your own mailing list as often as you like without having to pay for renting the names. For example, if you get started using the drop-shipping method, selling Company A's information, you can follow-up by selling to those buyers some other information. This information can be information from another drop-shipping company (Company B).

You can then follow-up for the second time with information in the form of reprint rights you purchased from another company (Company C). You can then follow-up for the third time, perhaps this time the follow-up information may be your own, self-published information.

The above scenario can be reversed. You can start with self-published information, then follow-up with information in the form of reprint rights or information from drop-shipping companies.

YOU CAN USUALLY GET A BETTER RESPONSE FROM YOUR OWN MAILING LIST

Another big advantage of using your own mailing list is that you can usually get a better response from it than any other list. The reason for this is that your previous customers have already dealt with you and, assuming you have been prompt and honest, they also trust you. Therefore, they are usually more likely to order from you again than the potential customers from other mailing lists.

My Experience With My Own Mailing List

I have a lot of experience in using my own mailing list. My accumulated experience has shown me that my own mailing list pulls at an average a 60% better response than most rental mailing lists. This is a significant difference in response.

I have greatly enjoyed having a profitable 3.0% rental list response become a highly profitable 4.8% response when I used my own mailing list. One word of caution however. In testing my own mailing list versus rental lists I have been very careful to test "like versus like." In other words, the average 60% better response has occurred when I have used my own "hot line" names versus rental "hot line names," my own six month old names versus rental six month old names and so on.

YOUR OWN MAILING LIST CAN EVENTUALLY BECOME YOUR BEST LIST

Naturally, when you first start you will not have your own mailing list. Then, in the very beginning, your mailing list will be relatively small. Obviously, you can make only so much money with a small mailing list, even if it is your own list. However, as time goes by your own mailing list can grow. As your own mailing list grows in size, it can eventually become your best mailing list because of the money you can make from it with follow-up business.

Remember, your own mailing list has two advantages over all other mailing lists. First, you can use your own mailing list as often as you like without having to pay for renting the names. Second, you can usually get a better response from your own mailing list than any other list.

Compiled Lists

Compiled lists come from previously printed sources. A list may be compiled from a telephone directory, government reports, memberships of associations and so on. Compiled lists are lists of names and addresses of people who have some factor in common. These types of lists are usually demographic and are compiled by a list compiler.

An example of a compiled list would be a list of accountants compiled by a list compiler who purchased the membership lists of various accounting organizations.

THE PROBLEM WITH COMPILED LISTS

The problem with compiled lists is that they are generally not as good as mail response lists and your own or "in-house" mailing list. In fact it is safe to say that compiled lists almost never work for selling information by mail.

Mail Response Lists

Mail response lists are lists of names and addresses of people who have responded to other company's mail order advertising. Mail response lists can be further broken down into two other categories: inquirers and actual buyers.

INQUIRY LISTS

Inquiry lists contain names and addresses of people who have reponded to display, direct mail or classified advertising but did not necessarily order anything. Let me describe how this typically works.

The advertisement offers "free details" regarding the product. The interested potential buyer, then writes the advertiser, asking for the "free details." When the advertiser receives his letter, the interested potential buyer becomes an "inquiry."

The advertiser then sends a direct mail package to all of his inquiries. Those who respond by ordering become buyers while those who do not order remain only inquiries.

Theoretically, inquiry lists can be useful since they list people who have at least expressed an interest in the type of product that was advertised. Practically, an inquiry list can never be as good as the same advertiser's buyer list.

ACTUAL BUYER LISTS

Buyer lists contain names and addresses of people who have actually ordered a particular product from a display, direct mail or classified advertisement. Buyer lists are therefore obviously much better than inquiry lists. Because of this buyer lists usually cost more than inquiry lists.

How To Choose Mailing Lists To Rent

As stated earlier in this chapter, choosing the mailing lists you will use is the single most important factor in achieving direct mail success. On the surface, this may seem like a difficult task when you consider the fact that there are literally tens of thousands of mail response mailing lists actually available.

In reality, choosing the mailing list you will use is a relatively simple task. The task is made relatively simple because of the information that is available. This information comes in two forms. One is published information and the other is the service available from professionals who are ready, willing and able to give you expert assistance at no cost to you.

STANDARD RATE AND DATA SERVICE

Standard Rate and Data Service publishes a two-volume "Direct Mail List Rates and Data," consumer lists, and business lists. The two-volume set organizes and classifies about every mailing list available for direct mail advertising.

A listing in the "Direct Mail List Rates and Data" is free, which is one reason why it contains about every mailing list available. Your public or nearby college library should have a copy or you may want to subscribe. Write to Standard Rate and Data Service, 3002 Glenview Rd., Wilmette, Illinois 60091.

MAILING LIST BROKERS, MAILING LIST MANAGERS AND MAILING LIST OWNERS

You do not have to subscribe to "Direct Mail List Rates and Data" or even go to the library and look for a copy. What you can do instead is what I do—I deal with mailing list brokers, managers and owners.

Mailing list brokers and managers provide me with an invaluable service by giving me their expert advice on which lists I should choose and how I should use them. They also teach me a lot about the mail order business in general just about every time I talk to them. And that is not all. Perhaps the best part is that they do all this for me for free.

Why would they do all this for free? The truth is that they do get paid, but not by me. They get their money from the mailing list owners. Their commission is typically twenty to thirty percent of the mailing list rental fee. I can not save that money by dealing with the mailing list owners directly because they simply pocket the commission.

There are several advantages to renting mailing lists directly from the owners. First, this can allow you to rent the latest names before they are marketed by mailing list brokers. Second, you can test the mailing list by renting a very small number of names. I have rented as few as 300 names in this manner. Note that before I test any mailing list, I ask the mailing list broker, manager or owner to give me names of other advertisers who successfully used that list and I contact them to verify how successful they were before testing it.

Let's discuss the difference between mailing list brokers and mailing list managers.

Mailing List Brokers

Mailing list brokers typically put the user of the list and the mailing list manager together for a brokerage fee. This fee is usually twenty percent of the mailing list rental fee. Mailing list brokers want you to succeed with the mailing lists they recommend because if you succeed the first time, you will order more mailing lists from them in the future and they will make more money.

Mailing List Managers

Mailing list managers manage an owner's mailing list for rental purposes. The mailing list manager handles all the inquiries, processes the orders and collects the rental fee for the lists he manages. Before he agrees to do all this work for the mailing list owner, he gets him to agree to a contract making the mailing list manager the exclusive list manager of the owner's list.

The mailing list manager arranges with *Standard Rate and Data Service* to have the owner's lists listed in "Direct Mail List Rates and Data." Then, mailing list brokers and anyone else interested in renting one of those lists contact the mailing list manager.

How Mailing List Brokers And Managers Get Paid

Typically the mailing list manager will offer mailing list brokers a twenty percent fee (broker's fee) for renting the lists he is managing. In that scenario, the mailing list manager retains a ten percent fee (management fee).

If the mailing list manager finds someone to rent the mailing list without the help of a mailing list broker, the mailing list manager then gets paid the twenty percent broker's fee plus he can still retain the ten percent management fee, for a total of thirty percent fee.

MAILING LIST BROKERS

Here are names, addresses and telephone numbers of some mailing list brokers.

Chilton Direct Marketing
1 Chilton Way
Radnor, PA 19089
215-964-4365

Hugo Dunhill Mailing Lists, Inc.
630 Third Avenue
New York, NY 10017
212-682-8030

R.L. Pork & Co.
6400 Monroe Blvd.
Taylor, MI 48180
313-292-3200

Edith Roman Associates, Inc.
253 West 35th Street
16th Floor
New York, NY 10001
212-695-3836

Dependable Lists
33 Irving Place
New York, NY 10003
212-677-6760

Macromark, Inc.
65 West Ninety-Sixth Street
New York, New York 10025
212-662-1170

List-Masters
Box 425
Mt. Sinai, NY 11766
800-356-8664

Advon
Drawer B3
Shelley, ID 83274
800-992-3866

Action Markets
1710 Highway 35
Ocean, NJ 07712
908-531-2212

Caldwell List Co., Inc.
4350 Georgetown Square
Suite #701
Atlanta, GA 30338
800-241-7425

American Business Lists, Inc.
5711 S. 86th Circle
P.O. Box 27347
Omaha, NE 68127
402-331-7169

LPM Associates
Box 9805
Coral Springs, FL 33075
305-344-8685

Mega Media Associates, Inc.
P.O. Box 4255
Balboa, California 92661
714-673-2290

Alvin B. Zeller
224 5th Avenue
New York, NY 10001
212-689-4900

Ed Burnett List Consultants
100 Paragon Drive S.
Montvalle, NJ 07645
201-476-2300

OTHER MAILING LIST BROKERS

You can check your local Yellow Pages or go to your local library and look through the two-volume "Direct Mail List Rates and Data" in order to get names of many more mailing list brokers.

Be Careful When Choosing Mailing Lists

Remember, choosing the mailing lists you will use is the single most important factor in achieving direct mail success. You should therefore be very careful when choosing the mailing lists you will use.

DO NOT RENT CHEAP LISTS

The current price for good mail response lists ranges between $65 and $100 per one thousand names and addresses. Beware of cheap lists costing less money. Many newspapers, magazines and different publications are full of ads offering mailing lists at bargain basement prices. Stay away from them.

Even some mailing list brokers and mailing list managers offer cheap mailing lists. Again, my advice remains the same. Stay away from cheap mailing lists.

ANOTHER MISTAKE I MADE

I made another mistake when I rented a mailing list without asking for two important items. First, I did not ask for a copy of the direct mail package or display advertisement which generated the names on the mailing list. Second, I did not ask the mailing list owner to give me names of other advertisers who successfully used that list so I could contact them to verify how successful they were before testing it. The mailing list was advertised in a magazine and if it had been at a bargain basement price I would have stayed away from it. However, the list was priced in the same range as many good mail response lists I had rented from my mailing list brokers. I thought I had found a mailing list they were not aware of and rented it.

TRADING MAILING LISTS

Sometimes competitors trade mailing lists. A potential problem with this practice is that there is no way you can be sure you are trading like-for-like. For instance, if you exchange 1,000 names of your newest buyers for 1,000 names of your competitor's inquiries or two year old buyers, you will get ripped off.

YOUR OWN MAILING LIST AND "HOT LINE" MAIL RESPONSE LISTS ARE THE BEST MAILING LISTS

As previously discussed, your own mailing list should always be your best mailing list. In addition to your own mailing list, the best mailing lists you can find are the "hot line" mail response lists.

"Hot line" mail response lists are usually names of mail order buyers who have made a purchase during the most recent 90 day period. "Hot line" lists are therefore usually names from the "latest available quarter." You should always test a company's "hot line" list before you rent its names from any of the previous quarters.

NINE RULES TO FOLLOW WHEN CHOOSING MAILING LISTS

I had to learn a lot of things the hard way, as you have probably noticed by now by reading about all the mistakes I have made. The following nine rules I have definitely had to learn on my own.

Note that Rules #1 through #6 are general rules and involve the relationship between you and mailing list brokers, managers and owners. Rules #7 through #9 are more specific rules.

Rule #1

Do not rent a single mailing list from any mailing list broker without first sending him a copy of your direct mail package. With your direct mail package in hand, the mailing list broker can do a much better job of recommending the best mailing lists for you to rent.

Rule #2

Always ask the mailing list broker or owner to send you a copy of the direct mail package or display advertisement which generated the names of a mailing list you are considering renting. Also, always ask the mailing list broker or owner to give you names of other advertisers who successfully used a list so you can contact them to verify how successful they were before testing it.

Rule #3

You can usually get the best results when you rent mailing lists of competitors whose advertising is very similar to yours.

Rule #4

When you first start direct mail advertising, do not rent a single mailing list for which your broker is unable to provide a copy of the direct mail package or display advertisement which generated the names of the mailing list he recommends.

Rule #5

After you have had a number of successful experiences renting names from a particular mailing list broker, you can carefully consider breaking Rule #4.

Your broker should explain to you why he is unable to provide a copy of the direct mail package or display advertisement which generated the names of the mailing list he recommends.

Also, your broker must provide you with very good reasons why you should rent the mailing list which will cause you to break Rule #4.

Rule #6

If, after careful consideration you decide to break rule #4, do the smallest test possible for that list. If you plan to order more names at the same time, make sure those names are from mailing lists that are proven winners so that you can spread your risk.

For a more detailed discussion on spreading risk, see "HOW TO SPREAD YOUR RISK" later in this chapter.

Rule #7

Always order and test up to 5,000 names from a company's "hot line" (latest quarter) list before you test any more of its "hot line" names and any of its older quarters.

Rule #8

After the results of the test under Rule #7 are conclusive (see "Projecting Direct Mail Results" later in this chapter), you can try another test, a continuation or take the remaining "hot line" names from each list which had a successful test result.

(For a more detailed discussion, including examples, see "Another Test, Continuation, Rolling Out, New Tests and Repetition" later in this chapter).

Rule #9

After you have successful, conclusive results from the test under Rule #8, you can test up to 5,000 names from the quarter immediately prior to the "hot line" quarter.

TEST YOUR DIRECT MAIL PACKAGE USING THE MAILING LISTS OF YOUR CHOICE

The fourth step to successful direct mail advertising is to test your direct mail package using the mailing lists of your choice. This is a very important step in achieving direct mail success.

Testing Your Very First Direct Mail Package

When you are ready to test your very first direct mail package, you should play it safe and test it using only one mailing list. Use the very best "hot line" mailing list you can find and test up to 5,000 names.

More Experienced Testing Of A Direct Mail Package

After you have some experience in direct mail advertising, you can test a direct mail package using more than one mailing list. However, no matter how many successful direct mail campaign experiences you have under your belt, you should always remember to stick by Rule #1: Always test up to 5,000 names from each list or quarter you want to rent (including "hot line").

The Nth Name Test

Since many lists will have more than 10,000 names, you can do what is called the Nth test. The Nth name test is when you rent a fraction of the names on a mailing list by incrementally taking every tenth or fifth or third name, etc. from the list.

The Nth name test ensures that the names you get will be totally random. With an Nth name test you should not get alphabetic or geographic groupings of names. Let's assume the list you will test has 20,000 names. A test of 2,000 names means that every 10th name will receive your package.

Key Codes

Use a key code printed on the mailing label even when testing only one mailing list. I usually use three digit key codes for my direct mail advertising. Not only do I give each list a separate key code, but if I am using different quarters of one list, each quarter gets a separate key code.

Let's use a more experienced test of a direct mail package as an example. Let's say I am testing 5,000 names each from List A, 3rd Quarter of 1991; List B, 3rd Quarter of 1991, List C, 3rd Quarter of 1991 and List C, 2nd Quarter of 1991. My key codes might be the following:

Example 11.1

101 - List A, 3rd Quarter of 1991
102 - List B, 3rd Quarter of 1991
103 - List C, 3rd Quarter of 1991
104 - List D, 3rd Quarter of 1991

After I have the results of the test, I may decide to rent the following lists and quarters and use the following key codes:

Example 11.2

105 - List A, 3rd Quarter of 1991
106 - List B, 3rd Quarter of 1991
107 - List B, 2nd Quarter of 1991
108 - List D, 3rd Quarter of 1991
109 - List D, 2nd Quarter of 1991
110 - List E, 3rd Quarter of 1991
111 - List F, 3rd Quarter of 1991

Note that despite the fact I used List A, 3rd Quarter of 1991 for the second time, I gave it a new key code, 105 instead of using the same one I gave it the first time, 101. I do this because I am extra careful.

If key code 101 yields a response that is significantly higher or lower than key code 105 (let's say 15% or more higher or lower), I will ask my mailing list broker why this happened. I like to ask questions because usually, when I ask questions, I learn something new.

Testing Direct Mail Advertisements

As noted in Chapter 4, "How To Write A Successful Advertisement," the headline is by far the most important element of an advertisement. To be more specific, the headline is perhaps 80% of the advertisement. All the other elements combined add up to perhaps only 20%.

In my opinion, this is true for direct mail advertisements also. Because of the importance of the headline, if you want to test elements of your direct mail advertisement, you should test the headline.

Some of the other elements of a direct mail advertisement you can test besides the headline include price, advertising copy, color and various elements of the direct mail package including the envelopes, circular and order form.

DO NOT TEST MORE THAN ONE DIRECT MAIL ADVERTISEMENT ELEMENT AT A TIME

As noted in Chapter 4, "How To Write A Successful Advertisement," if you want to test more advertisement elements than just the headline, make sure you do not test more than one element of the advertisement at a time, since you will not be able to determine how the different elements effected the results.

HOW TO TEST DIRECT MAIL ADVERTISEMENTS

The most widely used method of testing direct mail advertisements is the Nth name test. To test two advertisements, simply tell your mailing list broker that you want to do a test. Tell him that you want to send half of the mailing one advertisement, the other half the other advertisement.

My Experience In Testing The Elements Of The Direct Mail Package

I already described some of my experiences in testing the elements of the direct mail package earlier in this chapter ("PREPARE YOUR DIRECT MAIL PACKAGE"). The following are my remaining experiences in testing the elements of the direct mail package.

COLOR

I have tested various colors for my sales letters and other components of the direct mail package.

My Sales Letters

Since my sales letters are always printed on white paper, I often use a color to emphasize the headline, subheads and bold sentences in my sales letters. The color that has worked the best for my sales letters is red.

My Order Forms

I have tried many different colors for my order forms. I always use colored paper for the order form to make it stand out from the rest of my direct mail package. I prefer a light colored order form and I use a small amount of a second color (usually red) to emphasize the important points.

My Envelopes

My outside envelopes are often white with black and red print like my sales letters. My return envelopes are white with plain black print. I have seen no reason to spend extra money for color on the return envelopes.

FIRST CLASS VERSUS BULK RATE

Bulk rate saves a lot of money on postage over first class. For that reason I have used bulk rate for my direct mail advertising from the beginning. Later I read a number of articles by various direct mail marketing experts stating that mailing first class could actually save money over bulk rate because of high non-deliverability of bulk rate mail.

The idea was that my direct mail packages would be delivered to a much higher percentage of my potential customers if I used first class instead of bulk rate. Naturally, if this did happen, my response would be higher. I decided to do a test.

My Experience

My test results in the past did not convince me to use first class instead of bulk rate for my direct mail advertising. I got only a slightly better response with first class mail, but not enough to cover the extra cost of postage. However, my most recent experiences have convinced me that for me, first class now works better than bulk rate. In addition to making a greater profit, the orders have been arriving more quickly from the first class mailings because the potential customers are receiving my first class mailing pieces sooner.

BULK MAIL: POSTAGE METERED VERSUS STAMPED VERSUS PRINTED PERMIT

I have never liked the appearance of outside envelopes with printed bulk rate permits. To me they just look cheap. I also noticed that most of the biggest direct mail operators do not use them. I have never used printed bulk permits for the outside envelope of my direct mail package.

I have tested both postage metered and stamped outside envelopes. I could never discern a difference in response in favor of either. I think a stamped outside envelope looks more personal and a postage metered outside envelope looks more professional. Despite the fact that I usually prefer a personal look to my direct mail packages, recently I have been using the postage metered outside envelope.

Projecting Direct Mail Results

Projecting direct mail results is relatively easy for me, because I have a lot of direct mail experience and I have kept good records.

VARIABLES AFFECTING PROJECTIONS

How quickly your orders come in is a function of many variables. One variable is how you mail your direct mail packages to the potential customers. Obviously, if you use first class the orders you receive will come more quickly than if you use bulk rate.

In addition, since some areas of the United States are heavily populated while others are sparsely populated, your geographic location within the United States can also affect your results.

If you live in a heavily populated area and you send your mail out from there, your mail should reach more people more quickly than if you live in and send your mail out from a sparsely populated area. Therefore, orders should come in more quickly if you live in a heavily populated area.

The geographic variable can be further complicated if you live in one area, and you have your mail sent out from another area in the United States. Because of all these variables, my experience will probably slightly differ from yours.

MY EXPERIENCE

Figure 11.6, ten weeks of cumulative direct mail advertising results, has two columns. The first column is time—the days and weeks of receiving orders. The second column is the percentage of the total cumulative orders received from an average bulk rate mailing.

Please do not confuse the days and weeks of receiving orders with days and weeks after you sent your mail out. You may receive your first orders from a bulk rate mailing 12-14 days after the day you mailed it. With a first class mailing, you may receive your first orders five to seven days after the day you mailed it.

MY EXPERIENCE: AVOID THANKSGIVING AND CHRISTMAS HOLIDAYS

It has been my experience that Christmas and Thanksgiving holidays are not a good time for potential customers to receive a direct mail package offering business opportunity information for sale. I recommend a different strategy for each holiday.

For Thanksgiving, time your direct mailing so that you can expect to receive at least 60% to 70% of your orders before the holiday. For Christmas, time your direct mailing so that it arrives the first week in January. Otherwise, you can expect a significant drop off in orders immediately preceding and following Thanksgiving and Christmas holidays.

ANOTHER TEST, CONTINUATION, ROLLING OUT, NEW TESTS AND REPETITION

Once you have received enough results from your test to be able to safely project an eventual outcome of the test mailing, you are ready to deal with the final step to successful direct mail advertising. You are ready to decide what to do next.

To me, this is the most exciting step to successful direct mail advertising. I feel like a general planning war strategy. My objective is to devise a strategy which will bring me the greatest profits with a minimum risk both quickly and over a period of time. Let's look at the options available.

Time	% of cumulative orders
Day 1	.1%
Day 2	2%
Day 3	4%
Day 4	6%
Day 5	8%
Day 6	10%
Day 7	13%
Day 8	16%
Day 9	20%
Day 10	25%
Day 11	30%
Day 12	35%
3 Weeks	62%
4 Weeks	70%
5 Weeks	78%
6 Weeks	85%
7 Weeks	91%
8 Weeks	94%
9 Weeks	96%
10 Weeks	98%

Figure 11.6 Ten weeks of cumulative direct mail advertising results.

Another Test

If you use the Nth names test to test 5,000 names out of 30,000 names available from List A, 3rd Quarter of 1991, and your results are successful (see "A SUCCESSFUL DIRECT MAIL TEST," following), you may decide to minimize your risk and do another test.

This means you tell your mailing list broker you want another 5,000 Nth names test from List A, 3rd Quarter of 1991, omitting the previously tested 5,000 names. A different key code should be used for this second test.

A SUCCESSFUL DIRECT MAIL TEST

Remember from Chapter 4, "How To Write A Successful Advertisement," most mail order companies consider a test to be successful if they just break even—if the money they receive from their direct mail covers their costs. A reason is that they plan to make a lot of money on the "back end"—perhaps as much as $200 per customer. Back end means future profits to be made by the advertiser after the customer places the initial order.

IF YOU FIRST TEST USING ONLY YOUR OWN MAILING LIST

If you have already been in business for a while when you decide to test your direct mail package, you can use your own mailing list. Whenever you test a direct mail package using only your own mailing list, remember that my experience with my own mailing list has been that if the age of the lists is equal, my mailing list pulls at an average a 60% better response than most rental mailing lists.

Keep this in mind when you analyze the results of any test using only your own mailing list. It may turn out later that your own mailing list will pull at an average of 20% better response than most rental mailing lists, but to be safe, use my 60% figure to project the results using rental lists.

Continuation

Using the previous List A example, you might order a "continuation" instead of another test if your results were "very successful" instead of just "successful." To most mail order companies, a "very successful" test means a moderate profit from the test itself on top of the expected future back end profits from the customer names.

When doing a "continuation," you are taking more names than you would take for "another test" (omitting the previously tested names), but not all the remaining names from the quarter of the mailing list successfully tested. Using our previous List A example, you may tell your mailing list broker you want to take 10,000 names out of the 30,000 names available from List A, 3rd Quarter of 1991, omitting the previously tested 5,000 names.

ALWAYS CHECK YOUR BROKER'S ORDER

The mailing list broker you decide to use will be a human being just like you and everyone else. Human beings can make mistakes. This is why you should always check your mailing list broker's order when you get it in the mail, and compare it to your own notes of what you in fact ordered.

I almost made another mistake

One of my mailing list brokers once made a mistake and forgot to write "omit previous use" when he placed my order for a certain list. He forgot that my order was a continuation and not a test. I in turn almost made another mistake. I nearly forgot to check the order when he sent it to me in the mail.

If I had not checked the order and found the mistake, my direct mail package could have been sent to the exact same segment of the list I had just tested. Sending that same segment of the mailing list the same mailing piece so quickly would no doubt have cut my response rate in half if not worse. Always check your mailing list broker's order.

HOW I COMPOUNDED A MISTAKE I ALREADY MADE

Earlier in this chapter I mentioned a mistake I made when I rented a mailing list which was advertised in a magazine. Unfortunately, this was only the first mistake I made with that mailing list.

The Second Mistake I Made: I Broke Rule #7

The second mistake I made with that mailing list was that I broke Rule #7: "Always order and test up to 5,000 names from a company's "hot line" (latest quarter) list before you rent any more of its "hot line" names and any of its older quarters."

At that particular moment I had about a 20,000 surplus of all components of my direct mail package except the outside envelope (I had only 5,000 of those) so I decided to order and test 20,000 names plus I ordered 15,000 more outside envelopes. I knew that I should order and test only up to 5,000 names from one company's mailing list (as per Rule #7) but I convinced myself that it would be all right if I broke the rule this one time. My intention was to test 5,000 names first, and then to use the remaining 15,000 names if the test was very successful.

I was on a hot winning streak with my direct mail advertising, thinking I could do no wrong. Every mailing list I ordered, every test, every continuation and roll out turned into solid gold. I expected to have very successful results of the test before the 15,000 outside envelopes I ordered arrived at my mailing house.

Recapping The First Two Mistakes

To recap, my first mistake was ordering a mailing list advertised in a magazine. I will never do that again. I will always order mailing lists through mailing list brokers and mailing list managers.

My second mistake was breaking Rule #7 by ordering and testing more than 5,000 names from one company's mailing list. I rented an additional 15,000 names I never should have rented without first successfully testing up to 5,000 of the same company's names. I will never do that again either.

My Third And Biggest Mistake: I Did Not Make Myself Clear

My third and biggest mistake was that I did not make it clear to my mailing house that they should wait to receive the green light from me before mailing the remaining 15,000 names. They knew that I had never before ordered names that I did not use (I had never before broken Rule #7), so when the 15,000 outside envelopes I ordered arrived at their office, they sent out the last 15,000 names.

The next day I was able to project an unsuccessful test of the first 5,000 names, so I called the mailing house and told them to throw away the remaining 15,000 names. You can imagine my shock and anger when I heard that they had already sent them out.

Fortunately my anger did not last long. No mistake is really tragic if you learn from it, and I have definitely learned from these three mistakes. I hope you will too.

Rolling Out

Using the previous List A example, you might order a "roll out" instead of another test or a continuation if your results were "extremely successful" instead of just "very successful" or "successful." To most mail order companies, "extremely successful" results from a direct mail test mean excellent profits from the test itself on top of the expected future back end profits from the customers' names.

A "roll out" is when you take all the remaining names from the quarter of the mailing list you have successfully tested. Using our previous List A example, you tell your mailing list broker you want to take the remaining 25,000 names out of the 30,000 names available from List A, 3rd Quarter of 1991, omitting the previous use (test) of 5,000.

A word of caution. Some mail order experts define a "roll out" as taking all the remaining names from the mailing list you have successfully tested. Notice that my definition of a "roll out" stated ". . . when you take all the remaining names from the quarter of the mailing list you have successfully tested."

I believe in an aggressive yet conservative direct mail strategy. Taking all the remaining names from an entire mailing list when you have only tested the "hot line" or last quarter's names is too risky for my disposition.

Repetition

After you have successfully rolled out of a mailing list, you can consider repetition. Repetition is when you remail the same offer to the same mailing list. The optimum waiting period between mailings is usually two to three months.

However, even if you wait the optimum period, you should expect your results to drop off 25% to 60%, perhaps even more. Because of this potential drop off, and the resulting high risk involved, I recommend remailing to only your own, in-house mailing list and your very best rental mailing lists if your initial mailings indicated that you can suffer the remailings' 25% to 60% drop off and still make a profit. Always test up to 5,000 names from the latest quarter you have already mailed to when doing a remailing.

How To Spread Your Risk

The objective of every mailing is to maximize profit while minimizing risk. In order to do this you must spread your risk. To spread my risk I always use lists that are proven winners at the same time I am testing new, risky lists. This way I feel I am using a strategy which is aggressive yet conservative at the same time.

MAILING LIST "QUARTERS"

As I have already explained, the "hot line" lists are usually names of mail order buyers who have made a purchase during the most recent 90 day period, or quarter. Typically, companies will list their names by age or quarters: 3rd Quarter 1991, 2nd Quarter 1991, 1st Quarter 1991, 4th Quarter 1990, 3rd Quarter 1990 and so on.

The 1st quarter names are from January through March of a given year. The 2nd quarter names are from April through June. The 3rd quarter names are from July through September. And the 4th quarter names are from October through December.

Usually, a company's 1st quarter names become available to rent toward the end of April of that same year. 2nd quarter names usually become available in late July. 3rd quarter names usually become available in late October. 4th quarter names usually become available in late January.

If you call your mailing list broker in late October, the latest, "hot line" names he will have available from various companies will be the 3rd quarter names. You should always order and test up to 5,000 names from a company's "hot line" (latest quarter) list before you test any more of its "hot line" names and any of its older quarters. (See My Rule #7).

MY EXPERIENCE WITH DIFFERENT QUARTERS

My experience has shown me that most mailing lists drop off an average 20% per quarter. In other words, if you receive a 4% response on List D's 3rd Quarter of 1991 names, you can somewhat accurately project that you will receive a 3.20% response on List D's 2nd Quarter of 1991 names and 2.56% on its 1st Quarter of 1991 names.

The fact is, however that some mailing lists drop off more than 20% and others drop off less than 20% per quarter. I have even had a number of cases where an older quarter of a mailing list pulled as well or even better than the more recent quarter.

According to one of my mailing list brokers, this can happen as a result of other mail order companies shying away from renting certain quarters of mailing lists because they are afraid the names are too old. Since those names were no longer receiving my competitors offers, they have sometimes pleasantly surprised me.

HOW I CHART MAILING LIST PERFORMANCE BY QUARTERS

Figure 11.7 shows how I chart mailing lists' performance by quarters. The names of different mailing lists A, B, C, D, E, F, G, H, I, and J go along the top of the chart. The different quarters available for those lists are listed on the side, latest quarter available ("hot line") on top, the oldest on the bottom.

I fill out the percentage responses for a specific quarter of a specific list in the corresponding space on the chart as I am able to make my projections. With this chart in front of me I am able to make plans for my next mailing.

How To Use A Computer House

As soon as you rent more than one mailing list at the same time, you will need the services of a computer house. A computer house prints the names from the different mailing lists, sorts them by zip code and eliminates duplicate names.

There are always individuals who order by mail from more than one company. When your computer house eliminates duplicate names, you avoid sending more than one mailing piece to the same individual and thus save money on postage and printing of your mailing pieces.

	A	B	C	D	E	F	G	H	I	J
3rd Qtr 1991	4.1	5.4	2.3	4.4	2.7	5.1	3.6	4.6	3.4	3.3
2nd Qtr 1991	3.3	4.7		3.8		4.4	3.4	3.8	2.8	2.7
1st Qtr 1991	2.6	3.9		3.3		4.0	3.5	3.0		
4th Qtr 1990		3.5		2.8		3.4	2.8			
3rd Qtr 1990		2.7				3.5				
2nd Qtr 1990						3.1				
1st Qtr 1990						2.6				

Figure 11.7 How I chart mailing list performance by quarters.

LIST DUPLICATION

You simply tell your mailing list broker you want the names from each mailing list on separate "mag tapes." Mag tapes are special reel to reel magnetic tapes containing computer information. The mag tapes are then sent to a computer house which can do a "merge purge." In other words, the names from the two or more mailing lists are merged and the duplicate names are eliminated by the computer.

KEY CODING

If you rent two or more separate quarters from the same company you should always tell your mailing list broker you want the names from each quarter on separate mag tapes because you want each quarter to have a separate key code. This is the only way you will be able to chart mailing list performance by quarters.

NIXIES

Every time you do direct mail advertising, you will get a number of your mailing pieces back from the United States Postal Service, marked "Not Deliverable As Addressed," or "Moved—Forwarding Order Expired." This is inevitable in direct mail and you simply have to accept the fact that the more direct mail you send, the more "nixies" will come back to you.

The way to deal with nixies is to keep accurate records of your actual orders. When a mailing list makes me an excellent profit, I do not worry about the number of nixies. I simply accept the fact that this is the nature of direct mail. People move, and the older the names on a mailing list, the more nixies will come back.

SUPPRESS

As your own in-house mailing list grows in size, you should try to avoid mailing your offer to the individuals who have already ordered that particular offer. This is called "suppress" and computer houses know how to get this done. It is very important to use "suppress" if you are doing a repetition to either your own mailing list or a rental mailing list.

COMPUTER HOUSES

There are numerous computer houses all across the country. Your mailing list broker can recommend computer houses. You can compare prices and services of the following computer houses with your local computer houses.

Data Processing Enterprises
914 South Hoover Street
Los Angeles, CA 90006
213-380-7200

Mailing Data Services, Inc.
6055 East Washington Blvd.
Suite 1011
Commerce, CA 90040
213-724-8950

Enertex Computer Concepts
99 Madison Avenue, 10th Floor
New York, NY 10016
212-532-3115

Phoenix Systems
8800 Edgeworth Dr.
Capitol Heights, MD 20743
410-792-8118

Printronic Corp.
17 Battery Place, 13th Floor
New York, NY 10004
212-480-4000

Anchor Computer
1900 New Highway
Farmingdale, NY 11735
516-293-6100

Precise Data Service Inc.
7550 Plaza Court
Willowbrook, IL 60521
708-986-8880

Creative Mailings, Inc.
111 East Artesia Blvd.
Carson, CA 90746
310-637-7100

Acxiom Corp.
301 Industrial Blvd.
Conway, AR 72032
501-336-1000

MS Data Services, Inc.
151 Kalmuf Drive
Suite L-1
Costa Mesa, CA 92626
714-540-4430

Hallmark Data Systems
6201 West Howard
Niles, IL 60648
708-647-1200

Mailing Service Companies

Mailing service companies can label, insert and sort your direct mail. By sophisticated bulk mail sorting they can save you a lot of money on direct mail postage. There are numerous mailing service companies all across the country and here are some of them. Your mailing list broker can recommend mailing service companies.

Globe Mail Agency
541 West 25th Street
New York, NY 10001
212-675-4600

Brodie Advertising Service, Inc.
1140 W. Exchange Avenue
Chicago, IL 60609
312-254-2000

Lee Enterprises
17111 South Wallace
South Holland, IL 60473
708-596-7900

Hallmark Data Systems
6201 West Howard
Niles, IL 60648
708-647-1200

Quality Folding & Inserting
17600 Williams, Suite 5
Thornton, IL 60476
708-877-2700

You can also compare prices and services with your local mailing service companies and with the following printing and mailing service companies.

Printing And Mailing Service Companies

Here are companies which can both print and mail your direct mail package. You can also compare prices and services with your local printing and mailing service companies and with "Direct Mail Package Printers" listed earlier in this chapter.

Mailing & Printing Services
P.O. Box 748
Neenah, WI 54957-0748
414-722-2333

WCUL Services Corp.
10205 West Greenfield Ave.
West Allif, WI 53214
414-778-0877

Triway Printers & Mailers, Inc.
301 N. Frio
San Antonio, TX 78207
512-227-9185

Lelli Printing & Advertising
2650 Cr. 175
Loudonville, OH 44842
419-994-5302

Automatic Mail Services Inc.
3002 48th Avenue
Long Island City, NY 11101
718-361-3091

Precise Data Service Inc.
7550 Plaza Court
Willowbrook, IL 60521
708-986-8880

Chiappone Mail Enterprises, Inc.
P.O. Box 1152
West Babylon, NY 11704-1152
516-884-6309

Chapter 12

Classified Advertising

As was the case with display and direct mail advertising, the first step to successful classified advertising is to write a successful advertisement. See Chapter 4, "How To Write A Successful Advertisement," and "How To Write A Successful Classified Advertisement" later in this chapter.

The second step to successful classified advertising as well as display advertising is to target your potential customers by using the right publications to sell your information. To find out how to do this, see Chapter 7, "Display Advertising."

Various Classifications

Look in the classified advertisement section of publications you are interested in advertising in. You will find that advertisements dealing with information are being run under various classifications such as:

ADDITIONAL INCOME
BOOKS AND COURSES
BOOKS AND PERIODICALS
BUSINESS OPPORTUNITIES
BUSINESS SERVICES
CASH GRANTS
EDUCATION AND INSTRUCTIONS
FINANCIAL
GOVERNMENT SURPLUS
INCOME OPPORTUNITIES
INVENTIONS
LOANS BY MAIL
MONEY AVAILABLE
MONEYMAKING OPPORTUNITIES
MONEY WANTED
MULTI-LEVEL MARKETING

SELECT THE CLASSIFICATION YOU WANT TO USE

Select the classification you want to use to run your classified advertisement in. You should advertise where your successful competition advertises. See Chapter 7, "Display Advertising." Unless your information is unusual, that classification should exist in most if not all of the publications you will eventually advertise in.

If it turns out that the classification you selected does not exist in some publications, even better. Ask those publications to create a new classification just for your advertisement. If they agree to do so, your advertisement will probably be the only one under that classification the first time you run your advertisement. That is good for you because the odds are that more potential customers will see and read your advertisement.

Small, 1/2 Inch Or One Inch Display Advertisements

Sometimes you may discover that the right publications to use to sell your information do not accept classified advertisements but do accept small, 1/2 inch or one inch display advertisements. For these publications you can run a 1/2 inch or one inch display advertisement instead of your short (ten to twenty words) classified advertisement.

Key Codes

As was the case with display advertisements, use a different key code for every classified advertisement you run in every publication you run it in. For example, you can use key codes such as "101" and "102" tacked on at the end of your name or your company name.

The Two-Step Approach

The traditional approach to classified advertising is the "two-step" approach. First you run a short (ten to twenty words) classified advertisement offering free details about your information. Then, when potential customers write to you asking for the free details, you follow-up by mailing them a sales package.

The sales package you will be mailing should be the same as the direct mail package used for direct mail advertising. For more information about the sales package, read about the direct mail package in Chapter 11, "Direct Mail Advertising."

FREE DETAILS

When using the two-step approach, do not ask for $1 or $2 for postage and handling. Charging for postage and handling will reduce the number of inquiries you receive for two reasons.

First, the strength of the two-step approach is that it allows you to use an important magic word: "free." If you are charging for postage and handling you will not be offering "free details." Second, you will lose credibility if you state "free details" despite the fact that you are charging for postage and handling.

When using the two-step approach, do not ask the potential customers to send you a self-addressed stamped envelope (SASE) or a stamp to pay for your postage. Asking them to do this will reduce the number of inquiries you receive.

SPEED IS VITAL WHEN FOLLOWING UP ON AN INQUIRY

When using the two-step approach to classified advertising, it is vital that you get the sales package to your potential customers as soon as possible. Always use first class mail and send the sales package to the potential customers within 24 hours of receiving their inquiries.

If you are swamped with inquiries you may not be able to accomplish the 24 hour turn-around goal. In that case, a 48 hour turn-around becomes a must. Do not let your red hot potential customers wait too long to receive your sales package.

HERE IS THE INFORMATION YOU REQUESTED

You should have the words "Here is the information you requested" printed on your outside envelope for following up on inquiries. This way your potential customers will know that your envelope contains the information they are expecting.

HOW MANY TIMES SHOULD YOU FOLLOW-UP ON AN INQUIRY?

You should follow-up on an inquiry at least once after your initial follow-up. Many mail order companies follow-up on their inquiries from four to eight times.

How many times you follow-up after the second attempt depends on your offer. Only by testing can you find out what will work best for your offer. Obviously, as long as you make money each time you follow-up, continue to do so.

ORDERS, NOT INQUIRIES ARE IMPORTANT

When evaluating the effectiveness of your classified advertisement in different publications, consider the orders you receive, not only the inquiries. For example, you may receive 300 inquiries from publication "A" and only 100 inquiries from publication "B." If you keep record of only the number of inquiries, you would think that publication "A" is more effective than publication "B."

THE CONVERSION PERCENTAGE

In fact, this may not be the case at all, depending on the conversion percentage of each publication. Conversion is the act of changing an inquiry into a buyer.

Let's say you convert 5 percent of the inquiries you receive from publication "A" and 20 percent of the inquiries you receive from publication "B." That means that publication "A" produced 15 buyers and publication "B" produced 20. Those are the most important figures you should keep a record of and consider—the number of buyers each publication produces.

The One-Step Approach

Asking for the order in the classified advertisement is the one-step approach. This approach can be effective if your information is unique or inexpensive. If your information is expensive, the two-step approach should work better.

AN EXAMPLE OF SUCCESSFUL USE OF THE ONE-STEP APPROACH

Sam Pitts successfully sold information about credit cards for $5 using the one-step approach. He was able to achieve success despite the fact that his information was not unique because it was inexpensive. See Chapter 5, "The Greatest Business In the World," for more information about Sam Pitts' success story.

How To Write A Successful Classified Advertisement

The classified advertisement is like a tiny display or direct mail advertisement. The difference is that you are limited by the number of words you can use when writing a classified advertisement. The similarity is that despite limitation, you must state the most important benefit in order to get the reader's attention.

THE FIRST FEW WORDS MUST GET THE READER'S ATTENTION

The first few words of a classified advertisement are like the headline in a display or direct mail advertisement. They must get the attention of the potential customers so that they finish reading the entire advertisement. You should always make the first few words in CAPITALS or upper-case letters because this brings more attention to your classified advertisement.

EXAMPLES OF SOME ATTENTION-GETTING FIRST FEW WORDS

Here are some attention-getting first few words for classified advertisements:

CASH IN ON WALL STREET
MAKE BIG MONEY WITH HOME COMPUTER
NEED MONEY? GET FREE GRANTS
BE YOUR OWN BOSS!
GET PAID FOR READING BOOKS!
BEAT THE BANK
MONEY PROBLEMS?
LUCRATIVE HOME BUSINESS
MAKE BIG MONEY FIXING RUNDOWN HOUSES
LOANS BY MAIL
PERFECT HOME BUSINESS!
GET A SELF-LIQUIDATING LOAN
AMAZINGLY EASY MONEY MAKING PLAN
#1 MONEY MAKER
FREE CASH GRANTS
GOVERNMENT SEIZED VEHICLES FROM $100
FINANCIAL FREEDOM
MAKE EXTRA MONEY AT HOME
MAKE MONEY FROM FORECLOSURES
KNOWLEDGE IS POWER
BORROW MONEY BY MAIL TO $30,000 ON SIGNATURE
HOW TO FIND MONEY
HOME IMPORT MAIL ORDER BUSINESS
JANITORIAL BUSINESS MONEYMAKING SECRETS
VISA/MASTERCARD. SECURED.

CUT OUT EVERY WORD THAT IS NOT VITAL

After you write your classified advertisement, carefully go over every word to make sure that every word is vital to the success of the advertisement. The words which you decide are not vital are in fact unnecessary and should be cut out.

There are two reasons for this. First, a short advertisement consisting of only important and informative words will get more responses than a longer advertisement full of unnecessary and non-informative words. Second, a short advertisement will not only get more responses but will cost less because you pay for each word of a classified advertisement.

Therefore, your classified advertisement must have a few words that say a lot instead of a lot of words that say a little. Look at the two classified advertisements below and decide which would be more effective.

CLASSIFIED ADVERTISEMENT "A"

LET ME SHOW YOU HOW YOU CAN MAKE BIG MONEY! Information about at-home business available. Free details. Write Stephens & Associates, Dept. 101, 445 5th Street, Anytown, CA 00001.

CLASSIFIED ADVERTISEMENT "B"

YOU CAN MAKE BIG MONEY AT HOME! Free details. Stephens-102, 445 5th, Anytown, CA 00001.

ANALYSIS

If you picked classified advertisement "B" as the more effective, you are right. Notice that advertisement "B" starts out with a key word "you." This word gets the attention of the potential customers and leads to an important benefit. It is a very effective word.

Advertisement "A" has a lot of unnecessary words which are cut out in advertisement "B." Those words do little or nothing to persuade the potential customers to become inquiries—to write for free details. What is worse, you have to pay extra for each of those words and they only get in the way of the truly effective words such as the word "you" leading off advertisement "B."

Remember, when writing classified advertisements, use a few words that say a lot. For more examples of classified advertisements, see Figure 12.2 at the end of this chapter.

HOW TO COUNT THE WORDS

The preceding classified advertisement "A" has 29 words and advertisement "B" has only 15. Different publications use slightly different methods of counting words in classified advertisements but you can use the following rules as a guideline for counting words. Typically, each separate word counts as a word unless the separate words are the name of a city such as "San Francisco" for example. Then the two separate words count as only one word.

What is considered to be a "separate" word? Usually, if it is preceded and followed by a space, it is a separate word. If two words are joined together by a hyphen, each word is considered a separate word. For example, "at-home" is two words.

Many publications do not count the zip code as a word. Capitalized words usually cost extra per word but some publications automatically set the first few words of all classified advertisements in capitals free of charge.

How You Can Save Up To 17% Of Classified Advertising Costs

It is possible to save up to 17% of your classified advertising costs as well as your display advertising costs. For more details on this, see Chapter 9, "How I Save Up to 17% Of Display Advertising Costs" and the classified advertisement insertion order form, Figure 12.1 in this chapter.

Some publications may try to put up a resistance to your in-house advertising agency placing your classified advertising for you. Simply tell them that other publications are honoring your advertising agency and that if they want your classified advertising business you expect them to do the same.

If this strategy does not work and you decide you still want to advertise in a publication which will not honor your advertising agency, run your advertisement anyway, without the 17% savings. If the advertisement makes you money without the advertising agency savings, keep running it. What is important is not that you save up to 17% of your classified advertising costs in every publication you run in, but that you try to save the 17% every time.

CLASSIFIED INSERTION ORDER

Date: ____________________
To Publisher of: ____________________
Advertiser: ____________________
For (product): ____________________
Run Ad Under Classification: ____________________
Times: ____________________
Dates of Insertion: ____________________
Key: ____________________

Rate: ____ Words at ____ each ____________
____ Capitalized words at ____ each ____________
Agency Commission (   ): ____________
Discount (   ): ____________
NET: ____________

PLEASE ACKNOWLEDGE
After publication, please send one complete copy of this issue and two tear sheets
Order issued by: ____________________

Figure 12.1 Classified advertisement insertion order form.

ADDITIONAL INCOME

$1800 FROM $10 WOOD! Details plus sample $5—satisfaction guaranteed. Alcraft, Box 540-C2, Alexandria Bay, N.Y. 13607.

EASY Work! Excellent Pay! Assemble products at home. Call for information. 504-641-8003 Ext. 759

HOW TO MAKE UP TO $750.00 NEXT WEEKEND! Just $19.95—Guaranteed! Starritt Publishing, P.O. Box 8752, Chula Vista, CA 92010-8752.

AUTHOR'S SERVICE

PUBLISH YOUR BOOK! Join our successful authors. Publicity, advertising, beautiful books. All subjects invited. Send for fact-filled booklet and free manuscript report. Carlton Press, Dept. SME, 11 West 32 Street, New York 10001

LOOKING for a publisher? Learn how you can have your book published, promoted, distributed. Send for free booklet. HP-5, Vantage Press, 516 W. 34th., New York, NY 10001

AUTOMOBILES & MIDGET CARS

IS it true ... Jeeps For $44 Through The Government? Call For Facts! 1-312-742-1142 Ext. 4674

SAVE To 40% on your car insurance! Virtually everyone qualifies! Send for free valuable report. F. Vouche Industries, Box 948, Bensalem, PA 19020

GOVERNMENT SEIZED Vehicles from $100. Fords. Mercedes. Corvettes. Chevys. Surplus. Buyers Guide (1) 805-687-6000 Ext. S-20062

ALL NEW! $400.00 Daily wholesaling automobiles without investment! Details $2.00: Smith, Box 2085, Titusville, FL 32781

SEIZED IN GOVERNMENT NARCOTICS RAIDS!! Automobiles. Vans. Boats. Furniture. Thousands other items. Buy Dirt Cheap—Resell for Big Profits. Free information: 216-453-3000 Ext. A837

BOOKS & PERIODICALS

SUPERLEARNING! Triple learning speed through music! Develop Super-memory; Control stress; Tap potentials. Free book excerpt & catalogue. (Distributors Wanted). Superlearning, 450-Z5, Seventh Avenue, New York, NY 10123

FREEDOM FROM DEBT! Learn how with new book. Send $4.00 to: Reamy Publications, P.O. Box 238L, Cokedale, CO 81032

MAKE $200,000 every year for life! Our new book reveals extremely successful money making procedures. MONEY BACK GUARANTEE! Mail $11.95 to: Bell Business Group, 27595 Detroit Avenue, Westlake, Ohio 44145.

BUSINESS OPPORTUNITIES

VENDING MACHINES. No selling. Routes earn amazing profits. 32-Page Catalogue FREE. Parkway Corporation. 1930NO Greenspring Drive, Timonium, Maryland 21093.

GET RICH!! Secret law smashes debts—brings Cash. Credit! Details FREE! Wealthkit-V Box 4036, Pompano Beach, FL 33063

MAKE BALLOON ANIMALS. $400.00 Weekends! FREE SAMPLES/INSTRUCTIONS: Showcase—IO95, Box 250, Alexandria Bay, NY 13607

BUSINESS OPPORTUNITIES—Cont'd

BARGAINS! Buy Wholesale and Below! Name Brands. Appliances. Furniture. Sports Equipment. Televisions. Cameras. Watches. Jewelry. Thousands More. Free Details. Write Today. Bargainhunters Opportunities, Box 1409-IO, Holland, MI 49422

CLIP newspaper items—$2-$25 Each!! FREE report! Clippings -V, Box 6109, Pompano Beach, FL 33063

STAY HOME! MAKE MONEY ADDRESSING ENVELOPES. VALUABLE GENUINE OFFER 20¢. Write Lindco, 3636-DA Peterson Ave., Chicago, IL 60659

PROFITABLE GOLD FOIL PRINTER. Personalize business cards, pencils, matches. Free details. Gold, P.O. Box 24986(BC), Tampa, FL 33623.

"BUMPERSTICKER PRINTER. Cheap, Simple, Portable. Free Details. Bumper, POB 22791(BC), Tampa, FL 33622"

NEW IMPORTS: Foreign manufacturers offering direct. Free information. International Intertrade Newsletter, Box 636-AA, Newark, N.J. 07101

MAKE Rubber Stamps. Highly Profitable. Free Details. STAMPER, P.O. Box 22809(BC), Tampa, FL 33622.

FREE DEALERSHIP—SELL MAILING LISTS! Complete Program Free! Write Today: PCW, Box 1302-IN59, Valley Stream, N.Y. 11582

BUSINESS LOANS: Start-up and Venture Capital our specialty. No Collateral, Co-signers, Interviews. Write: Associates-DB, C.S. 9008, Baldwin,NY 11520-9008

TAKE PICTURES for profit. Try our unique methods. Write: Camera Ventures, Box 771, Lamar, CO 81052

$24,000 IN BACKYARD! Growing new specialty plants. Start with $60. Free information. Growers, Box 988-IN, Friday Harbor, WA 98250

$1,000's Weekly!! Processing Mail! Start immediately! Free supplies/Postage! No experience! No Obligation! JRB, Box 3349-IO, Danbury, CT 06813

$200-$500 weekly—AT Home!! No gimmicks—Details FREE!! Homeworkers-V, Box 636679, Margate, FL 33063

FREE REPORT: Earn $7,000 monthly as Loan Broker without experience/investment. Financial, Box 3578-N, Anaheim, CA 92803

TAKE CATALOG ORDERS. We dropship 2955 best selling specialty products. Lowest below wholesale prices. Immediate delivery. Spectacular home business opportunity. FREE BOOK. SMC, 9401 De Soto Avenue, Dept. 155-05, Chatsworth, CA 91311-4991

START profitable home business without investment/experience. TWT, IO5, 755 Date Street, Brea, California 92621

GET PAID for reading books! Write: Pase-CK8, 161 Lincolnway, North Aurora, IL 60542

CLIP NEWSPAPER items for cash! $3 to $25 each. Free Details: Enterprises. Box 3128-N, West Anaheim, CA 92803

ALUMINUM Scrap—Recycle Yourself—Make up to $25.00/Pound! Free Information: Industrial—IO95, Box 127, Alexandria Bay, New York 13607

BUSINESS OPPORTUNITIES—Cont'd

MILLIONS NEED LOANS, CREDIT! Cash in with your own prestigious money consulting business. No educational requirements. Start part-time. 10-year old national firm, provides training, support. FREE valuable report. PFA, Box 697-DN, Dana Point, CA 92629. (714) 240-0405. X104-DN

CONCRETE Block Machines. Excellent Income. Catalog $1.00. Carlayne Company, Route One, Box 3740, Rapid City, South Dakota 57702-3740

MAKE HOMEMADE BOOKLETS. I've earned $187,000 with mine. Free information. Raven, P.O. Box 5320, Sevierville, TN 37864

1400% PROFIT. SELL—120 ROLLS KODAK FILM 12 cents roll. FREE Coupon Book. Central Film, Box 692E, Grover City, CA 93433

STARTING YOUR OWN BUSINESS. FREE Subscription to Opportunity Magazine tells how. Write: Opportunity, Dept. P35, 6 N. Michigan, Chicago, IL 60602

GOOD MONEY! Weekly! Processing Mail! Free Supplies, Postage! Bonuses! Information? Rush stamped envelope! Foodmaster-MDC, Burnt Hills, NY 12027

MAKE HIGH PROFIT, HOT SELLING License Plates, Signs. VACUMAGIC, P.O. Box 24986(BC), Tampa, FL 33623.

MAILORDER BOOKS. Distributors Needed. Wide Selection. Free Report. Mascor, Dept. IM, Box 7367, Silver Spring MD 20907

FREE INFORMATION. Start and Run 10 of the Most Profitable Home Businesses. Send $1.00 for Postage. Info Dep. 1, 1102 Maple Heights Road, Quesnel, B.C., Canada V2J 3X3

MAKE $15,000 in 30 days! Easy! No investment. Free Details: McDowell, Box 5529-N, Diamond Bar, CA 91765.

HOME Import Mail Order Business. Start without capital. Free Report. Mellinger, Dept. C1736 Woodland Hills, California 91367

MINIATURE GOLF COURSES—Outdoors, Indoors. Financing. Immediate Installation. Starting $4,900. MINI-GOLF, INC., Dept. O, Bridge Street, Jessup, PA 18434 (714) 489-8623.

MAKE BIG MONEY Repairing Windshields & Plate Glass! Up to $75,000 yearly! Call Toll Free for valuable report. 1-800-321-2597. Glas-Weld Systems, Box 5755I, Bend, OR 97708

CREDIT CLINIC OWNERSHIP UNDER $300. FREE report. Equal Opportunity Foundation, Box 2335-I, Laguna Hills, CA 92653

$5,000 MONTHLY GUARANTEED with Part Time Business. Exciting details free with SASE. PC Group, 4807 Bethesda Avenue-Suite 116T, Bethesda, MD 20814

SCREEN PRINT T-SHIRTS. Inexpensive kits. Free Details. T-Printer, P.O. Box 23991(BC), Tampa, FL 33623

$400 daily recycling "Free Tires?" Yes! (Free) Information. Winans, 771NC, Battle Ground, Washington 98604-0771

DEALERS WANTED! $5,000 Weekly Earnings Possible Distributing Credit Cards. No experience or Franchise Fees Required. (305) 360-9467 (24 Hours)

NEED MONEY? Get Free Grants, signature loans, business loans—without collateral. Free Details. Action, Box 5499-NN, Diamond Bar, CA 91765

Figure 12.2 Examples ofclassified advertisements.

GENERAL INTEREST

We want to help you make money! Here at National Publications, we would like to introduce you to a new program we're offering. We will PAY you to talk to us. If you've ever purchased a money-making opportunity AND have been successful at it, we want to hear from you! If you've ever received financial assistance from the government, we'd like to hear from you! If you've ever been the recipient of a grant from a foundation, we can do business together! Please write to us and tell us your success stories. If we use your testimonials, we will PAY you cold, hard cash! Please write to us at: 6150 Mission Gorge Rd., Suite -22, San Diego, CA 92120, attn: Consultants. (No phone calls, please.)

GOVERNMENT SURPLUS

Government seized/surplus vehicles as low as $100. BMW'S, Cadillacs, Chevys, Fords, Mercedes, Porsches, plus trucks and vans. Amazing recorded message reveals details. 303-965-7041. Ext. 108

HELP WANTED

$208.00—$417.00 Weekly! Homeworkers needed Nationwide! For application, rush large addressed-stamped envelope to: Jobs-26, Box 70, Earlton, NY 12058

HOMEWORKERS NEEDED—TOP PAY! These words can mean FRAUD! Profitable homework is possible but don't get taken! FREE report. Send long SASE to Consumer Affairs Dept-F, Box 8135, St. Paul, MN 55108

$300 A DAY! TAKING PHONE ORDERS. People call you 513-271-2820

AIRLINES PASSENGER SERVICE Earn $9.00 to $14.00 an hour. (203) 623-2929, Ext. 111, 2pm-9pm

WORK AT HOME. $1,359.47 or more per week. Assembling OUR products. Apply now! (415) 257-5090, Ext 11

INVENTORS/INVENTIONS

How to get your invention marketed and produced on a royalty basis for under $500.00. Complete Kit $9.95. Capital Publishing Company, P.O. Box 265, Madison, Wisconsin 53701-0265

LOANS BY MAIL

Signature, Business, Commercial. Real Estate loans. Visa, purchase mortgage/trust deeds. Call (414) 633-9135

MAILING LISTS

NEW "HOT" NAMES DAILY! FIRST ORDER "TRIPLED FREE"! Opportunity Seekers. 200/$8; 500/$14; 1,000/$25; 2,000/$39; 5,000/$75; 10,000/$139. List-Masters, Box 750-CM, Wantagh, NY 11793. Visa/MC/COD-800-356-8664

Mail Lists Guaranteed. Opportunity seekers 2,000/$30.00 Categories: 1,000/$35.00 Visa/MC/AMEX. Compu-Lists, 1270 Slayton Dr., Manteca, CA 95336. Info (209) 823-7002. order 1-800-331-6339

EAGER MAILORDER BUYERS! Adhesive labels! 200/$4 500/$7 1,000/$12. 2,000/$19. 5,000/$45 10,000/$79 20,000/$119. 50,000/$249. Quality Lists Box 1305-LR Seaford, NY 11783 Visa/MC/COD—800-356-6392

MAILING LISTS

Hottest-Freshest computerized names. Opportunity seekers/buyers in zip code order less than 30 days old, peel & stick labels. Shipped UPS. 200/$18, 500/$24, 1000/$40, 5,000/$124. Successful Communications, P.O. Box 6, Dept 121, McKenzie, AL 36456. (205) 374-2783

Highest quality mailing lists. 100/$5.00; 200/$8.00; 500/$12.00 Tri-Star Communications, 285 Duck Ct., Foster City, CA 94404

MAIL ORDERS

$500/day. $1.00 + SASE to B.A. Hudson, 2908 Adams, DesMoines, IA 50310

MISCELLANEOUS

BUGGING. WIRETAPPING. Emergency Locksmithing Investigative Technology, False Documents. Weapons, Covert Sciences: Free brochure. Mentor, Drawer 1549-D, Asbury Park, NJ 07712

POSTAL JOBS Secrets for getting hired fast! Free report Unlimited, Box 295-SJ, San Juan, PR 00902. USA

MONEYMAKING OPPORTUNITIES

CASH PAID for taking pictures everyday. I have been doing it for years. I'll show you how you can start making thousands of dollars with just a snap of your camera. Call (619) 280-5050. Ext 9600

Unique Packages Make You Wealthy. Premier, 105 Plaza Trail D-22, Virginia Beach, Virginia 23452

Lovely Ladies pay you for your "special" personal services. Make money. Have fun. Details, $1.00. Special Services, PO Box 100046-SOC, Fort Lauderdale, FL 33310

REPAIR YOUR CREDIT RATING! Plus FILL YOUR BANK ACCOUNT WITH CASH! Free details. Wattley, PO Box 514 New York, NY 10025

GOVERNMENT SEIZED VEHICLES. BMW's, Porsches Mercedes, Corvettes. Buy dirt Cheap, resell for big Profits! Or Keep it yourself! Insiders guide to Big Profits. Call (619) 280-5050, Ext 3000

Make $750.00 Next Weekend Premier, 105 Plaza Trail D-22 Virginia Beach, VA 23452.

LIFETIME INCOME! RELAX-GET RICH working at home Exciting free details! Charleen Gore-SO6, Box 103, Prineville, OR 97754

BREAKTHROUGH OPPORTUNITY Make $800 or more daily No tricks, surprises, or silly schemes. Free report! MR1. 829 Woodgate Trail, Longwood, FL 32750

WATCH T.V. and make Big Money. Just turn on your TV and with my simple procedure you'll make thousands. Companies pay you to WATCH. Call (619) 280-5050, Ext. 9500

YOUR CHOICE! 34 GUARANTEED MONEYMAKERS. Each repeatedly proven profitable. Rush SASE for FREE details Victor Marketing, 6418 West Rose, Glendale, AZ 85301

Average $140/100 stuffing envelopes. Self addressed stamped envelope—Cunningham's, Box 1131SO, Parsons, KS 67357

Home Assembly Opportunities! Easy work, excellent pay! Rush S.A.S., Homework-SFO, Box 520, Danville, NH 03819

WANT CASH QUICK?Send $5 to Cash Enterprises, 16 Western Ave. Suite3, Waterville, ME 04901, for EZ details

MONEYMAKING OPPORTUNITIES

UNUSUAL OPPORTUNITY! Earn MEGA BUCKSwith this government supported program. $10,000 monthly could be yours. Isn't it time you chose a plan and got started? For your complete, ready-to-initiate package send $15.00+$3.00 s/h to FMN Services, P.O. Box 4070, HR, CO 80126

PAYING CASH FOR BOXTOPS, COUPONS. Nichols-176, Box 27788, Memphis, TN 38127

$100,000 REFUNDS FROM UNCLE SAM. With just one letter you can start receiving refunds from the U.S.Government. You don't even have to be a citizen. Thousands of people every week are receiving yours. (619) 280-5050, Ext.8000

$500,000 can be yours every year. Learn the inside secrets of how one man made a fortune without working. I'll show you how to do the same. Send $2.00 for details to Leforce & Associates, 5341 E. Zion Pl., Tulsa, OK 74115

Can you stuff 1000 envelopes for $500.00 weekly? Send six 25 cent stamps. Winston's, Box 866714, Plano, Texas 75086

Hundreds daily - Simple unique $5 Action, Box 243, Roll, MO 65401

Make $25.00 DAILY GUARANTEED SEND $1.00 and S.E.S.L.E. to Box 73316, Metairie, LA 70003

$100,000+ YEAR! Easy, new. The ultimate opportunity Powerful FREE details. IFS, 28131-SO Mission Viejo, CA 92692 or call (800) 242-6660

AMAZING NEW PRODUCT can make you rich. Recorded message reveals details 405-436-3460 Publishers, 1139D Highschool, Ada, OK 74820

HOW TO START and operate your own profitable business at home. FREE details. Ranco, Box 2057-S2, CA 92955

OWN YOUR OWN BUSINESS FOR $45.00. Publications/Magazines/Videos/CDs 919-867-1548, Ext L-18

Make millions in '89/'90. Phenomenal, easy, new program Guaranteed. Send $19.00 + $2 shipping & handling to Imperial Marketing, 7 Elm St., Garden City, NY 11530

BIG MONEY selling Nu Face Skin System. Send $5.00: DARR Cosmetics, Box 8040, Jonesboro, AR 72403

Make money selling imitation car telephone. $2.00: Margo Lanier, Post Office 720384, Houston, TX 77272

MAKE MILLION$ off Pepsi, Coca-Cola, Miller, Budweiser! Write: Press-S, Pembroke, NC 28372-0014

BIG PROFIT HOME BUSINESS! Little or no investment. Valuable report from Larry's, 649 N 13th, #5, Lake Arthur, NM 88253

Become a professional jeweler! Gold jewelry repairing, gemstone setting. V.H.S. Video Courses shows how! Info 501-562-9226

HOTTEST MONEYMAKING SYSTEMS EXPOSED! FREE DETAILS! Autumnbrook Research, P.O. Box 3189, Hutchinson, KS 67504-3189

"No-Nonsense Way to $500 A Day!" $1 + SASE to Ward's, 301 Bradford Dr., Salisbury, NC28144

GET RICH READING ADS! Free report! DJM-A, 665 Sioux, Perris, CA 92370

LOOK - If you want an easy, honest and proven money maker, you're going to love this offer! No products to stock or sell! Details, $2.00. Golden Opportunities, Box 64242, Virginia Beach, VA 23464

Figure 12.2 (Continued)

Chapter 13

Free Publicity

Publicity is a form of advertising, like display, classified and direct mail advertising. The difference between publicity and other forms of advertising is that publicity is free. You do not have to pay publications anything for publicity regardless of how much money their publicity brings you.

Publicity is making something known to the general public on a local, state or national level. Almost everybody uses publicity. Politicians, celebrities, book publishers, movie distributors, manufacturers and service businesses all use publicity.

Publicity is free and it is available, ready for you to grab it. You should try to get as much publicity as you can. You do not have to be an expert or have any particular experience to get publicity. The more publicity you get, the more money it can generate for you.

How To Prepare For Your Free Publicity Campaign

The first step to a successful publicity campaign is to write a press release. The second step is to target your potential customers by using the right publications to sell your information. To find out how to do this, see Chapter 7, "Display Advertising." The third step is to send your press release to the right person. The fourth step is to exploit the first publicity you get.

Once your press release is written and you find the right publications, send them your press release and you can be on your way to making a lot of money from publicity.

WHY PUBLICATIONS GIVE AWAY PUBLICITY

Publications give away publicity for several reasons. First, they always need interesting information or news with which they can fill up their publications. Of all publications, newspapers are the most news-hungry because they have to supply their readers with new material 365 days a year. This is one reason why I included Appendix A, a listing of names and mailing addresses of some of the newspapers in the United States.

Second, publications which do not use your press release will have to fill up the space in their publication some other way. This usually means that if they pass up on your press release, they will have to spend time and money on having either their own staff writers or a free-lance writer write another story. Of course, if they use your press release they will save the time and the cost of another story.

Third, some editors give away publicity hoping that the publicity will produce good results for you because then you will be encouraged to place paid advertising in their publication. They have seen this happen before and they know it could happen again with you. However, keep in mind that most editors do not care about obtaining paid advertising so do not make a mistake of hinting at this third reason either in writing or on the phone.

SEND YOUR PRESS RELEASE TO THE RIGHT PERSON

The success of your publicity campaign depends to a large extent on your ability to send your press release to the right person. If you send your press release to the wrong person, they may trash it instead of forwarding it to the right person in the organization.

If you want to send your press release to a local, small town newspaper, you should send it to the "features editor." Find out this person's name and send them your press release. Even better, call them first and tell them you are sending the press release. This way they will be expecting it.

Large city newspapers have various sections and before you make contact, you should decide which section you would like your press release to appear in. If your offer is information regarding sports, ideally you want the press release to go in the sports section.

If your information has to do with travel, the travel section is the perfect place for your press release. Once you decide on the section of the newspaper, send your press release to the editor of that section. If you decide to make contact first, call the editor of that section or their assistant if the editor is not available.

Trade publications and magazines are also an excellent source of publicity. If they have a special section for new products or information, send your press release to the editor of that section. If not, send it to the editor of the section you think is appropriate for your press release.

HOW FAR CAN YOU GO WITH PUBLICITY

The answer to the question: "How far can you go with publicity?" is simple. If you have not guessed already, the answer is: how far do you want to go?

Everything has a beginning and your publicity campaign has to start somewhere. Once you start your publicity campaign, it can take off like a rocket. If you start your publicity campaign locally, you can then take it to the state level and then to the national level. You can also start your publicity campaign on the national level instead of the local level.

EXPLOIT THE FIRST PUBLICITY YOU GET

You should fully exploit the first publicity you get regardless of how and where you plan to start your publicity campaign. In other words, use your first publicity again and again to get still more publicity.

Publicity Can Be More Effective Than Paid Advertising

One of the most interesting features of publicity is that it can be more effective than paid advertising. In other words, as an example, a 1/3 page press release can bring more orders than a 1/3 page advertisement run in the same publication. There are several reasons for this.

First, a press release looks like an editorial and studies have shown that readers notice and read editorial material five times as much as advertising. This only makes sense if you think about it. Most people subscribe to or purchase a publication on the newsstands to read the editorials and articles in that publication. They read advertisements only if the headline gets their attention.

Second, readers believe editorials more than advertisements and are thus more likely to order as a result of reading an editorial.

There are several types of publicity you can use—press releases, feature stories and reviews. In the following pages I will discuss all of them.

Press Releases

Press releases are also known as news releases or publicity releases. They can go to just one publication or a number of publications at once.

HOW TO WRITE A PRESS RELEASE

Your press release should be written in such a way that it appears to educate the readers of the publications (potential customers) about your product. The best way to achieve this effect is to write in third person, as if you are a reporter and not the writer, advertiser or publisher of your information.

In other words, do not write: "send us $20 plus $2 for postage and handling and we will rush you the book by first class mail." Instead, write: "the book is available for $20 plus $2 for postage and handling."

Go to your local library and closely read articles from various newspapers. Study product reviews in magazines such as Popular Mechanics, Car and Driver, Motor Trend and Road & Track. Study book reviews on the back covers of books in the local library or bookstores.

Study the style and the words the writers use to express themselves. Note how they try to keep their articles and reviews fast paced, useful, newsworthy and interesting. Use the work of others to stimulate your mind and get your own ideas for writing the press release.

THE APPEARANCE OF THE PRESS RELEASE

Type your press release on 8 1/2" by 11" paper, double spaced. The press release should be up to one page long. Keep in mind that your press release may be published exactly as it is received by the publications you sent it to.

Put your name, address, the name of your book and the price of your book on the top left portion of your press release. You can also include your telephone number with your name and address if you like.

"FOR IMMEDIATE RELEASE" AND THE HEADLINE

Below your name and address and in full capital letters type FOR IMMEDIATE RELEASE. Then, in capital letters, type either the headline of your advertisement or the title of your information. This will be the headline of your press release.

HOW TO START THE PRESS RELEASE

Always start the body of your press release with the most important benefit of your information. Explain this benefit thoroughly. Then you can go on to less important benefits.

The reason for this approach is that some editors may print your press release just as you wrote it except that they may cut out parts of it to fit the space they have available. If they do this, they are unlikely to cut out the beginning of the press release.

INCLUDE ORDERING INFORMATION

You want to receive orders from press releases so you should include ordering information, including the price of your book and your address and telephone number in another place besides the top of your press release. Place this information somewhere in the middle of the press release, but never at the end because it could get cut out.

Publications are not likely to exclude your ordering information from the press release on purpose, but anyone can make a mistake. By having your ordering information in two places, you are greatly reducing the chance of that type of a mistake.

KEY CODE EACH PRESS RELEASE

Key code your address so you can track how many orders you receive from each publication which gives you publicity. You should do this because publicity is a great, free way to test the effectiveness of publications you are interested in placing paid advertising in. To be safe, you should key code your address at the top of the press release and in the middle, with the ordering information.

INCLUDE A PHOTOGRAPH WITH YOUR PRESS RELEASE

If at all possible, include a photograph or a line drawing with your press release because this may get you more space in the publication. Editors and readers love photographs and even line drawings and most of the time they will be run with your press release.

Send only glossy black and white photographs. Most publications can not use any other type of photograph, so take no chances and always include only glossy photographs. Write the name of your book and your company name on the back of the photograph. This will make it less likely that someone in the publication will make a mistake and run your photograph with someone else's press release.

Always send only one photograph to each publication because they will rarely use more than one photograph for each press release. The ideal size photograph for press releases seems to be 3" by 5", so you should submit photographs of only that size.

SAY "THANK YOU" OR SEND "THANK YOU" CARDS

Editors rarely receive a "thank you" for including a press release in their publication as publicity. You should always do this, but wait for two to three weeks after you start receiving orders. If you key coded the press release, you will be able to project the results of the publicity by that time.

When you are sure of good results, call the editor of the publication or send a "thank you" card. Thank them, including your press release, and tell them about the good results. Editors will be glad to hear this because they chose to include your press release in the publication and the fact that you received a good response from the readers proves that they picked a winner.

Feature Stories

Local newspapers and local organizations such as churches, colleges and alumni publications are always searching for interesting stories regarding people in their community. If you wrote your own information, or published a ghostwriter's work, the local newspapers or organizations may be interested in doing a feature article on you and your business. Send them your press release (to the attention of the "features editor") and a few days later call to see if they would like to interview you.

Reviews

Look at the back cover of books. Many books have reviews quoted on the back cover. These reviews are a form of publicity. So are positive movie reviews that you can see quoted on the advertisements for many movies. Positive reviews can ensure the successful sale of the information you are offering.

While researching your information you should come across various people who are considered to be experts in that field. While studying your target market you should come across various publications which appeal to the potential customers for your information.

Send the experts and the editors of publications copies of your information and ask them to review it. See Figure 13.1. You may be surprised by the positive response.

Since the editors are often busy, you can include your own "sample review." Keep your review at least somewhat objective. Many editors may print your "sample review" in their publication just as you wrote it.

The Pet Rock Craze And Other Examples Of Free Publicity

Do you remember the pet rock craze? This is a classic example of a highly successful free publicity campaign which made millions of dollars.

Mr. Gary Dahl created the pet rock and sold one million of them without spending a penny on advertising. How did he do this? By using free publicity.

Mr. Dahl sent out press releases which talked about the interesting phenomenon known as the pet rock craze. He wrote about the pet rocks as if they were living, breathing pets, like the kind of pets people traditionally buy at the local pet stores. The point Mr. Dahl ingeniously stressed in his press releases was how much easier it was to keep a pet rock rather than other pets, such as a cat or a dog.

Mr. Dahl's press release was picked up by a popular national magazine, *Newsweek*. Mr. Dahl got almost a full page write-up in *Newsweek* which led to hundreds of interviews on radio and television and over one thousand stories

Dear ______________________________:

I would appreciate it if you could give me a review for the enclosed book "____"

I would like your permission to use all or any portion of your review for promotional purposes. Let me know in writing how you would like me to list your name.

Please send your review as soon as possible to ________________________

____

Sincerely,

Figure 13.1 An example of a letter you can use to obtain reviews for your information.

written about the pet rock in publications world wide. His publicity campaign started in *Newsweek* and took off like a rocket.

Peter McWilliams

Peter McWilliams wrote a book about word processing and called it, simply, "The Word Processing Book." He charged $10 per book and sold over 500,000 copies in about a year. That is $5,000,000 in one year. How did Peter McWilliams do this? By using free publicity.

Jim Everroad

Jim Everroad was an athletic coach with a pot belly. He flattened his stomach using exercises he developed on his own. Next he wrote a small 24 page booklet entitled *"How To Flatten Your Stomach."* He received free publicity in the form of a book review from a local newspaper in Columbus, Indiana and sold 500 copies of his booklet in one week.

Jim Everroad did not stop there. He went on to sell 35,000 copies through free publicity. By then he had created enough waves that a large publishing company called Price, Stearn & Sloan contacted him about publishing *"How To Flatten Your Stomach."*

He made a royalty deal with them and the booklet became a number one best seller. Over three million copies of "How To Flatten Your Stomach" have been sold. He went on to write another, similar book called *"How To Trim Your Hips and Shape Your Thighs."* This book also made it to the best seller lists. Such great success and it all started with only one book review in a local newspaper.

Let me give you more examples of how some smart people have been taking advantage of free publicity offered by one of the country's leading opportunity magazines, *Income Opportunities.*

Income Opportunities has a regular department called "Mail Order Pipeline." It provides a forum for people to share information with the readers of *Income Opportunities*, and it is used to an extent by people starting mail order businesses who are looking to get publicity.

$10 BOOKLETS FOR SALE

I am looking at "Mail Order Pipeline" of the July/August 1991 issue of *Income Opportunities.* I see a letter offering booklets for *Income Opportunities* readers interested in starting a business with little or no capital. The person who wrote this letter really knew how to target his or her market because most readers of *Income Opportunities* are in fact interested in starting a business with little or no capital. The price of the booklets is $10 each.

FOLLOWING UP ON LAST YEAR'S SUCCESS

In the same issue I saw a letter from a lady from Canada who is thanking *Income Opportunities* for publishing her letter a year earlier about a directory she sells for $10. In her letter the lady states that the response to her letter last year was great and that she is already putting together an updated version of her directory.

Her directory lists United States and Canadian mail receiving, forwarding and processing contacts. I am really impressed with this lady's ingenuity. She is touching all the bases.

In her "Mail Order Pipeline" letter she is not only offering her directory for sale but is also offering a free listing for any of the readers who forward mail and would like to be listed in her directory for free. This way she is not only using publicity to sell her information, but she's also obtaining listings to update her information!

"WHOLESALE DIRECTORY" FOR $14.95

In the same issue I see a letter offering a "Wholesale Directory" for $14.95 plus $3 for shipping and handling. The directory lists hundreds of sources for almost any product made, at wholesale or below prices. The price of the directory is $19.95, but the company is offering it at a $5 discount to the readers of *Income Opportunities.*

ANOTHER BOOKLET

I also see a letter from a person who is using a slightly different approach than the previously mentioned letters. He is offering his booklet for only $1. He apparently usually charges more for his booklet because he urges the readers who order to mention "Pipeline" with their order.

If his booklet is short and if he is using an inexpensive printer he may even make a profit on the front end. But he is obviously looking to make a lot more money on the back end.

His booklet has a generic title "How To Start A Profitable Home-Based Business" so he can follow-up the original order with any number of his own or drop-shipped business opportunity information sales packages. As discussed in Chapter 4, "How To Write A Successful Advertisement," it is not unusual for a mail order company's average customer to purchase more than $200 worth of additional information after the initial sale.

Chapter 14

Postscript

You have finished reading "My Amazing Discovery." What has it done for you?

A purpose of the first three chapters is to persuade you to start believing in yourself. I am convinced that belief in myself has been an absolutely necessary ingredient to my success.

Fear of suffering setbacks keeps many people from taking action which they must do in order to achieve their goals. Chapter 3, "The Power Of Belief" shows you how you can face setbacks and achieve your goals.

Believe In Yourself

If you are still not sure that you believe in yourself, go back and read the first three chapters again. Believe in yourself! Think to yourself: "If he could do it and he could not read, speak or write English well, then I can do it!" Remember, believing in yourself is a key to making your dreams come true. Once you believe in yourself, anything is possible.

Take Action To Overcome Fear of Setbacks

You must believe in yourself and you must take action in order to be successful. If you are like most people, you will have to overcome fear of setbacks before you can get started. Fear of setbacks stops most people before they even get started.

I faced the same problem before I got started. I learned that taking action is a key to overcoming fear, a key to getting started. Let this knowledge release you from the fear trap so that you too can take the first all important steps on the road to financial freedom.

A purpose of the remainder of this book, starting with Chapter 4, "How To Write A Successful Advertisement," is to teach you how to make large amounts of money by using my amazing discovery.

Read This Book From Cover To Cover

Review this book often. Please read it from cover to cover, perhaps more than once, so you can get the complete benefit of my experiences and knowledge. Refer to the index (Appendix E) and the table of contents whenever you want to review a specific topic.

The End, And The Beginning

Although this is the end of "My Amazing Discovery," it is also the beginning—your beginning. Financial freedom and personal satisfaction can be yours.

I can not think of any other money making opportunity where the money making potential is so big and can be done by anyone, young or old, male or female, from any walk of life. It does not matter what your background is and it does not even matter if you live in a big city, the smallest town or somewhere in between.

I have shared with you all the information about my secret, my amazing discovery, what it is, what I have learned since I got started and the mistakes I made so that you do not have to repeat them. It will be rewarding for me to know that "My Amazing Discovery" is helping you achieve your dreams. I wish you the greatest financial and personal success and rewards.

Part III

APPENDIXES

Appendix A

Newspapers

The following newspaper listings are only a small fraction of newspapers in the United States. They are listed in alphabetic order, by state. Newspaper names, mailing addresses and telephone numbers are listed so that you can contact them in writing or by telephone.

These newspapers are not necessarily recommended for you to advertise in or to seek free publicity from. They are listed here to give you a starting point. You can pick a state or an area of the country and get started by contacting the newspapers listed here.

There are literally thousands of newspapers which are not listed here because of space limitation. You can go to your local library and ask a librarian to show you reference books with listings of all the newspapers and magazines published in the United States.

If you do not want to do your own research, you can write to Bacon's Publishing Company, 332 South Michigan Avenue, Suite 900, Chicago, IL 60604. Ask for information on the Bacon's Publicity Checker for all the daily and weekly newspapers and magazines published in the United States.

ALABAMA

Birmingham Post Herald
P.O. Box 2553
Birmingham, AL 33202
205-325-2222

ALASKA

Anchorage Daily News
P.O. Box 149001
Anchorage, AK 99514
907-257-4200

ARIZONA

Phoenix Republic
Gazette
120 E. Van Buren
Phoenix, AZ 85004
602-271-8000

Tempe News
120 W. 1st Street
Mesa, AZ 85210
602-898-6414

Tuscon Citizen
P.O. Box 26887
Tuscon, AZ 85726
602-573-4400

ARKANSAS

Arkansas Democratic
Gazette
P.O. Box 2222
Little Rock, AR 72203
501-378-3400

Benton Courier
P.O. Box 207
Benton, AR 72015
501-778-8228

Fayetteville NW
Arkansas Times
Drawer D
Fayetteville, AR 72701
501-442-1777

Hot Springs Sentinel
P.O. Box 580
Hot Springs, AR 71902
501-623-7711

Jacksonville News
116 W. Hickory
Jacksonville, AR 72076
501-982-6506

Springdale News
P.O. Box 7
Springdale, AR 72765
501-751-6200

CALIFORNIA

Corona Independent
823 Main Street
Corona, CA 91720
714-737-1234

Glendale News-Press
111 N. Isabel
Glendale, CA 91206
818-241-4141

Los Angeles Daily News
P.O. Box 4200
Woodland Hills, CA 91365
818-713-3131

Los Angeles Journal
915 E. 1st Street
Los Angeles, CA 90012
213-625-2414

Martinez News-Gazette
615 Estrudillo
Martinez, CA 94553
510-228-6400

Napa Register
P.O. Box 150
Napa, CA 94559
707-226-3711

Oakland Tribune
P.O. Box 24304
Oakland, Ca 94623
510-645-2521

Palo Alto Peninsula
Times
245 Lytton Avenue
Palo Alto, CA 94301
415-853-1200

Pasadena Star-News
525 E. Colorado
Pasadena, CA 91109
818-578-6532

The Sacramento Bee
P.O. Box 15779
Sacramento, CA 95852
916-321-1000

San Bernardino Sun
399 D. Street
San Bernardino, CA 92401
714-889-9666

San Clemente Sun-Post
1541 N. El Camino
San Clemente, CA 92672
714-492-5121

San Diego Union/Tribune
P.O. Box 191
San Diego, CA
92112-4106
619-299-3131

San Diego County
Blade-Tribune
1722 S. Hill Street
Oceanside, CA 92054
619-433-7333

San Francisco Chronicle/
Examiner
925 Mission Street
San Francisco, CA 94103
415-777-5700

San Jose Mercury News
750 Ridder Park Drive
San Jose, CA 95190
408-920-5000

Santa Ana Register
625 N. Grand Avenue
Santa Ana, CA 92701
714-835-1234

Santa Barbara News-Press
P.O. Box 1359
Santa Barbara, CA
93102-1359
805-966-7171

Santa Cruz Sentinel
207 Church Street
Santa Cruz, CA 95061
408-423-4242

Santa Maria Times
P.O. Box 400
Santa Maria, CA 93456
805-925-2691

Santa Rosa Press Democrat
P.O. Box 569
Santa Rosa, CA 95402
707-546-2020

Tahoe Tribune
P.O. Box 1358
South Lake Tahoe, CA
96156
916-541-3880

Vista Press
P.O. Box 2168
Vista, CA 92085-2168
619-724-7161

COLORADO

Boulder Camera
P.O. Box 591
Boulder, CO 80306
303-442-1202

Colorado Springs Gazette
Telegraph
P.O. Box 1779
Colorado Springs, CO
80901
719-632-5511

Denver Post
1560 Broadway
Denver, CO 80202
303-820-1421

Grand Junction Sentinel
P.O. Box 668
Grand Junction, CO
81502
303-242-5050

Greeley Tribune
P.O. Box 1138
Greeley, CO 80632
303-352-0211

Pueblo Chieftan
P.O. Box 4040
Pueblo, CO 81003
719-544-3520

Rocky Mountain Post
400 W. Colfax Avenue
Denver, CO 80204
303-892-5411

CONNECTICUT

Bridgeport Post
410 State Street
Bridgeport, CT 06604
203-384-1158

Hartford Courant
285 Broad Street
Hartford, CT 06115-2510
1-800-524-4242

Norwalk Hour
346 Main Street
Norwalk, CT 06851
203-846-3281

DELAWARE

Delaware State News
P.O. Box 737
Dover, DE 19903
302-674-3600

DISTRICT OF COLUMBIA

Times
3600 New York Avenue, N.E.
Washington, D.C. 20002
202-636-3028

Washington Post
1150 15th Street, N.W.
Washington, D.C. 20071
202-334-6000

FLORIDA

Daytona Beach Journal
P.O. Box 2831
Daytona, FL 32120
904-252-1511

Fort Lauderdale Sun-Sentinel
101 N. New River Drive
Fort Lauderdale, FL 33302
305-761-4000

Miami Herald
1 Herald Plaza
Miami, FL 33132
305-376-2820

Naples News
1075 Central Avenue
Naples, FL 33940
813-262-3161

Orlando Sentinel
633 N. Orange Avenue
Orlando, FL 32801
407-420-5266

Pensacola News-Journal
1 News Journal Plaza
Pensacola, FL 32501
904-433-0041

Sarasota Herald-Tribune
801 S. Tamiami Trail
Sarasota, FL 33578
813-953-7755

St. Petersburg Times Independent
P.O. Box 1121
St. Petersburg, FL 33731
813-893-8111

Tampa Tribune
P.O. Box 191
Tampa, FL 33601
813-272-7450

GEORGIA

Atlanta Journal-Constitution
72 Marietta Street N.W.
Atlanta, GA 30303
404-526-5183

Brunswick News
P.O. Box 1557
Brunswick, GA 31521
912-265-8320

Columbus Ledger
711 W. 12th Street
Columbus, GA 31994
404-324-5526

Dalton Citizen
P.O. Box 1167
Dalton, GA 30720
404-278-1011

Thomasville Times Enterprise
P.O. Box 650
Thomasville, GA 31799
912-226-2400

HAWAII

Hawaiian Newspaper Agency
605 Kapiolani Blvd.
Honolulu, HI 96813
808-538-6397

IDAHO

Idaho Statesman
P.O. Box 40
Boise, ID 83707
208-377-6200

Twin Falls Times-News
P.O. Box 548
Twin Falls, ID 83303
208-733-0931

Idaho State Journal
P.O. Box 431
Pocatello, ID 83204
208-232-4161

ILLINOIS

Chicago Tribune
435 N. Michigan Avenue
Chicago, IL 60611
312-222-3232

Peoria Journal-Star
1 News Plaza
Peoria, IL 61643
309-686-3078

Pontiac Leader
318 N. Main Street
Pontiac, IL 61764
815-842-1153

Springfield State Journal
P.O. Box 219
Springfield, IL 62705
217-788-1354

INDIANA

Anderson Bulletin
P.O. Box 1090
Anderson, IN 46015
317-643-5371

Bloomington-Bedford
Herald Telephone
P.O. Box 909
Bloomington, IN 47402
812-332-4401

Fort Wayne Journal
600 W. Main Street
Fort Wayne, IN 46806
219-461-8488

Gary Post-Tribune
1065 Broadway
Gary, IN 46402
219-881-3187

Indianapolis Star News
307 N. Pennsylvania
Indianapolis, IN 46204
317-633-1240

Muncie Star
P.O. Box 2408
Muncie, IN 47307-2408
317-747-5700

Decatur Democrat
P.O. Box 1001
Decatur, IN 46733
219-724-2121

IOWA

Cedar Rapids Gazette
500 3rd Avenue S.E.
Cedar Rapids, IA 52401
319-398-8211

Des Moines Register
715 Locust Street
Des Moines, IA 50309
515-284-8046

Sioux City Journal
P.O. Box 118
Sioux City, IA 51102
712-279-5026

Waterloo Courier
P.O. Box 540
Waterloo, IA 50704
319-291-1400

KANSAS

Coffeyville Journal
8th & Elm Street
Coffeyville, KS 67337
316-251-3300

Junction City Union
P.O. Box 129
Junction City, KS 66441
913-762-5000

Kansas City Kansans
901 N. 8th Street
Kansas City, KS 66101
913-371-4300

Topeka Capital-Journal
616 Jefferson Street
Topeka, KS 66607
913-295-1247

Wichita Eagle
825 E. Douglas
Wichita, KS 67202
316-268-6545

KENTUCKY

Bowling Green News
813 College Street
Bowling Green, KY
42101
502-781-1700

Henderson Gleaner
P.O. Box 4
Henderson, KY 42420
502-827-2000

Lexington Herald Leader
100 Midland Avenue
Lexington, KY 40508
606-231-3345

The Louisville Times
525 W. Broadway
Louisville, KY 40202
502-582-4703

Richmond Register
P.O. Box 99
Richmond, KY 40475
606-623-1669

LOUISIANA

Baton Rouge Advocate
P.O. Box 588
Baton Rouge, LA 70821
504-383-1111

Lafayette Advertiser
P.O. Box 3268
LaFayette, LA 70502
318-235-8511

Lake Charles American
Press
P.O. Box 2893
Lake Charles, LA 70602
318-433-3000

New Orleans Record
P.O. Box 53367
New Orleans, LA 70153
504-581-4926

Times-Picayune
3800 Howard Avenue
New Orleans, LA 70140
504-826-3075

Shreveport
Journal-Times
222 Lake Street
Shreveport, LA 71130
318-459-3200

MAINE

Brunswick Times
P.O. Box 10
Brunswick, ME 04011
207-729-3311

MARYLAND

Record
111 E. Saratoga Street
Baltimore, MD 21202
301-752-3849

The Baltimore Sun
501 N. Calvert Street
Baltimore, MD 21278
301-332-6363

Easton Star
P.O. Box 600
Easton, MD 21601
301-822-1500

MASSACHUSETTS

Boston Globe
P.O. Box 2378
Boston, MA 02107
617-929-2000

Boston Herald
P.O. Box 2096
Boston, MA 02106
617-426-3000

Springfield Union
1860 Main Street
Springfield, MA 01102
413-788-1050

MICHIGAN

Big Rapids Pioneer
502 N. State Street
Big Rapids, MI 49307
616-796-4831

Cadillac News
130 N. Mitchell Street
Cadillac, MI 49601
616-775-6565

The Detroit News
615 LaFayette Blvd.
Detroit, MI 48226
313-222-2332

The Grand Rapids Press
155 Michigan Street
N.W.
Grand Rapids, MI 49503
616-459-1567

Kalamazoo Gazette
401 Burdick Street
Kalamazoo, MI 49007
616-345-3511

MINNESOTA

Duluth News-Tribune &
Herald
424 W. 1st Street
Duluth, MN 55802
218-723-5220

Minneapolis Star &
Tribune
425 Portland Avenue
Minneapolis, MN 55488
800-328-4674

St. Paul Pioneer Press &
Dispatch
345 Cedar Street
St. Paul, MN 55101
612-222-5011

MISSISSIPPI

Commercial Dispatch
P.O. Box 511
Columbus, MS
39703-0511
601-328-2424

Corinthian
P.O. Box 119
Corinth, MS 38834
601-287-6111

Jackson Clarion-Ledger
P.O. Box 40
Jackson, MS 39205-0040
601-961-7000

MISSOURI

Columbia Missourian
P.O. Box 507
Columbia, MO 65205
314-442-3161

Tribune
P.O. Box 798
Columbia, MO 65205
314-449-3811

Independence Blue
Springs Examiner
P.O. Box 459
Independence, MO
64051
816-254-8600

The Kansas City Times
1729 Grand
Kansas City, MO 64108
816-234-4125

Macon Chronicle-Herald
P.O. Box 7
Macon, MO 63552
816-385-3121

St. Louis Globe
Democrat
710 N. Tucker Blvd.
St. Louis, MO 63101
314-342-3031

Springfield News
Leader & Press
P.O. Box 798
Springfield, MO 65801
417-836-1100

MONTANA

Butte-Anaconda
Montana Standard
25 W. Granite Street
Butte, MT 59701
406-496-5500

Great Falls Tribune
P.O. Box 5468
Great Falls, MT 59403
406-761-6666

NEBRASKA

Columbus Telegram
P.O. Box 648
Columbus, NE 68602
402-564-2741

Fremont Tribune
P.O. Box 9
Fremont, NE 68025
402-721-5000

Lincoln Journal & Star
926 "P" Street
Lincoln, NE 68508
402-473-7448

Omaha World Herald
14th & Dodge
Omaha, NE 68102
402-444-1000

NEVADA

Carson City Nevada Appeal
P.O. Box 2288
Carson City, NV 89702
702-882-2111

Las Vegas Review Journal
P.O. Box 70
Las Vegas, NV 89125
702-383-0211

Reno Gazette Journal
P.O. Box 22000
Reno, NV 89520
702-788-6200

NEW HAMPSHIRE

Concord Monitor
P.O. Box 1177
Concord, NH 03302
603-224-5301

Portsmouth Herald
P.O. Box 119
Portsmouth, NH 03802
603-436-1800

Manchester Union Leader
P.O. Box 985
Manchester, NH 03108
603-668-4321

NEW JERSEY

Jersey Journal
30 Journal Square
Jersey City, NJ 07306
201-653-1000

Newark Star-Ledger
1 Star Ledger Plaza
Newark, NJ 07101-1200
201-877-4141

Trenton Times
500 Perry Street
Trenton, NJ 08618
609-396-3232

NEW MEXICO

Albuquerque Journal Tribune
P.O. Drawer J-T
Albuquerque, NM 87103
505-823-3390

Carlsbad Current Argus
P.O. Box 1629
Carlsbad, NM 88220
505-887-5501

Clovis News Journal
P.O. Box 1689
Clovis, NM 88101
505-763-3431

NEW YORK

Albany Times-Union Knickerbocker News
Box 15000, News Plaza
Albany, NY 12212
518-454-5680

Buffalo News
One News Plaza
P.O. Box 100
Buffalo, NY 14240
716-849-5440

Glen Falls Post Star
P.O. Box 2157
Glen Falls, NY 12801
518-792-3131

Ithaca Journal
123 West State Street
Ithaca, NY 14850
607-272-2321

Daily News
220 E. 42nd Street
New York, NY 10017
212-210-2100

New York Post
210 S. Street
New York, NY 10002
212-815-8000

New York Times
229 W. 43rd Street
New York, NY 10036
212-354-3900

Wall Street Journal
420 Lexington Avenue
New York, NY 10170
212-808-6700

Rochester Democrat & Chronicle Times-Union
55 Exchange Blvd.
Rochester, NY 14614
716-232-7100

Utica Press Observer-Dispatch
221 Oriskany Plaza
Utica, NY 13501
315-792-5000

NORTH CAROLINA

Charlotte Observer
P.O. Box 32188
Charlotte, NC 28202
704-358-5000

Concord-Kannapolis Tribune
P.O. Box 608
Union Street S.
Concord, NC 28025
704-782-3155

Fayetteville Observer & Times
P.O. Box 849
Fayetteville, NC 28302
919-323-4848

Raleigh News & Observer Times
215 McDowell
Raleigh, NC 27602
919-829-4620

Roanoke Rapids Herald
P.O. Box 520
Roanoke Rapids, NC 27870
919-537-2505

Winston-Salem Journal
418 N. Marshall Street
Winston-Salem, NC 27102
919-727-7418

NORTH DAKOTA

Bismarck Tribune
P.O. Box 1498
707 E. Front Avenue
Bismarck, ND 58502
701-223-2500

The Forum
P.O. Box 2020
Fargo, ND 58107
701-241-5412

OHIO

Bowling Green
Sentinel-Tribune
300 E. Poe Road
Bowling Green, OH
43402
419-352-4611

Cincinnati Post Enquirer
617 Vine Street
Cincinnati, OH 45202
513-721-2700

Cleveland Plain Dealer
1801 Superior Avenue
N.E.
Cleveland, OH 44114
216-344-4970

Columbus Dispatch
34 S. Third Street
Columbus, OH 43215
614-461-5000

Dayton-Springfield News
Journal-Herald
Fourth & Ludlow Streets
Dayton, OH 45402
513-225-2085

Norwalk Reflector
P.O. Box 71
Norwalk, OH 44857
419-668-3771

Youngstown Vindicator
P.O. Box 780
Youngstown, OH
44501-0780
216-747-1471

OKLAHOMA

Edmond Sun
P.O. Box 2470
Edmond, OK 73083
405-341-2121

Lawton Press
Constitution
P.O. Box 2069
Lawton, OK 73502
405-353-0620

Norman Transcript
Drawer 1058
215 E. Comanche Street
Norman, OK 73070
405-321-1800

Oklahoman
P.O. Box 25125
Oklahoma City, OK
73125
405-475-3311

Seminole Producer
P.O. Box 431
Seminole, OK 74818
405-273-4200

Tulsa Tribune/
Tulsa World
P.O. Box 1770
Tulsa, OK 74102
918-581-8555

OREGON

Eugene Register-Guard
P.O. Box 10188
Eugene, OR 97440
503-485-1234

The Oregonian
1320 S.W. Broadway
Portland, OR 97201
503-221-8280

Salem Stateman-Journal
280 Church Street N.E.
Salem, OR 97309
503-399-6808

PENNSYLVANIA

The Morning Call
101 6th Street
Allentown, PA 18105
215-820-6646

Altoona Mirror
P.O. Box 2008
Altoona, PA 16603
814-946-7411

Bethlehem Globe Times
P.O. Box 1067
Bethlehem, PA
18015-1067
215-867-5000

Gazette
P.O. Box 671
Bedford, PA 15522
814-623-1151

Gettysburg Times
18 Carlisle Street
Gettysburg, PA 17325
717-334-1131

Harrisburg Patriot News
P.O. Box 2265
Harrisburg, PA 17105
717-255-8100

Philadelphia
Inquirer-News
440 N. Broad Street
Philadelphia, PA 19131
215-854-2000

Pittsburgh Press
Post Gazette
34 Blvd. of Allies
Pittsburgh, PA 15222
412-263-1100

RHODE ISLAND

Newport News
101 Malbone Road
Newport, RI 02840
401-849-3300

Providence
Journal-Bulletin
75 Fountain Street
Providence, RI 02902
401-277-7172

SOUTH CAROLINA

Beaufort Gazette
P.O. Box 399
Beaufort, SC 29901
803-524-3183

Sun News
P.O. Box 406
Myrtle Beach, SC 29578
803-626-8555

Sumter Item
P.O. Box 1677
Sumter, SC 29151
803-775-6331

SOUTH DAKOTA

Brookings Register
P.O. Box 177
Brookings, SD 57006
605-692-6271

Rapid City Journal
P.O. Box 450
Rapid City, SD 57709
605-394-8300

TENNESSEE

Chattanooga News-Free
Press Times
P.O. Box 1447
Chattanooga, TN
37401-1447
615-756-6900

Herald Citizen
P.O. Box 2729
Cookeville, TN 38502
615-526-9715

Kingsport News
310 E. Sullivan
Kingsport, TN 37660
615-246-4800

Knoxville Journal
News Sentinel
P.O. Box 59038
Knoxville, TN 37950
615-523-3131

Memphis Commercial
Appeal
495 Union Avenue
Memphis, TN 38103
901-529-2211

Times News
701 Lynn Garden Drive
Kingsport, TN 37662
615-246-8121

TEXAS

Amarillo Globe
Times News
P.O. Box 2091
Amarillo, TX 79166
806-376-4488

Arlington News
1000 Ave H East
Arlington, TX 76011
817-695-0500

Austin American
Statesman
305 S. Congress
Austin, TX 78704
512-445-3745

Beaumont Enterprise
P.O. Box 3071
Beaumont, TX 77704
409-833-3311

Big Spring Herald
710 Scurry
Big Spring, TX 79720
915-263-7331

Corpus Christi Caller
Times
820 Lower N. Broadway
Corpus Christi, TX
78401
512-886-3644

Dallas Morning News
508 Young St.
Dallas, TX 75202
214-977-8222

El Paso Herald Post
Times
Times Plaza
El Paso, TX 79901-1470
915-546-6260

Fort Worth Star Telegram
P.O. Box 1870
Fort Worth, TX 76101
817-390-7400

Galveston Daily News
P.O. Box 628
Galveston, TX 77553
409-744-3611

Garland News
P.O. Box 461587
Garland, TX 75046-1587
214-272-6591

Grand Prairie News
P.O.Box 1289
Grand Prairie, TX 75050
214-262-5141

Houston Chronicle
P.O. Box 4260
Houston, TX 77210
713-220-7171

Houston Post
4747 Southwest Freeway
Houston, TX 77210
713-840-5600

Lubbock
Avalanche-Journal
Box 491
Lubbock, TX 79408
806-762-8844

Midland Reporter
Telegram
P.O. Box 1650
Midland, TX 79702
915-682-5311

Odessa American
P.O. Box 2952
Odessa, TX 79760
915-337-4661

San Angelo Standard Times
P.O. Box 6111
San Angelo, TX 76901
915-653-1221

San Antonio Express News
Box 2171
San Antonio, TX 78297
512-225-7411

San Antonio Light
P.O. Box 161
San Antonio, TX 78291
512-271-2700

Texarkana Gazette
P.O. Box 621
Texarkana, TX 75504
903-794-3311

UTAH

Ogden Standard-Examiner
455 23rd Street
Ogden, UT 84401
801-394-7711

Provo Herald
1555 North 200
West Provo, UT 84603
801-373-5050

Salt Lake City Tribune
P.O. Box 45838
Salt Lake City, UT 84145
801-237-2721

VERMONT

Newport Express
P.O. Box 347
Newport, VT 05855
802-334-6568

Rutland Herald
P.O. Box 668
Rutland, VT 05702
802-775-5511

VIRGINIA

Manassas Journal Messenger
9009 Church St
Manassas, VA 22110
703-368-3101

Richmond News Leader Times Dispatch
P.O. Box 85333
Richmond, VA 23293
804-649-6000

Suffolk News-Herald
P.O. Box 1220
Suffolk, VA 23434
804-539-3437

Winchester Star
2 N. Kent Street
Winchester, VA 22601
703-667-3200

WASHINGTON

Seattle Journal of Commerce
P.O. Box 11050
Seattle, WA 98111
206-622-8272

Spokane Chronicle Spokesman Review
P.O. Box 2160
Spokane, WA 99201
509-459-5045

WEST VIRGINIA

Charleston Gazette Mail
1001 Virginia Street E.
Charleston, WV 25301
304-348-5105

Clarksburg Exponent Telegram
P.O. Box 2000
Clarksburg, WV 26301
304-624-6411

WISCONSIN

Baraboo News-Republic
219 1st Street
Baraboo, WI 53913
608-356-4808

Green Bay News-Chronicle
133 S. Monroe
Green Bay, WI 54301
414-432-2941

Press-Gazette
P.O. Box 19430
Green Bay, WI 54307-9430
414-435-4411

Milwaukee Journal-Centinal Inc.
P.O. Box 661
Milwaukee, WI 53201
414-224-2000

Racine Journal Times
212 Fourth Street
Racine, WI 53403
414-634-3322

Press
122 W. 3rd Street
Ashland, WI 54806
715-682-2313

WYOMING

Casper Star-Tribune
P.O. Box 80
Casper, WY 82602
307-266-0500

Wyoming Tribune-Eagle
702 W. Lincolnway
Cheyenne, WY 82001
307-634-3361

Laramie Boomerang
314 S. 4th Street
Laramie, WY 82070
307-742-2176

Appendix B

IRS Taxpayer Education Coordinators

The following Internal Revenue Service Taxpayer Education Coordinators can provide you with information regarding locally scheduled Small Business Tax Education Programs (STEP). These programs include workshops and business tax seminars.

The IRS Taxpayer Education Coordinators are listed in alphabetic order, by state. Their mailing addresses and telephone numbers are listed so that you can contact them in writing or by telephone. The telephone numbers listed are not toll free and will involve long distance charges to callers outside of the local calling area. Contacts by mail should be made to the attention of the "Taxpayer Education Coordinator."

If you need other assistance from the IRS, check for the telephone number of the IRS office closest to you in your local telephone book or call, toll free, 1-800-829-1040.

ALABAMA

500 22nd St., S.,
Stop 117
Birmingham, AL 35233
205-731-0403

ALASKA

949 E. 36th Ave.
Anchorage, AK
99508-4328
907-271-6231

ARIZONA

2120 N. Central,
Stop 6610-PX
Phoenix, AZ 85004
602-379-3861

ARKANSAS

P.O. Box 3778, Stop 603
Little Rock, AR
72203-3778
501-378-5685

CALIFORNIA

Laguna Niguel
Chet Holifield Fed. Bldg.
P.O. Box 30210
Laguna Niguel, CA
92607-0210
714-643-4060

Los Angeles
300 N. Los Angeles St.
Room 5202
Los Angeles, CA 90012
213-894-4574

Sacramento
P.O. Box 2900,
Stop SA5650
Sacramento, CA 95812
916-978-4083

San Francisco
1221 Broadway, 5th Floor
Oakland, CA 94612-1808
415-273-4233

San Jose
P.O. Box 100,
Stop HQ-6300
San Jose, CA
95113-2397
408-291-7114

COLORADO

600 17th Street,
Stop 6610-DEN
Denver, CO 80202
303-844-3340

CONNECTICUT

135 High Street,
Stop 115
Hartford, CT 06103-1185
203-240-4149

DELAWARE

P.O. Box 28
Wilmington, DE 19899
302-573-6270

DISTRICT OF COLUMBIA

P.O. Box 538
Baltimore, MD 21203
202-488-3100 Ext. 2222

FLORIDA

Jacksonville
400 W. Bay St.,
Stop 6250
Jacksonville, FL
32202-0045
904-791-2514

Ft. Lauderdale
One. N. University Dr.
Stop 6030
Building A, Room 270
Ft. Lauderdale, FL
33324-2019
305-424-2438

GEORGIA

Peachtree Summit Bldg.
401 W. Peachtree St.
526, Stop 902D
Atlanta, GA 30385
404-331-3808

HAWAII

PJKK Federal Buildling
P.O. Box 50089
Honolulu, HI 96850
808-541-3329

IDAHO

550 W. Fort St., Box 041
Boise, ID 83724
208-334-9153

ILLINOIS

Chicago
P.O. Box 1132, DNP 7-5
Chicago, IL 60604-1132
312-886-4609

Springfield
P.O. Box 19201, Stop 8
Springfield, IL
62794-9201
217-492-4386

INDIANA

P.O. Box 44211, Stop 60
Indianapolis, IN 46244
317-226-6543

IOWA

P.O. Box 1337, Stop 30-2
Des Moines, IA
50305-1337
515-284-4870

KANSAS

412 S. Main Street
Stop 6610-WIC
Wichita, KS 67202
316-291-6610

KENTUCKY

P.O. Box 1216, Stop 531
Louisville, KY 40201
502-582-6259

LOUISIANA

600 S. Maestri Place,
Stop 21
New Orleans, LA 70130
504-589-2801

MAINE

P.O. Box 1020
Augusta, ME 04332
207-622-8328

MARYLAND

31 Hopkins Plaza,
Room 615A
Baltimore, MD 21201
410-962-2222

MASSACHUSETTS

JFK Federal Building
P.O. Box 9088
Boston, MA 02203
617-565-1645

MICHIGAN

P.O. Box 330500,
Rm. 1196
Detroit, MI 48232-6500
313-226-3674

MINNESOTA

316 North Robert Street
Stop 6500
St. Paul, MN 55101-1474
612-290-3320

MISSISSIPPI

100 W. Capitol Street
Room 101A, Stop 30
Jackson, MS 30200
601-965-4142

MISSOURI

P.O. Box 1147, Stop 612
St. Louis, MO
63188-1147
314-539-3660

MONTANA

Federal Building,
301 S. Park
Drawer 10016
Helena, MT 59626-0016
406-449-5375

NEBRASKA

106 S. 15th, Stop 27
Omaha, NE 68102-1676
402-221-3501

NEVADA

4750 W. Oakey Blvd.
Las Vegas, NV 89102
702-455-1029

NEW HAMPSHIRE

80 Daniel Street
Portsmouth, NH 03801
603-433-0519

NEW JERSEY

425 Raritan Ctr. Pkwy.
Edison, NJ 08818
201-417-4075

NEW MEXICO

517 Gold Ave., S.W.
Stop 6610-ALB
Albuquerque, NM 87102
505-766-2537

NEW YORK

Manhattan
P.O. Box 3036
Church Street Station
New York, NY
10008-3036
212-264-3310

Brooklyn
P.O. Box 606, RM G-14
Brooklyn, NY
11202-0013
718-780-4000

Albany
Leo O'Brien Federal Bldg.
Clinton & N. Pearl Streets
Room 421
Albany, NY 12207-2378
518-472-3636

Buffalo
P.O. Box 606
Cheektowaga, NY
14225-0606
716-685-8328

NORTH CAROLINA

320 Federal Place,
Room 128
Greensboro, NC 27401
919-333-5620

NORTH DAKOTA

P.O. Box 2461
Fargo, ND 58108-2461
701-239-5105

OHIO

Cincinnati
P.O. Box 3459
Cincinnati, OH 45201
513-684-2828

Cleveland
P.O. Box 99184
Cleveland, OH 44199
216-522-3414

OKLAHOMA

200 Northwest 4th Street
Stop 6610-OKC
Oklahoma City, OK
73102
405-231-4989

OREGON

P.O. Box 2709
Portland, OR 97208
503-326-6565

PENNSYLVANIA

Philadelphia
600 Arch St., Room 6424
Philadelphia, PA 19106
215-597-0512

Pittsburgh
P.O. Box 2488,
Room 1117
Pittsburgh, PA 15230
412-644-6504

RHODE ISLAND

P.O. Box 6627
Providence, RI 02940
401-528-4276

SOUTH CAROLINA

Strom Thurmond
Fed. Bldg.
1835 Assembly St.,
Room 408
Columbia, SC 29201
803-253-3031

SOUTH DAKOTA

P.O. Box 370
Aberdeen, SD
57402-0370
605-226-7230

TENNESSEE

801 Broadway, MDP 46
Nashville, TN
37203-3836
615-736-2280

TEXAS

Austin
300 E. 8th Street
Stop 6610-AUS
Austin, TX 78701
512-499-5439

Houston
8701 S. Gessner
Stop 6610 HAL
Houston, TX 77074
713-541-7610

Dallas
1100 Commerce Street
Stop 6610-DAL
Dallas, TX 75242
214-767-1428

UTAH

465 South 400 East Street
Stop 6610-SLC
Salt Lake City, UT 84111
801-524-6095

VERMONT

Courthouse Plaza
199 Main Street
Burlington, VT
05401-8345
802-860-2089

VIRGINIA

P.O. Box 10049
Room 5223
Richmond, VA 23240
804-771-2289

WASHINGTON

915 Second Ave.,
MS-425
Seattle, WA 98174
206-553-4230

WEST VIRGINIA

P.O. Box 1138,
Stop 2019
Parkersburg, WV 26102
304-420-6612

WISCONSIN

P.O. Box 493
Milwaukee, WI
53201-0493
414-297-3302

WYOMING

308 W. 21st Street
Stop 6610-CHE
Cheyenne, WY 82001
307-772-2325

PUERTO RICO

Mercantil Plaza Bldg. GF
Taxpayer Service
Division
Avenida Ponce de Leon
Stop 27 1/2
Hato Rey, PR 00918
809-498-5946

Appendix C

Three-Digit Zip Code Prefixes

The following three-digit zip code prefixes include the first three digits of each assigned group of zip codes and the areas associated with these digits. The prefixes are listed in numeric order, from 006 to 999.

If you have a problem reading the name of the city on your customer's order form or envelope because the handwriting is illegible, look up the first three digits of the zip code in this appendix. To the right of the first three digits of the zip code you should find the name of the city. If you do not, you can go to your local post office and in their lobby you should find a large book of five-digit zip codes which should be able to solve your problem.

006-009 PUERTO RICO AND VIRGIN ISLANDS

006 San Juan
007 San Juan
008 San Juan (Virgin Islands)
009 San Juan

010-027 MASSACHUSETTS

010 Springfield
011 Springfield
012 Pittsfield
013 Springfield
014 Worcester
015 Worcester
016 Worcester
017 Worcester
018 Middlesex-Essex
019 Middlesex-Essex
020 Brockton
021 Boston
022 Boston
023 Brockton
024 Brockton
025 Buzzards Bay
026 Buzzards Bay
027 Providence, RI (Massachusetts Offices)

028-029 RHODE ISLAND

028 Providence
029 Providence

030-038 NEW HAMPSHIRE

030 Manchester
031 Manchester
032 Manchester
033 Concord
034 Manchester
035 White River Junction
036 Brattleborro, VT (New Hampshire Offices)
037 White River Junction, VT (New Hampshire Offices)
038 Portsmouth

039-049 MAINE

039 Portsmouth, NH (Maine Offices)
040 Portland
041 Portland
042 Auburn
043 Augusta
044 Bangor
045 Portland
046 Bangor
047 Bangor
048 Portland
049 Waterville

050-059 VERMONT

050 White River Junction
051 Brattleboro
052 Brattleboro
053 Brattleboro
054 Burlington
055 Middlesex-Essex, MA
056 White River Junction
057 White River Junction
058 White River Junction

059 White River Junction

060-069 CONNECTICUT

060 Hartford
061 Hartford
062 Hartford
063 New Haven
064 New Haven
065 New Haven
066 Bridgeport
067 Waterbury
068 Stamford
069 Stamford

070-089 NEW JERSEY

070 Newark
071 Newark
072 Elizabeth
073 Jersey City
074 Paterson
075 Paterson
076 Hackensack
077 Red Bank
078 Paterson
079 Summit
080 South Jersey
081 Camden
082 South Jersey
083 South Jersey
084 Atlantic City
085 Trenton
086 Trenton
087 Trenton
088 New Brunswick
089 New Brunswick

004-149 NEW YORK

004 Mount Vernon
090-098 Military (AE)
100 New York
101 New York
102 New York
103 Staten Island
104 Bronx
105 Westchester
106 White Plains
107 Yonkers
108 New Rochelle
109 Rockland
110 Queens
111 Long Island City
112 Brooklyn
113 Flushing
114 Jamaica
115 Western Nassau
116 Far Rockaway
117 Hicksville
118 Hicksville
119 Riverhead
120 Albany
121 Albany
122 Albany
123 Schenectady
124 Poughkeepsie
125 Poughkeepsie
126 Poughkeepsie
127 Mid Hudson
128 Glens Falls
129 Plattsburgh
130 Syracuse
131 Syracuse
132 Syrecuse
133 Utica
134 Utica
135 Utica
136 Watertown
137 Binghamton
138 Binghamton
139 Binghamton
140 Buffalo
141 Buffalo
142 Buffalo
143 Niagara Falls
144 Rochester
145 Rochester
146 Rochester
147 Jamestown
148 Elmira
149 Elmira

150-196 PENNSYLVANIA

150 Pittsburgh
151 Pittsburgh
152 Pittsburgh
153 Pittsburgh
154 Pittsburgh
155 Johnstown
156 Greensburg
157 Johnstown
158 Du Bois
159 Johnstown
160 New Castle
161 New Castle
162 New Castle
163 Oil City
164 Erie
165 Erie
166 Altoona
167 Bradford
168 Altoona
169 Williamsport
170 Harrisburg
171 Harrisburg
172 Harrisburg
173 Lancaster
174 York
175 Lancaster
176 Lancaster
177 Williamsport
178 Harrisburg
179 Pottsville
180 Lehigh Valley
181 Allentown
182 Wilkes-Barre
183 Lehigh Valley
184 Scranton
185 Scranton
186 Wilkes-Barre
187 Wilkes-Barre
188 Scranton
189 Southeastern
190 Philadelphia
191 Philadelphia
192 Philadelphia
193 Southeastern
194 Southeastern
195 Reading
196 Reading
213 Philadelphia

197-199 DELAWARE

197 Wilmington
198 Wilmington
199 Wilmington

200-205 DISTRICT OF COLUMBIA

200 Washington
202-205 Government

206-219 MARYLAND

206 Southern
207 Southern
208 Suburban
209 Silver Spring

210 Baltimore
211 Baltimore
212 Baltimore
214 Annapolis
215 Cumberland
216 Easton
217 Frederick
218 Salisbury
219 Baltimore

220-246 VIRGINIA

220 Northern Virginia
221 Northern Virginia
222 Arlington
223 Alexandria
224 Richmond
225 Richmond
226 Winchester
227 Culpeper
228 Harrisonburg
229 Charlottesville
230 Richmond
231 Richmond
232 Richmond
233 Norfolk
234 Norfolk
235 Norfolk
236 Newport News
237 Portsmouth
238 Richmond
239 Farmville
240 Roanoke
241 Roanoke
242 Bristol
243 Roanoke
244 Charlottesville
245 Lynchburg
246 Bluefield, WV (Virginia Offices)

247-268 WEST VIRGINIA

247 Bluefield
248 Bluefield
249 Lewisburg
250 Charleston
251 Charleston
252 Charleston
253 Charleston
254 Martinsburg
255 Huntington
256 Huntington
257 Huntington
258 Beckley
259 Beckley
260 Wheeling
261 Parkersburg
262 Buckhannon
263 Clarksburg
264 Clarksburg
265 Clarksburg
266 Cassaway
267 Cumberland, MD (West Virginia Offices)
268 Petersburg

270-289 NORTH CAROLINA

270 Greensboro
271 Winston-Salem
272 Greensboro
273 Greensboro
274 Greensboro
275 Raleigh
276 Raleigh
277 Durham
278 Rocky Mount
279 Rocky Mount
280 Charlotte
281 Charlotte
282 Charlotte
283 Fayetteville
284 Fayetteville
285 Kinston
286 Hickory
287 Asheville
288 Asheville
289 Asheville

290-299 SOUTH CAROLINA

290 Columbia
291 Columbia
292 Columbia
293 Greenville
294 Charleston
295 Florence
296 Greenville
297 Charlotte, NC (South Carolina Offices)
298 Augusta, GA (South Carolina Offices)
299 Savannah, GA (South Carolina Offices)

300-319 GEORGIA

300 North Metro
301 North Metro
302 North Metro
303 Atlanta
304 Swansboro
305 North Metro
306 Athens
307 Chattanooga, TN (Georgia Offices)
308 Augusta
309 Augusta
310 Macon
311 Atlanta
312 Macon
313 Savannah
314 Savannah
315 Waycross
316 Valdosta
317 Albany
318 Columbus
319 Columbus

320-349 FLORIDA

320 Jacksonville
321 Daytona Beach
322 Jacksonville
323 Tallahassee
324 Panama City
325 Pensacola
326 Gainsville
327 Mid-Florida
328 Orlando
329 Orlando
330 South Florida
331 Miami
332 Miami
333 Fort Lauderdale
334 West Palm Beach
335 Tampa
336 Tampa
337 Saint Petersburg
338 Lakeland
339 Fort Myers
340 Military (AA)
342 Manasota
346 Tampa
347 Orlando
349 West Palm Beach

350-369 ALABAMA

350 Birmingham
351 Birmingham
352 Birmingham
354 Tuscaloosa
355 Birmingham
356 Huntsville
357 Huntsville
358 Huntsville
359 Gadsden
360 Montgomery
361 Montgomery
362 Anniston
363 Dothan
364 Evergreen
365 Mobile
366 Mobile
367 Montgomery
368 Montgomery
369 Meridian, MS (Alabama Offices)

370-385 TENNESSEE

370 Nashville
371 Nashville
372 Nashville
373 Chattanooga
374 Chattanooga
376 Johnson City
377 Knoxville
378 Knoxville
379 Knoxville
380 Memphis
381 Memphis
382 McKenzie
383 Jackson
384 Columbia
385 Cooksville

386-397 MISSISSIPPI

386 Memphis, TN (Mississippi Offices)
387 Greenville
388 Tupelo
389 Grenada
390 Jackson
391 Jackson
392 Jackson
393 Meridian
394 Hattiesburg
395 Gulfport
396 McComb
397 Columbus

400-427 KENTUCKY

400 Louisville
401 Louisville
402 Louisville
403 Lexington
404 Lexington
405 Lexington
406 Frankfort
407 London
408 London
409 London
410 Cincinnati, OH (Kentucky Offices)
411 Ashland
412 Ashland
413 Campton
414 Campton
415 Pikesville
416 Pikesville
417 Hazard
418 Hazard
420 Paducah
421 Bowling Green
422 Bowling Green
423 Owensboro
424 Evansville, IN (Kentucky Offices)
425 Somerset
426 Somerset
427 Elizabethtown

430-458 OHIO

430 Columbus
431 Columbus
432 Columbus
433 Columbus
434 Toledo
435 Toledo
436 Toledo
437 Zanesville
438 Zanesville
439 Steubenville
440 Cleveland
441 Cleveland
442 Akron
443 Akron
444 Youngstown
445 Youngstown
446 Canton
447 Canton
448 Mansfield
449 Mansfield
450 Cincinnati
451 Cincinnati
452 Cincinnati
453 Dayton
454 Dayton
455 Springfield
456 Chillicothe
457 Athens
458 Lima

460-479 INDIANA

460 Indianapolis
461 Indianapolis
462 Indianapolis
463 Gary
464 Gary
465 South Bend
466 South Bend
467 Fort Wayne
468 Fort Wayne
469 Kokomo
470 Cincinnati,OH (Indiana Offices)
471 Louisville, KY (Indiana Offices)
472 Columbus
473 Muncie
474 Bloomington
475 Washington
476 Evansville
477 Evansville
478 Terre Haute
479 Lafayette

480-499 MICHIGAN

480 Royal Oak
481 Detroit
482 Detroit
483 Royal Oak
484 Flint
485 Flint
486 Saginaw
487 Saginaw
488 Lansing
489 Lansing
490 Kalamazoo
491 Kalamazoo
492 Jackson
493 Grand Rapids
494 Grand Rapids
495 Grand Rapids

496 Traverse City
497 Gaylord
498 Iron Mountain
499 Iron Mountain

500-528 IOWA

500 Des Moines
501 Des Moines
502 Des Moines
503 Des Moines
504 Mason City
505 Fort Dodge
506 Waterloo
507 Waterloo
508 Creston
509 Des Moines
510 Sioux City
511 Sioux City
512 Sheldon
513 Spencer
514 Carroll
515 Omaha, NE (Iowa Offices)
516 Omaha, NE (Iowa Offices)
520 Dubuque
521 Decorah
522 Cedar Rapids
523 Cedar Rapids
524 Cedar Rapids
525 Ottumwa
526 Burlington
527 Rock Island, IL (Iowa Offices)
528 Davenport

530-549 WISCONSIN

530 Milwaukee
531 Milwaukee
532 Milwaukee
534 Racine
535 Madison
537 Madison
538 Madison
539 Portage
540 Saint Paul, MN (Wisconsin Offices)
541 Green Bay
542 Green Bay
543 Green Bay
544 Wausau
545 Rhinetander
546 La Crosse
547 Eau Claire
548 Spooner
549 Oshkosh

550-567 MINNESOTA

550 Saint Paul
551 Saint Paul
553 Minneapolis
554 Minneapolis
555 Minneapolis
556 Duluth
557 Duluth
558 Duluth
559 Rochester
560 Mankota
561 Windom
562 Willmar
563 Saint Cloud
564 Brainerd
565 Detroit Lakes
566 Bemidji
567 Thief River Falls

570-577 SOUTH DAKOTA

570 Sioux Falls
571 Sioux Falls
572 Watertown
573 Mitchell
574 Aberdeen
575 Pierre
576 Mobridge
577 Rapid City

580-588 NORTH DAKOTA

580 Fargo
581 Fargo
582 Grand Forks
583 Devils Lake
584 Jamestown
585 Bismark
586 Dickinson
587 Minot
588 Williston

590-599 MONTANA

590 Billings
591 Billings
592 Wolf Point
593 Miles City
594 Great Falls
595 Havre
596 Helena
597 Butte
598 Missoula
599 Kalispell

600-629 ILLINOIS

600 North Suburban
601 North Suburban
602 Evanston
603 Oak Park
604 South Suburban
605 South Suburban
606 Chicago
609 Kankakee
610 Rockford
611 Rockford
612 Rock Island
613 La Salle
614 Galesburg
615 Peoria
616 Peoria
617 Bloomington
618 Champaign
619 Champaign
620 St. Louis, MO (Illinois Offices)
622 St. Louis, MO (Illinois Offices)
623 Quincy
624 Effingham
625 Springfield
626 Springfield
627 Springfield
628 Centralia
629 Carbondale

630-658 MISSOURI

630 Saint Louis
631 Saint Louis
633 Saint Louis
634 Hannibal
635 Kirksville
636 Flat River
637 Cape Girardeau
638 Sikeston
639 Poplar Bluff
640 Kansas City
641 Kansas City
644 Saint Joseph
645 Saint Joseph

646 Chillicothe
647 Harrisonville
648 Joplin
650 Mid-Missouri
651 Jefferson City
652 Mid-Missouri
653 Mid-Missouri
654 Springfield
655 Springfield
656 Springfield
657 Springfield
658 Springfield

660-679 KANSAS

660 Kansas City
661 Kansas City
662 Shawnee Mission
664 Topeka
665 Topeka
666 Topeka
667 Fort Scott
668 Topeka
670 Wichita
671 Wichita
672 Wichita
673 Independence
674 Salina
675 Hutchinson
676 Hays
677 Colby
678 Dodge City
679 Liberal

680-693 NEBRASKA

680 Omaha
681 Omaha
683 Lincoln
684 Lincoln
685 Lincoln
686 Columbus
687 Norfolk
688 Grand Island
689 Hastings
690 McCook
691 North Platte
692 Valentine
693 Alliance

700-714 LOUISIANA

700 New Orleans
701 New Orleans
703 Thibodaux
704 Hammond
705 Lafayette
706 Lake Charles
707 Baton Rouge
708 Baton Rouge
710 Shreveport
711 Shreveport
712 Monroe
713 Alexandria
714 Alexandria

716-729 ARKANSAS

716 Pine Bluff
717 Camden
718 Texarkana, TX (AR Offices)
719 Hot Springs National Park
720 Little Rock
721 Little Rock
722 Little Rock
723 Memphis, TN (AR Offices)
724 Jonesboro
725 Batesville
726 Harrison
727 Fayetteville
728 Russelville
729 Fort Smith

730-749 OKLAHOMA

730 Oklahoma City
731 Oklahoma City
734 Ardmore
735 Lawton
736 Clinton
737 Oklahoma City
738 Woodward
739 Liberal, KS (Oklahoma Office)
740 Tulsa
741 Tulsa
743 Tulsa
744 Muskogee
745 McAlester
746 Oklahoma City
747 Durant
748 Oklahoma City
749 Poteau

750-799 TEXAS

750 North Texas
751 Dallas
752 Dallas
753 Dallas
754 Greenville
755 Texarkana
756 Longview
757 Tyler
758 Palestine
759 Lufkin
760 Fort Worth
761 Fort Worth
762 Denton
763 Wichita Falls
764 Fort Worth
765 Waco
766 Waco
767 Waco
768 Abilene
769 Midland
770 Houston
771 Houston
772 Houston
773 North Houston
774 North Houston
775 North Houston
776 Beaumont
777 Beaumont
778 Bryan
779 Victoria
780 San Antonio
781 San Antonio
782 San Antonio
783 Corpus Christi
784 Corpus Christi
785 McAllen
786 Austin
787 Austin
788 San Antonio
789 Austin
790 Amarillo
791 Amarillo
792 Childress
793 Lubbock
794 Lubbock
795 Abilene
796 Abilene
797 Midland
798 El Paso
799 El Paso
885 El Paso

800-816 COLORADO

800 Denver
801 Denver
802 Denver

803 Boulder
804 Denver
805 Longmont
806 Brighton
807 Brighton
808 Colorado Springs
809 Colorado Springs
810 Pueblo
811 Alamosa
812 Salida
813 Durango
814 Grand Junction
815 Grand Junction
816 Glenwood Springs

820-831 WYOMING

820 Cheyenne
821 Yellowstone National Park (Montana Office)
822 Wheatland
823 Rawlins
824 Worland
825 Riverton
826 Casper
827 Gillette
828 Sheridan
829 Rock Springs
830 Rock Springs
831 Rock Springs

832-838 IDAHO

832 Pocatello
833 Twin Falls
834 Pocatello
835 Lewiston
836 Boise
837 Boise
838 Spokane, WA (Idaho Offices)

840-847 UTAH

840 Salt Lake City
841 Salt Lake City
842 Salt Lake City
843 Salt Lake City
844 Ogden
845 Provo
846 Provo
847 Provo

850-865 ARIZONA

850 Phoenix
852 Phoenix
853 Phoenix
855 Globe
856 Tucson
857 Tucson
859 Show Low
860 Flagstaff
863 Prescott
864 Dingman
865 Gallup, NM (Arizona Offices)

870-884 NEW MEXICO

870 Albuquerque
871 Albuquerque
872 Albuquerque
873 Gallup
874 Farmington
875 Sante Fe
877 Las Vegas
878 Socorro
879 Truth or Consequences
880 Las Cruces
881 Clovis
882 Roswell
883 Carrizozo
884 Tucumcari

889-898 NEVADA

889 Las Vegas
890 Las Vegas
891 Las Vegas
893 Ely
894 Reno
895 Reno
897 Carson City
898 Elko

900-966 CALIFORNIA

900 Los Angeles
901 Los Angeles
902 Inglewood
903 Ingelwood
904 Santa Monica
905 Torrance
906 Long Beach
907 Long Beach
908 Long Beach
910 Pasadena
911 Pasadena
912 Glendale
913 Van Nuys
914 Van Nuys
915 Burbank
916 North Hollywood
917 Alhambra
918 Alhambra
920 San Diego
921 San Diego
922 Palm Springs
923 San Bernardino
924 San Bernardino
925 Riverside
926 Santa Ana
927 Santa Ana
928 Anaheim
930 Oxnard
931 Santa Barbara
932 Bakersfield
933 Bakersfield
934 Santa Barbara
935 Mojave
936 Fresno
937 Fresno
938 Fresno
939 Salinas
940 San Francisco
941 San Francisco
942 Sacremento
943 Palo Alto
944 San Mateo
945 Oakland
946 Oakland
947 Berkeley
948 Richmond
949 North Bay
950 San Jose
951 San Jose
952 Stockton
953 Stockton
954 North Bay
955 Eureka
956 Sacramento
957 Sacramento
958 Sacramento
959 Marysville
960 Redding
961 Reno, Nevada (California Offices)
962-966 Military (AP)

967-968 HAWAII

967 Honolulu
968 Honolulu

969 GUAM

969 Agana, Guam

970-979 OREGON

970 Portland
971 Portland
972 Portland
973 Salem
974 Eugene
975 Medford
976 Klamath Falls
977 Bend
978 Pendleton
979 Boise, Idaho (Oregon Offices)

980-994 WASHINGTON

980 Seattle
981 Seattle
982 Everett
983 Tacoma
984 Tacoma
985 Olympia
986 Portland, OR (Washington Offices)
988 Wenatchee
989 Yakima
990 Spokane
991 Spokane
992 Spokane
993 Pasco
994 Lewiston, Idaho (Washington Offices)

995-999 ALASKA

995 Anchorage
996 Anchorage
997 Fairbanks
998 Juneau
999 Ketchikan

Appendix D

Glossary

Note that a glossary is an alphabetically arranged list of words with definitions peculiar to the subject of the book. Some of the terms listed in this glossary may have other, additional or different meanings when their definitions are not confined to mail order as they are here.

Acknowledgements — A list of everyone the author thanks for assisting in the preparation of the book. It is placed in the front matter of the book.
Acronym — An artificial or coined word formed from the initial letters of a phrase.
Active Buyer — A person (consumer) who has actually ordered something by mail within the last 12 month period.
Active Purchaser — A term used interchangeably with "active buyer."
Address Correction Requested — Printed in the upper left-hand corner under the return address of a piece of mail. It authorizes the United States Postal Service to provide the known new address on the mailing piece. A fee may be charged for this service.
Advertisement — A solicitation or a notice designed to attract the attention of potential customers and to obtain orders.
Advertisement Copy — The part of the advertisement below the headline which is used to communicate the offer to the potential customers.
Advertiser — A person, company or business running an advertisement.
Advertising Agency — A business which, for an agency commission, operates as a middleman between an advertiser (client) and publications the advertiser runs his advertisements in. (See also "in-house advertising agency").
Advertising Space — The actual space the display advertisement occupies in a publication.
Agate Line — A line of type in a publication such as a magazine or a newspaper. It is used to determine advertising rates. There are fourteen agate lines of type per inch.
Agate Type — Type of 5 1/2 points per em. It is commonly used in classified advertisements and set solid.
Agency Commission — Payment made by a publication to an advertising agency when advertisements are placed by that advertising agency. It is usually 15% of regular advertising rate.
Another Test — After a "successful" test, the mailer decides to minimize his risk by taking the same number of names from the quarter of the mailing list successfully tested, omitting the previously tested names.
Appendix — Contains important lists, graphs and charts and may be divided into several sections for easy reference. It is placed in the back matter of the book. Books with a large appendix often are used as a valuable reference tool.
Art — Consists of photographs, graphs and line drawings.
Artwork — A term used interchangeably with "art."
Audience — The number of potential customers reached by a specific advertisement.
Back Door — A term used interchangeably with "back end."
Back End — Activities to be performed and future profits to be made by the advertiser after the customer places the initial order.

Back Matter — Consists of the reference material placed at the end of the book, after the last chapter. It often contains the glossary, index and resources.

Balanced Advertisement — Ad with a balanced or worse, symmetrical layout. Ad layout should be unbalanced.

Benefits — What the product or information can do for the potential customer.

Bibliography — Lists the research material used in writing the book. It is placed in the back matter of the book.

Black-And-White — A term used for printing black type on white paper or one-color printing.

Blanket — A material used in the offset printing process which accepts ink from the printing plate and transfers it to paper. It is part of an offset printing press.

Blank Outside Envelope — An outside envelope left blank except the potential customer's name and address and perhaps the mailer's return address.

Body Of The Advertisement — A term used interchangeably with "advertisement copy."

Bold Face or Bold Type — A typeface which is heavier than regular type. The terms in this glossary are bold type.

Book — A publication of 49 or more pages which is not a serial or a periodical.

Booklet — A small book, usually with less than 48 pages. The material used for its cover can be the same or different from the paper used for its inside pages.

Book Rate — United States Postal Service's postage rate for books.

Bowker's Books in Print — Lists all books still in print by subject, author and title.

Bulk-Mail — A category of Third Class Mail which must meet various requirements in order to qualify at bulk rate. All the mail must be sorted into zip code sequence and must meet specific mailing requirements regarding bundling, labeling and sacking. A bulk rate mailing permit is required before this reduced rate can be used.

Bullet — A round, solid dot used to set off lists or separate phrases used in print. Measured in points.

Burning In — An offset printing term used to describe a process by which an offset plate is exposed to light through a negative.

Business Reply Mail — A card or an envelope supplied by the mailer to potential customers. It allows the customers to mail the card or envelope without paying for the postage because the postage payment is guaranteed by the mailer. The mailer must obtain a permit from the United States Postal Service in order to use business reply mail.

Buyer — A person (consumer) who has actually ordered something by mail.

C/A — Acronym for "change of address."

Camera-Ready — The complete copy, artwork or mechanical which is ready for printing.

Capitals — Upper-case letters.

Caption — The line of text accompanying an illustration.

Card Stock — Cardboard or very thick paper.

Carrier Route Pre-Sort — Mail sorted into a nine digit zip code sequence. This enables the mail to be sorted directly to the carrier who will deliver the mail to the addressee. It is more cost-effective than five digit zip code sequencing.

Cash On Delivery — The customer pays for the product when it is delivered to him, not before.

Cash With Order — The customer is required to pay for the product when he places the order. He is not allowed cash on delivery, credit or payment terms but he may be allowed to order with a credit card.

Catalog — A publication containing lists and descriptions of items for sale.

Catalog Buyers — Customers who have purchased products or services from a catalog.

Character — The generic term for an uppercase or lowercase letter, number, punctuation mark, symbol or space in printed matter. There are three types of characters: serif, sans serif and decorative.

Character Count — The number of characters (letters and blank spaces) that fill a specified area in a printed piece.
Cheshire Label — Labels containing names and addresses placed onto accordion fold, fanfold or rolled paper for the purpose of attaching them (mechanically or by hand), one at a time, to an envelope.
Circular — Printed advertising material separate from the sales letter.
Circulation — The number of copies of a publication sold and distributed. This figure usually includes newsstand sales, subscribers and samples.
Cleaning — A term used interchangeably with "mailing list cleaning."
Clip Art — Ready-made commercial line drawings on a large variety of subjects which you can use without permission of the artists. They can be cut out and pasted up.
Cloth Binding — A method used for binding hard cover books. It consists of Smyth sewing the stacked pages together and gluing them between two hard paper boards.
C.O.A. — Acronym for "change of address."
C.O.D. — Acronym for "cash on delivery."
Cold Composition — Preparation of copy by typewriter, computer or photocomposing machine as opposed to setting type in metal.
Collate — To assemble the pages in a book or booklet in proper numerical or logical sequence before binding. Also, the various components of a direct mail package can be assembled in a specific sequence prior to being placed into the outside envelope.
Column Inch — Space one inch high and one column wide. It is used to describe the amount of space in a display advertisement.
Commission — A percentage of the sale. Mailing list brokers and managers charge a commission based on the mailing list rental fee.
Commission Deal — A term used interchangeably with "per-inquiry deal."
Compiled List — Names and addresses of people who have some factor in common. It comes from previously printed sources such as telephone directories, government reports, membership of associations and so on. In contrast to a mail response list, a compiled list does not promise any sort of past purchasing activity by the people on its list.
Computer House — A company which prints the names and addresses from different mailing lists, sorts them by zip code and eliminates duplicate names.
Condensed Type — Typeface with letters narrower than normal for that particular typeface. The narrower typeface allows more letters to be set in the same amount of space.
Confidential Outside Envelope — An outside envelope with the word "confidential" or "personal" printed on it.
Consumer — A term used interchangeably with "buyer."
Continuation — After a "very successful" test, the mailer takes more names than he would take for "another test" (omitting the previously tested names), but not all the names from the quarter of the mailing list successfully tested.
Conversion — The act of changing an inquiry into a buyer.
Co-op Mailing — Two or more offers are mailed in the same envelope with each participating mailer sharing the costs.
Copy — A term used interchangeably with "advertisement copy."
Copy Block — A block of advertisement copy or body copy.
Copyright — The right to retain or sell copies of artistic works which you have produced. Legal protection to authors and artists.
Copyright Notice — The word placed on the copyright page such as "Copyright 1992, John Doe."
Copyright Page — Follows the title page and lists the name and address of the publisher, the edition of the book, the copyright notice, the Library of Congress Cataloging in Publication data, the International Standard Book Number (ISBN) and "printed and bound in the United States of America."
Coupon — The order form printed on a display advertisement which makes it easier for the customer to place an order.

Crop Marks — The lines used to define where an illustration or a photograph is to be reproduced.

Customer — A term used interchangeably with "buyer."

DBA — Acronym for "doing business as." A business operated in another name.

DMA — Acronym for Direct Marketing Association.

Decorative — A character intended for a headline or other special use.

Decoy — Names inserted in a mailing list meant to prevent unauthorized use of the list.

Dedication Page — Usually consists of a short statement of praise by the author for a family member, spouse, a friend or some other third party. It is placed in the front matter of the book.

Demographic Information — A detailed description of the readers of a publication found in the media kit. This information includes the average age, income and education of the readers.

Desktop Publishing — An inexpensive method of producing high quality (resolution of 300 or more dots per inch or "dpi") in-house laser typesetting using a computer, word processing or page layout software and a laser printer.

Direct Mail — A solicitation is sent directly by mail to the potential customers homes or place of business.

Direct Mail Package — Sales literature used in direct mail including sales letter, order form, circular and self-addressed envelope.

Direct Marketing — Soliciting orders directly from the potential customers using mail order, telemarketing, personal sales, direct mail or direct response.

Direct Marketing Association — The largest and oldest trade association having to do with mail order.

Direct Response — Solicitations are made to potential customers in publications, by direct mail or on radio or TV. Customers respond directly by placing orders.

Disclaimers — Often found on the copyright page. They are a form of legal protection for the author and the publisher regarding the use, content or subject matter of the material in the book.

Display Advertisement — The advertisement in a publication such as a newspaper or a magazine.

Drop-Shipping — An advertiser obtains orders for a product and a third party (the drop-shipper) produces, stores and mails the product to the customer.

Dummy — A preliminary "mock-up" of the book, booklet, pamphlet or any printed piece folded to the exact size of the finished job. It is used to verify its correct appearance and size.

Dummy Names—A term used interchangeably with "decoy" names.

Duplication Elimination — A name and address is accepted only once by a mailer, no matter how many times it appears on a list or on how many different lists it appears on.

Durosheen — A lacquer or UV book cover coating. It is dried with ultraviolet light and does not crack like a varnish coating might.

Editing — Adding to, deleting from and polishing the book.

Em — A square whose dimensions in points are identical with a particular type size.

Em Dash — A dash the width of an "M."

En Dash — A dash the width of an "N."

Exacto Knife — An inexpensive knife used for artwork and found in art stores.

Excerpt — A passage extracted from a book or an article and quoted in a new book. The author or publisher of the new book must obtain written permission to do this from the author, publisher or news syndicate of the original work.

Expanded Type — Typeface with letters wider than normal for that particular typeface. The wider typeface allows for less letters to be set in the same amount of space. Also called "extended type."

Face Trimming — Cutting a book's uneven edges off to produce a smooth and even right edge.

Family — The group name of a typeface which identifies the typeface's distinctive style or shape.
First Class Mail — United States Postal Service affords priority treatment to this type of mail. Most personal letters are sent via first class mail.
Flier — A printed announcement.
Follow-Up Advertising — A direct mail package is sent to each purchaser of one offer in an effort to obtain an order for another offer from the same purchaser.
Font — A typeface in a particular point size.
Foreword — Is written by someone other than the author and it is on an odd numbered page of the front matter. It is in fact a pitch for the book and the name of the person making the pitch appears at the end of the foreword.
Front End — The activities which take place before a buyer makes a purchase. Also, the profits made from the buyer's initial purchase.
Front Matter — Consists of the material placed in the beginning of the book up to Chapter One.
Fulfillment — The process of order processing, packing and shipping a customer's order.
General Interest Topics — Appeal to a large audience and include fitness and health, moneymaking opportunities, career opportunities, child rearing, human relationships, personal finance, etc.
Ghostwriter — A writer who produces work for others.
Glossary — An alphabetically arranged list of words with definitions peculiar to the subject of the book. It is placed in the back matter of the book.
Glossy — A photograph with a smooth, shiny, slick surface.
Graphic Arts — The printing term used to denote all creative work in designing and composing printed matter.
Graphics — Photos, artwork, special typefaces and other illustrative material used to enhance printed matter.
Guarantee — The promise of satisfaction to the consumer.
Gutter — The center of a newspaper or magazine where the two facing pages meet.
Halftone — A printing process in which a piece of art such as a photograph is broken up by a screen and printed as a series of dots.
Halftone Screen — A screen placed in front of the negative material in the process camera in order to break up the continuous tone image into dots of black and white to produce a halftone.
Headline — The large bold caption at the top of an advertisement. It is the most important element of the advertisement.
Hot Line List — A mailing list of mail order buyers who have made a purchase during the most recent quarter or 90 day period.
Index — An alphabetically arranged list of words giving the page numbers on which each item is mentioned. It is placed in the back matter of the book.
In-House Advertising Agency — A company set up by an advertiser in order to save the 15% agency commission when placing advertisements in publications.
In-House Mailing List — A mail order operator's own mailing list or a list of the names and addresses of all the people who have ordered from the operator. Also called "House List."
Inquiry — A person who has responded to a display, direct mail or classified advertisement offering "free details" but did not necessarily actually place an order.
Insert — A flier included in a mailing to a potential customer or inserted into a newspaper as an addition, not as part of the newspaper.
Insertion — The appearance of an advertisement in any one issue of any periodical.
Insertion Order Form — The form used by Advertising Agencies and In-House Advertising Agencies to submit advertisements to publications. Also known as "media insertion order."
International Standard Book Number — A unique number issued by R.R. Bowker which identifies the edition and publisher of a book.

Introduction — Where the author tells the reader why he wrote the information. It can come before Chapter One in which case it is part of the front matter. Or, it can be Chapter One as it is in this book, in which case it is part of the text.
ISBN — The acronym for International Standard Book Number.
Italic Typeface — Type with a right hand slant.
Junior Page — A 2/3 of a page advertisement.
Justified — A block of copy which has both left and right margins aligned or even. This eliminates the ragged right margin.
Key Code — A method used for identifying the specific publication or advertising source which generated a display or classified advertisement order. It is usually printed on the display advertisement coupon as a "Dept." followed by a code after the address of the mailer. In direct mail advertising it is usually printed on the address label and it is used to identify different mailing lists including different quarters of the same mailing list which generated the order.
Label — A slip or piece of paper containing a name and address. It is affixed to an order form or outside envelope for mailing purposes. Also called "mailing label."
Lacquer — A book cover coating that is applied like an ink.
Laminate — A thin plastic film book cover coating that is rolled off a roll and applied with heat.
Layout — The overall design of printed matter including artwork. The positioning of the headline, text, subheads and artwork.
Leading — Extra space between lines of type, usually measured in points. It increases legibility.
Lettershop — A term used interchangeably with "mailing service company."
Library Of Congress — The national library serving the U.S. Congress.
Library of Congress Catalog Card Number — A unique title control number assigned by the Library of Congress to a given work.
Line Drawing — A black and white drawing without any shading.
Line Rate — The price charged by a publication for each line of an advertisement.
Line Work — A term used interchangeably with "line drawing."
Linotronic Printing — Higher than 1250 dots per inch printing produced by a machine which uses a light-beam laser to expose the copy onto a special RC paper.
List Broker — A term used interchangeably with "mailing list broker."
List Manager — A term used interchangeably with "mailing list manager."
List Rental — An agreement between the owner of a mailing list and the mailer for only a one-time use of the mailing list.
Lowercase — Alphabet letters which are not capital letters.
Mag tapes — Special reel to reel magnetic tapes containing computer information. Used in "merge purge."
Mail House — A term used interchangeably with "mailing service company."
Mailing List — A collection of names and addresses of people who have something in common. It can be a compiled list, a mail response list or an in-house list.
Mailing List Broker — Puts the user of a mailing list and the mailing list manager or the owner of the mailing list together for a commission or a brokerage fee.
Mailing List Cleaning — The process of keeping the names and addresses on mailing lists current. When mailing lists are "cleaned," the names and addresses are corrected and/or eliminated.
Mailing List Maintenance System — A system which keeps a mailing list clean.
Mailing List Manager — Manages an owner's mailing list for rental purposes for a commission. Handles all the inquiries, processes the orders and collects the rental fee for the lists he manages.
Mailing Piece — A term used interchangeably with "direct mail package."
Mailing Service Company — Labels, inserts and sorts direct mail. Also called "mail house" or "lettershop."
Mail Order — You offer a product or a service to potential customers, they order by mail and you or a drop-shipper fulfill your customers' orders by mail.

Mail Order Buyer Lists — Lists of the names and addresses of customers who have actually purchased something through the mail.
Mail Order Inquiry Lists — Lists of the names and addresses of people who have responded to a "free details" offer through the mail but did not necessarily actually make a purchase.
Mail Response List — Names and addresses of people who have responded to other company's mail order advertising. Mail response lists can be further broken down into two other categories: inquirers and actual buyers. Also called "mail responsive list."
Manual — A reference book containing instructions.
Mechanical — The complete copy or artwork which is ready for printing.
Media Kit — Contains valuable information about the publication including a detailed demographic description of its readers.
Media Package — A term used interchangeably with "media kit."
Merge Purge — A computer house merges names from two or more mailing lists together and eliminates the duplicate names.
Multi-Buyer — A person (consumer) who made a purchase more than once from the same company.
Negative — A paper or film copy of a mechanical or artwork with black and white areas reversed. It is used to prepare offset plates.
News Release — A term used interchangeably with "press release."
Nixie — A piece of mail returned to the sender by the United States Postal Service due to an incorrect or undeliverable address.
Nth Name — When a mailer tests a mailing list by renting a fraction of the names on the mailing list by incrementally taking every tenth or fifth or third name, etc. from the list.
Offer — The offer presented to a potential customer. It includes the price, the delivery terms, the guarantee terms and any other terms for the product.
Official Outside Envelope — An outside envelope designed to give the appearance of an official letter.
Offset Plate — The metal or paper master plate used to print by the offset printing method.
Offset Printing — A method of printing where the image or the impression from the offset plate is transferred to a blanket and then to the paper.
Opportunity Seekers — People interested in improving their lot in life by pursuing a new idea or a business.
Optimum Price — The selling price which produces the highest profit.
Order Form — The "order blank" or "order card" used in a direct mail package which makes it easier for the customer to place an order.
Outside Envelope — The window or regular envelope containing the direct mail offer.
Pamphlet — A small booklet.
Paste-up — A term used interchangeably with "mechanical."
Perfect Binding — A method of binding books done by stacking the pages, folding the cover around the pages and gluing the pages and the cover at the spine.
Perforated Order Form — An order form with small holes, similar to the holes between postage stamps. The holes allow for easy separation.
PI Deal — Acronym for "per-inquiry deal."
Per-Inquiry Deal — A deal an advertiser makes with a publication. The advertiser does not pay anything for the advertisement, only for actual inquiries or orders the advertisement generates.
Periodical — Any newspaper, magazine or other publication published on a repetitive schedule
Photo Offset — A term used interchangeably with "offset printing."
Photostat — The complete copy, artwork or mechanical which is ready for printing.
Plastic Comb Binding — A method of book binding similar to spiral wire binding except that plastic instead of wire is used to bind the book.
Point — A vertical measurement of type equal to 1/72 of an inch.

Postage Meter — An office machine used to print prepaid postage notices directly on envelopes or on gummed tape.
Postage Scale — An accurate scale used for weighing mail in order to determine the correct postage.
Postscript — A personal message from the author to the reader, often wishing the best of luck. Usually it is the last chapter of the text, prior to the back matter.
Preface — A term used interchangeably with "introduction."
Press Release — An announcement sent to a periodical in an effort to obtain publicity. Also known as "news release" and "publicity release."
Pressure Sensitive Label — A type of label which peels off for direct attachment.
Printing And Mailing Service Company — Both prints and mails direct mail.
Proofreading — Proofing your book for spelling, punctuation and grammar.
Publication — Same as a periodical, but includes other printed material such as books, booklets and pamphlets which are not printed on a repetitive schedule.
Publicity — A form of advertising which is free.
Publicity Release — A term used interchangeably with "press release."
Purchaser — A term used interchangeably with "buyer."
Quarter — Mailing lists are often divided into 90 day periods or 1st, 2nd, 3rd and 4th quarters of a given year. A mailer should always test a company's "hot line" or most recent quarter list before testing any of its older quarters.
Ragged — A block of type uneven or unjustified at one or both margins.
Rate Card — The magazine or newspaper card which lists the costs, per agate line, for advertising in that publication. Publications usually include the rate card with their media kit.
Reader's Guide to Periodical Literature — Lists magazine articles on many topics.
Readership — Some publications claim that up to five or six different people read every copy of every issue of their publication.
Remainder Books — Books which usually did not sell well when they were originally published and consequently the publisher is trying to get rid of them. Also known as "bargain books."
Remnant Space — The unsold pages of advertising space in a publication. Usually available for sale at a reduced rate.
Rental Lists — Mailing lists which can be rented for a one-time use from the mailing list owner or the mailing list manager.
Repetition — When a mailer remails the same offer to the same mailing list.
Reply Envelope — A term used interchangeably with "self-addressed envelope."
Reprint Rights — Purchasing the rights to reprint or reproduce a book, booklet or pamphlet from a publisher.
Research — A close, careful study of a particular topic. It involves reading, taking notes and rearranging information.
Resources — Reference material in the back matter of a book. Supports or aids the information in the text.
Response — The percentage rate of orders received from a mailing.
Return Envelope — A term used interchangeably with "self-addressed envelope."
Reverse — To print an image white on black instead of black on white.
Review — An evaluation of a book, booklet or pamphlet.
Roll Out — After an "extremely successful" test, the mailer takes all the remaining names from the quarter of the mailing list successfully tested.
Royalty — A share paid to the author by the publisher out of the proceeds resulting from the sale of the author's book. The royalty is usually around 10% of the price of each hard cover book sold.
Saddle Stitching — An inexpensive method of binding softcover books using staples. It is done by laying out the book with the cover and the pages of the book collated, then stapling (usually in two places) and folding over to make a book.
Sales Tax — A required tax a mail order operator must collect from the customers who live in his state.

Sample Direct Mail Package — A mailing list owner or manager may request a sample of the direct mail package which the mailer wishes to mail to their list.

Sample Mailing Piece — A term used interchangeably with "sample direct mail package."

Sans Serif — A character without serifs. From the French "sans," meaning "without."

Screen — A term used interchangeably with "halftone screen."

Seeding — Putting in decoy names on a mailing list.

Self-Addressed Envelope — An envelope enclosed in a direct mail package which is used by the customer when placing an order.

Self-Mailer — A mailing piece designed so that it can be sent through the mail without being enclosed in an envelope.

Serif — A character with small lines or "tails" that project from the ends of the strokes. The text in this book is set in serif type.

Side Stitching — An inexpensive method of binding books using staples. It is done by laying out the book with the cover and the pages of the book collated, then stapling (usually in two places) from the front to the back cover without folding the pages over as in saddle stitching.

Slip — A single sheet of paper usually printed with an advertising message.

Soft Name — A term used interchangeably with "decoy."

Solicitation — A term used interchangeably with "advertisement."

Solicitor — A person, company or a business running an advertisement.

Source — The publication or the mailing list which generated the buyer or the inquiry. It is tracked by the key code.

Special Interest Topics — Appeal to a narrow audience and include topics such as sailing, parachuting, canoeing, various ethnic cooking methods, flying, handwriting analysis, skiing, etc.

Spike — A term used interchangeably with "decoy."

Spine — The part of the book which connects the front cover to the back cover. It usually contains the title, the name of the author and a logo of the publishing company.

Spiral Wire Binding — A book binding method using a coil of wire wound through the holes on the back edge of the book.

Split Run — The most widely used method of testing display advertisements. Half of the magazine or newspaper copies contain ad "A" and the other half contain ad "B." Both ads are key coded so results can be measured.

Standard Rate and Data Service — Catalogs magazines by different categories in a monthly publication called Consumer Magazine and Farm Publication Rates and Data. Also publishes a book dealing with newspapers: Newspaper Rates and Data.

Stat — The complete copy, artwork or mechanical which is ready for printing.

Subhead — A short line of print usually set apart from the rest of the advertisement copy.

Suppress — Avoiding mailing an offer to an individual who has already ordered that particular offer. Done by a computer house.

Syndicate — An agency which sells articles for publication in various newspapers and magazines at the same time.

Table Of Contents — Should start on an odd numbered page (on the right-hand side). It will include the number of each chapter, the title of each chapter and the beginning page number of each chapter.

Teaser Outside Envelope — An outside envelope with a phrase related to the offer printed on it.

Testimonial — A statement by an expert or a previous customer about a product or a book.

Text — Consists of the main portion of the book. It starts with Chapter One and ends with the last chapter. The majority of the information contained in the book is in the text.

Till-Forbid Order — An advertising term which tells the publication to run an advertisement until the advertiser orders them to stop running it.

Title Page — Lists the title and the subtitle (if there is one) of the book. It is on an odd numbered page — on the right-hand side. It may also list the name of the author, the publisher and the location of the publisher.

Trim Size — The final size of the book or booklet after it is cut to a specified size after printing and binding.

Typeface — A distinctive style of a set of characters. Numerous and varied typefaces are available.

Typesize — A term used by printers to depict the number of points to an inch of print.

Unbalanced Advertisement — Ad with a unbalanced, non-symmetrical layout. Ad layout should be unbalanced.

Uni-Binding — A method of binding books which uses a process similar to perfect binding to produce clear plastic covers with black or white spines.

Universe — An entire mailing list.

Uppercase — Capital letters. Opposite of lowercase.

Use Tax — A tax contingent upon the location of the mail order operator's "place of business."

Velo-Binding — A method of binding books using two hard plastic strips applied at the spine of the book.

Velox — A positive print of a photograph or line art which is ready for paste-up.

White Space — The portion of an advertisement which does not have type on it.

Wire Stitching — A term used interchangeably with "saddle stitching."

X-Acto Knife — A brand name of a knife which is shaped like a pencil and widely used in graphic arts.

Zip Code — A specified set of numbers consisting of five digits, beginning with 00000 and ending with 99999, which designate state and geographic locations within the United States.

Zip Code + Four — An additional four digits which can be added to the five digit zip code for greater time and postage savings.

Zip Code Sequence — The arrangement of names and addresses on a mailing list in the order of the zip code, beginning with 00000 and ending with 99999.

Index